Contents

Acknowledgement

I should like to acknowledge how much of the work in the organisation of the Bristol conference and in the preparation of this book was done by Dr David Reisman, editor of the Section F Series, and by his colleagues on the Section F Committee.

A.W.

Notes on the Contributors

Martin Buxton is a Senior Research Fellow and Director of the Health Economics Research Group at Brunel University where he was responsible for the major study of the costs and benefits of heart-transplant programmes in the UK. Prior to that he was an Economic Adviser at the Department of Health and Social Security.

Michael Drummond is Professor of Health Services Management and Director of the Health Services Management Centre, University of Birmingham. He is author of a number of books on the economic evaluation of health care programmes, including *Principles of Economic Appraisal in Health Care* (1980), *Studies in Economic Appraisal in Health Care* (1981) and *Methods for the Economic Evaluation of Health Care Programmes* (1986). He has also undertaken many empirical studies in this field.

Hugh Gravelle is Reader in Economics at Queen Mary College, University of London. He is the author (with Ray Rees) of *Microeconomics* (1981). In addition to health economics, his research interests include the economics of law and public sector economics.

Raymond Illsley is a Professorial Fellow at the University of Bath. From 1981–1985 he was Chairman, Social Affairs Committee, Economic and Social Research Council; and he has held a number of other positions in public service and at universities in Britain and abroad. His many publications include *The Health Burden of Social Inequalities* (1986) (with P.-G. Svensson).

Julian Le Grand is a Senior Research Fellow at the Suntory–Toyota International Centre for Economics and Related Disciplines, London School of Economics, where he is co-director (with A. B. Atkinson) of the Centre's Welfare State Programme. He previously taught at the University of Sussex and the London School of Economics Department of Economics, of which he is still a member. He is the author of many journal articles, and several books on the welfare state, including *The Economics of Social Problems* (with Ray Robinson, 1984) and *The Strategy of Equality* (1982).

Alistair McGuire is a Research Fellow at the Health Economics Research Unit, Department of Community Medicine, University of Aberdeen. He has worked in the areas of regional and energy economics as well as in the area of health care economics. He has also acted as a consultant for the World Health Organization. He is a graduate of Heriot-Watt and Aberdeen Universities.

Alan Maynard is Professor of Economics and Director of the Centre for Health Economics at the University of York. He has written widely on many topics in social economics and the economics of human resources.

John Mohan is an ESRC Postdoctoral Research Fellow in the Health and Health Care Research Centre, Queen Mary College, London. His research interests are in geographical aspects of health-service provision and he is currently working on spatial implications of restructuring in the health sector in England.

Gavin Mooney is Professor of Health Economics at the Institute of Social Medicine, University of Copenhagen. He has worked as an Economic Adviser in the Department of the Environment (1969–72) and the Department of Health and Social Security (1972–4). He was Director of the Health Economics Research Unit, University of Aberdeen, from 1977 until 1985. He is a member of the Copenhagen Collaboration Center for the study of regional variations in health care.

Joy Townsend is an economist and research scientist at the Medical Research Council's Epidemiology and Medical Care Unit, Harrow. She is widely known for her work on the epidemiology and economics of smoking.

Peter Townsend is Professor of Social Policy at the University of Bristol and visiting Professor of Sociology at the University of Essex. He is author of *Poverty in the United Kingdom* (1979) and co-author of the Black Report: *Inequalities in Health* (1980). His recent and current research deals predominantly with two themes: the relationship of ill-health to deprivation, and national and international theories of poverty.

Alan Williams is a (part-time) Professor of Economics at the University of York, mainly working on the appraisal of public expenditure in various fields. His interests in health care have been reflected in his membership of the DHSS Chief Scientist's Research Committee, the Royal Commission on the NHS, and the SSRC Panel on Health and Health Services Research, and in his publications on the application of economic analysis to medical care systems. Besides his interests in health and medical care, he has also worked on problems of water resource development (he was a member of the Yorkshire Water Authority and of the National Water Council) and on evaluating the effectiveness of police and criminal justice systems for the Council of Europe (he was formerly a member of the SSRC's Social Science and Law Committee).

Introduction

ALAN WILLIAMS

Economists, like doctors, are seeking to extend life and relieve misery. In the case of doctors, the premature mortality and the misery is due to disease. In the case of economists, it is due to scarcity. Health economics stands at the interface between those two important fields of human endeavour. It is a relatively young sub-discipline of economics, not really amounting to any significant volume of work until about 1970, and at that time mostly concentrated in the USA.

British health economists drew, and still draw, on the work of American colleagues, but the political and institutional frameworks within which health care is provided in the USA are so different from those in the UK (and in many other European countries), that it was necessary for the subject to develop along rather different lines in order that it could offer ideas, and empirical results, that are relevant to the much more egalitarian ideologies, and much heavier reliance on tax funding, which characterise health care provision in most European countries.

In such a rapidly developing field it is difficult to know just when to offer your wares to the public for appraisal and comment, but the enormous interest in public policy suggests that anyone with something useful to contribute should not hold back. We health economists think we have something useful to contribute, so in this volume we have offered up some of our wares for public inspection and discussion. In this enterprise we have been joined at one point by a medical sociologist, and at another by a social geographer, features which emphasise the undoubted fact that other disciplines, besides economics, will also have something to say on the topics addressed in this volume. We neither seek nor claim an exclusive franchise!

The volume opens with my own presidential address, which attempts to sketch out the whole territory in which health economists operate, even though only a selection of their work can be included here. Those who want a much more comprehensive picture of the scope of the subject should consult C. A. Blades *et al.*, *An International Bibliography of Health Economics* (1986), which contains annotations on over 5000 published works in the English language going back as far as 1914! It should satisfy even the most voracious appetite! The principle adopted for selecting topics for inclusion here was to span a wide *range* of topics, and to show that there is more to health economics than the economics of health services.

The broadest issues addressed are those concerned with inequality and injustice (Illsley and Le Grand; Peter Townsend; Mooney and McGuire; and Mohan), since these place health and health care in the context of socio-economic inequalities more generally, and pose fundamental questions about the potential role of the health-care system as a countervailing force. It is an important area of debate in which even the underlying facts, and the causal mechanisms at work, are in dispute. No-one familiar with the literature can seriously doubt that there is a major social problem to be addressed. The differences show up when one tries to decide exactly what notion of justice we are seeking to put into effect, and where it would lead us, and with what effect. It is to be hoped that the contributions offered here will help clarify the issues and put them in perspective.

There are also two papers on the relationships between unemployment and health, and on the economics of reduced smoking, both of which deal with issues that go beyond concern with the health care system itself. Gravelle demonstrates the intricacies of establishing causal links between phenomena which, however strongly related they may seem at first glance, may be the result of a variety of complex mechanisms, each of which would have different implications for policy. Joy Townsend works her way through the implication of reduced smoking showing the various ramifications of that trend, which seems currently to be the specific behavioural change which would do more than anything else to improve people's health. She shows that many of the claimed deleterious side-effects on the economy, and on the public finances, are, at the very least, exaggerated, and quite probably non-existent. It is a challenging analysis.

Thus, coming closer to the health service and its problems, we have the papers by Buxton, Drummond and Maynard. Drummond's contribution concentrates on the general methodological stance that underlies the economists approach to evaluative work, and argues in favour of a more significant role for the discipline of economics in both the formulation of problems and in the range of data collected when controlled clinical trials are being planned. This will make the findings much more relevant to the world in which health services operate. Buxton's work on the economics of the heart transplant programme is an excellent example of this kind of evaluative work. It also illustrates the role of health economists in a multi-disciplinary enterprise, where they are able to play a significant role in both problem formulation and data collection and analysis, but are nevertheless sensitive to the interests, expertise and knowledge of non-economists, and, at the end of the day, have to interpret their findings so as to address a public policy issue in terms that make sense to the policy-makers themselves. Finally, Maynard considers the incentive structure generated by the manner in which health services are financed, and suggests that many of the more persistent problems (and conflicts) which seem to be so intractable within the NHS might be more readily resolved with the more imaginative use of 'internal' markets (so that the time costs of different activities are made visible to the decision maker – often a doctor – and that person has an appropriate incentive to seek to minimise them).

All in all, it is a varied menu, but one which certainly does not exhaust all the possibilities. The potential of health economics to improve the lot of struggling humanity has so far scarcely been tapped, and if this volume enables non-economists to come to a better appreciation of its scope and methods, I shall be well satisfied.

1 Health Economics: The Cheerful Face of the Dismal Science?

ALAN WILLIAMS

Economics is usually a rather doom-laden subject, and in this respect is linked indirectly with medicine through the observation that the only two things in life that are certain are death and taxes. And if you wanted to take the gloomiest possible view of the subject matter of health economics, I guess you could say that that statement sums it up perfectly . . . it is all about death and taxes. But though death and taxes may be inescapable, they are, fortunately, not immutable, and if you wanted to take a more cheerful view of the subject matter of health economics you could say that it is all about *postponing* death and *reducing* taxes. Broadly speaking, this is the view I take, though I hope to show you that there is more to life than postponing death, and more to costs than shows up in taxes, so that too simple-minded a view will not in fact carry us very far in understanding what health economists are trying to do.

Before I expose to you the scope and content of health economics, I must explain the important distinction I wish to draw between a *discipline* and a *topic*. Economics is both a discipline and a topic, and that leads to confusion when people hear economists claiming expertise in areas which are not regarded by others as anything to do with economics (e.g. the practice of medicine). By economics *as a topic* I mean taking the economic system as the subject to be investigated, and the presumption then is that economists have (or should have) special expertise in helping us to understand that topic. This special expertise will have accumulated from sustained thinking over several centuries about how different economic systems work and develop, in

1

the course of which it will have proved useful to use certain concepts and structural relationships, to ask certain questions, and to collect certain kinds of data. All of this then comes to constitute the corpus of knowledge transmitted from one generation of investigators to the next, with increasing specialisation and internal subdivision of expertise as that corpus grows in volume and complexity. This 'special expertise', or characteristic mode of thinking, is what I see as the *discipline* of economics.

But although the relationship of the discipline of economics to the topic of economics may be a special and dominant one, it is not an exclusive one. It is not exclusive in two respects: firstly, the topic may be investigated by other disciplines, and secondly, this discipline may be used to investigate other topics. Let me illustrate each case in turn.

The topic of inflation is clearly within the ambit of economics, and it is one on which the discipline of economics is much utilised. But it is also very enlightening and fruitful to see inflation as a political or sociological or moral problem, and to apply the special expertise of those subjects to its analysis and clarification. In other words economic *topics* are not the exclusive preserve of one discipline, not even of the discipline with a special, and perhaps dominant, relationship to them.

Conversely, the discipline of economics will have something to contribute to topics which are not conventionally classified as 'economic' problems, for example, whether or not particular types of crime should attract the penalty of imprisonment or be tried by jury, how stringent fire and other safety regulations should be, or how many doctors we need. In other words, the *discipline* of economics is not exclusively focused on economic *topics*.

What is true of economics in general is equally true of health economics in particular, for it too has the property of being both a topic and a discipline. Its topic area is readily seen as being that of the provision of health care, but it is really much broader than that, for it is also about the many other factors which may affect health (for better or worse), for instance smoking, unemployment, income levels, education, geographical location, etc., all of which will be receiving attention from my co-authors in this volume.

To clarify the nature of the potential contribution of health economics to thinking about health care I have constructed a crude schematic representation of the main elements in health economics, which you will find set out in Figure 1.1. I should like to comment on its contents, so as to help you interpret its rather terse terminology.

An unkind critic once said that if you taught a parrot to say 'supply

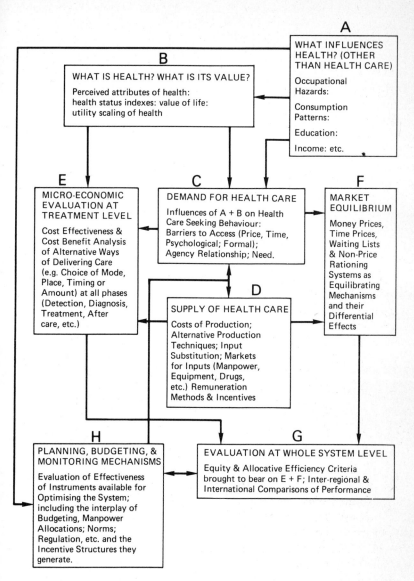

FIGURE 1.1 *Schematic presentation of the main elements in health economics*

and demand' it would give a passable imitation of an economist, so let me lend some credence to that caricature by starting in the middle of my chart, with the two boxes *C* and *D*, labelled respectively 'DEMAND FOR HEALTH CARE' and 'SUPPLY OF HEALTH CARE'. Taking the supply side first, our interests here are in the costs of delivering health care, in comparing the costs of different ways of delivering care (e.g. primary care versus hospital care, domiciliary versus institutional, surgery versus drugs), in the possibilities of substituting capital for labour, or one kind of labour for another, in the markets for these inputs (doctors, nurses, drugs, equipment, etc.) and how they work, and in how different remuneration systems affect the behaviour of suppliers of health care. In this kind of work one tries to see how much of what has been learned about other production systems could be used to advantage in the very complex and sensitive business of producing health care (which should be interpreted as including much of the care provided by local authority social services and voluntary organisations as well as by the health service).

If things are complicated on the supply side, they are even more complicated on the demand side, for here we find ourselves in territory which cannot so straightforwardly be made analogous to what we do in economics generally. The first of our difficulties stems from the fact that over large tracts of the health care field we do not want 'demand' to be based on willingness and ability to pay, but on 'need' (a concept to which I shall return shortly). In order to give effect to that objective, health care is typically provided 'free' (or at a nominal price) at the point of consumption. But even very rich countries cannot provide all the health care that people would like to have if it really were 'freely' available, so in practice it never really is. Some of the non-price barriers to access are simply there 'in nature' as it were (e.g. the time and trouble costs of getting to and from a consultation) whilst others are created as deliberate rationing devices (e.g., rules about eligibility, or priority assessments based on 'need'). Need is a central concept in this debate, but an unclear and ambiguous one, which I think essentially means some 'expert's' assessment of how much benefit someone would get from a particular 'treatment'. It will thus depend on (a) how effective the treatment is (b) how the 'expert' perceives the value to the patient of that effect. It is therefore, in principle, partly a factual and partly a (paternalistically) evaluative statement. This brings me to the second major difficulty on the demand side, which is that patients do not usually 'demand' health care the way they 'demand' apples or pears. It is as if we go shopping knowing only that we feel hungry, with not much knowledge as to *why* we feel hungry, or whether our hunger will go away all by itself in due course, or whether there is anything that can be done to assuage it, and, if so, what the most (cost-) effective way of doing that might be. For information on all these matters for health care we rely on the very same people who make a living by providing the goods in question, the doctors. Imagine what a heyday the foodsellers would have if we were in the same situation with them! In health economics this reliance on doctors is called the 'agency relationship' to denote the awkward fact that the suppliers of health care are often simultaneously the 'agents' of the demanders, with a potential for role conflict which I am sure needs no spelling out. Its analytical awkwardness for the *discipline* (as opposed to the topic) of economics is that it blurs the sharp distinction we try to draw between demand side influences and supply side influences. This happens elsewhere in economics in handling the role of advertising, where producers are clearly (despite their protestations to the contrary) trying to manipulate demand, rather than regarding 'preferences' as 'autonomous' and consumers as 'sovereign'. Could it be the same with health care?

Let me pass quickly on to where the consumers' own demand for health care comes from, which takes me to the top of Figure 1.1, and to Boxes *A* and *B*. We are here concerned with the demand for *health*, which is obviously prior to the demand for *health care*, and distinct from it. Clearly our health is strongly influenced by what might broadly be called our life-style, and this will depend quite a lot on our own particular niche in society. If we are well-informed, prudent, moderately well-off, in a non-hazardous occupation, leading a happy and interesting life, with a balanced diet, neither eating nor drinking to excess, and not smoking at all, our demand for health care is likely to be quite low, even though our demand for health may be quite high. The unfortunate people whose experiences and attitudes are the very opposite of those I just mentioned will present a very different pattern of demand for health care, mediated partly by their circumstances and partly by their own perceptions of the importance of life (i.e., whether they value a good quality of life now more than extra years of life later). If society generally wishes to maintain its members in a good state of health (i.e., maximise their quality-adjusted years of life-expectancy) we need some way of measuring and valuing health, and economists have been active (with others) in tackling those fundamental (but very difficult) problems too.

Let us next turn to how the market for health care is likely to resolve the tensions created by balancing the demands for health care against the available supply, which is the content of Box *F* on the right hand side of Figure 1.1. In textbook markets money prices play the central role in bringing supply and demand into balance, and in giving the appropriate signals to suppliers as to whether they should expand or contract capacity (by comparing prices with production costs). In health care we have the production costs, but, for the perfectly good reasons explained earlier, we don't have any prices (or, more precisely, not any market-clearing prices). We therefore need to work with more complex notions such as time prices, waiting time, and non-price priority-setting rules, all of which play the role of rationing devices which would otherwise be played by money prices. It is an interesting area of study as to what the differential effect on utilisation is of these different ways of impeding access to a nominally 'free' service.

The next logical step is to move from the 'positive' analysis of what actually happens to the 'normative' analysis of what we regard as 'better' or 'worse' ways of doing things. This is the content of Box *E* on the left-hand side of my chart, and takes us into the realm of cost-effectiveness and cost-benefit analysis. If 'effectiveness' or 'benefit' is to relate to how patients themselves perceive health and how they value it, then work of this kind must clearly draw on the material in Box *B* of Figure 1.1. It also needs to consider the many options contained in Boxes *C* and *D*, concerning alternative ways of delivering care (choice of mode, place, timing or amount) at all phases in the process (detection, diagnoses, treatment, care, etc.). This is where the bulk of the work of British health economists seems to be located, and it is the area in which we find ourselves collaborating with doctors, nurses, remedial professions, ancillary staff, managers and finance personnel, since this kind of evaluative work touches many people's interests, activities and expertise. It has great potential for the death-postponing tax-reducing aspect of health economics to which I alluded at the outset.

But the planning, budgeting and monitoring mechanisms of the health care system are worthy objects of study in themselves, and constitute the content of Box *H* in the bottom left-hand corner. Here we are not so much concerned with whether drugs or surgery are the most cost-effective ways of treating angina, but with whether the budgeting and planning systems are so designed as to give people an incentive to seek out and implement the most cost-effective way of treating angina. Would it help if clinicians became budget-holders and were allowed to retain some fraction of any efficiency savings they generated by more cost-effective practice, and spend those retained savings on service developments which they thought important, without the need to get authority from higher management? At present we rely either on people's public spiritedness, or on rather arbitrary cuts (or both), to generate a drive for greater efficiency. Is there not a more constructive incentive structure to be thought out and implemented?

Finally we come to Box *G* at the bottom right hand corner of my chart, which is labelled 'evaluation at whole system level'. In this we try to look in a more Olympian way at the performance of health care systems, testing them against broad equity principles as well as against tests of allocative efficiency. In that kind of work it is often instructive to make interregional or international comparisons of the impact of different structures, although the more dissimilar the societies and their objectives the more difficult it is to draw relevant conclusions from such comparisons. I fear too that it is often an enterprise in which the grass seems all-too-frequently to grow greener on the other side, so that while some people in this country look hopefully for a 'free market' model elsewhere in the world which they fondly imagine will deal once and for all with our 'waiting list' problems, those plagued with the very *unfree* market systems, which are what one actually observes in some parts of the world, are looking to us for the secret of our success in 'cost-containment'. Without a deeper understanding of the dynamics of priority-setting and resource allocation mechanisms in different systems, it is very dangerous to think that you can graft selected bits of one system onto another and assume that the rest of the system will 'accept' the transplant and otherwise behave as before.

So much for the very wide scope of health economics as a topic, but what grounds do I have for encouraging people to be *cheerful* about the role of health economics, rather than being hostile or suspicious, which might be their more natural reactions.

I think a lot of the suspicion about health economics, and about health economists, is the belief that our view of people is simply that they are (potentially) productive resources, that their value stems solely from that attribute, and therefore that the most cost-effective way of caring for the elderly (or the mentally or physically handicapped) is to kill them off as quickly and cheaply as possible. If that were in fact our position, we should undoubtedly deserve any hostility or suspicion that came our way, but fortunately it isn't.

The general objective, in normative micro-economics, is to ensure that the value of what people get from an activity is greater than the value of what they have to sacrifice in order that it be pursued. Since a sacrifice is fundamentally a benefit forgone, then our objective can alternatively be seen as trying to ensure that benefits gained outweigh benefits forgone. This is also the objective of normative health economics, and formulating it in that way puts benefit valuation, quite properly, at the centre of our attention. The benefits to be derived from health care are better health, by which I mean both improved quality of life and improved length of life. Some of this improved health may be used by people to earn money (i.e., for work), but it may equally be used simply to enjoy life (and lucky indeed are the people – like me – who find their work enjoyable in itself, for they have the best of both worlds). So our starting point is that health is valued 'for its own sake', not just as a source of income. This fundamental aspect of health can be measured in terms of quality-adjusted life years, when the 'quality-adjustment' might take the following form: suppose that a year of healthy life expectancy is worth 1, then a year of unhealthy life expectancy will be worth less than 1, and will be rated lower the worse is the person's quality of life. Quality of life could be rated in terms of physical mobility, capacity for self-care, absence of pain and distress, ability to perform normal social roles, etc., and, if being dead is rated as 0, it is not uncommon to find that some people rate some very bad states as worse than dead (i.e., on the above scale they would have *negative* values). So if we were measuring the cost-effectiveness of alternative patterns of health care provision for the elderly, we would measure effectiveness by the expected gain in quality-adjusted life years (or QALYs, for short), not by anything as crass as their contribution to GNP, which might be nil throughout.

But you don't normally get anything for nothing in this world, and it is likely that extra QALYs lead to extra costs. The notion of cost is a tricky one here, because in economics it is a much broader concept than expenditure. Expenditure simply means money spent, and the raising and spending of money is the subject matter of accountacy and finance. The subject matter of economics is the deployment of real resources, whether they cost money or not. Health services do not pay for the use of patients' time, yet it is an essential input into the health care system, and is generally a resource with valuable alternative uses (except for the pathological cases who regard undergoing medical treatment as the most enjoyable way to spend your life!). Perhaps if health services *did* pay for the use of patients' time we should see a welcome reform in the way outpatient clinics and GPs' and dentists' appointments systems are organised. But let me not be deflected further from my main theme, which is that the economist's notion of cost is much broader and deeper than the accounting notion of expenditure, hence it is rather more difficult to measure and value.

Suppose we have solved all these knotty problems, however, and were in a position to say that, at the margin (e.g., if we expanded some treatment activity by a small amount) the cost of a QALY (quality-adjusted life year) for a range of activities was something like this:

Activity *A*	£15000 per QALY gained
Activity *B*	£ 8000 per QALY gained
Activity *C*	£ 3500 per QALY gained
Activity *D*	£ 2000 per QALY gained
Activity *E*	£ 1000 per QALY gained
Activity *F*	£ 750 per QALY gained
Activity *G*	£ 200 per QALY gained

Does it then not seem natural to say that if we want to improve people's health as much as possible (i.e., maximise the number of QALY's gained) we should first of all expand Activity *G* to the limit, then *F*, then *E*, and so on, and when we run out of resources, stop. Suppose we got as far as Activity *C* before we ran out of resources, then we would *implicitly* be saying that we think a QALY is worth £3500 (because at that level we are not willing to put more resources into health care). Note that this cut-off point has nothing to do with people's productivity, for the beneficiaries of Activity *C* might be utterly 'useless' from the narrow viewpoint of their contribution to GNP.

There are, of course, some barely hidden complications in this simple-minded view of the world. The first of these is that one QALY is assumed to be of equal value to everybody. This is obviously a convenient analytical assumption, but it has to be judged not in those terms, but whether you believe that to be the appropriate ethical position for a health service to adopt. If not, what position do you think it should adopt? More complex ethical positions will of course require more complex calculations, but that is a minor matter. Secondly, as you expand an activity, and take on less and less promising cases for treatment, the effectiveness of treatment falls, hence cost per QALY rises, so the above table of numbers may well change as activity rates change. Thirdly, costs-per-QALY may change if the resources used in them become more or less expensive, so the cost-effectiveness of a treatment depends on 'economic' as well as on 'medical' considerations. So, it may be that expanding an activity generates economies of scale which more than outweigh the reduced effectiveness of the activity on marginal patients (i.e., costs fall faster than effectiveness). Fourthly, it may be that activities such as *A* and *B*, though very expensive in terms of cost-per-QALY *now*, are subject to rapid development, either of an effectiveness-improving kind or of a cost-reducing kind, and need to be kept going (on a small scale at any rate) to allow this development work to proceed. Here one is essentially investing resources now in *future* cost-effectiveness. This argument has two important corollaries however, firstly that it is inapplicable to rather stable activities with little prospect of technological breakthrough, and secondly that it implies that the activity should be conducted as a pursuit of knowledge (not as a proven therapy) hence be subject to proper research protocols, full disclosure of data, and evaluated for its cost-effectiveness by independent researchers, *not* by the protagonists of the activity.

In fact the activities I listed above are as follows:

A   hospital haemodialysis
B   heart transplantation
C   kidney transplantation
D   coronary artery bypass grafting
E   pacemaker implantation
F   hip replacement
G   GPs trying to persuade every smoker who visits them to stop smoking

The estimates are a bit rough and ready, and the costs are mainly service costs. It may be of interest to note that Activity *B* is regarded as experimental, but Activity *A* not! In looking again at that data you may also like to bear in mind that the *average* amount of GNP per head available to keep each of us going for a whole year is about £5500.

So we come back to GNP again, as of course we must, but not in order to grade people in order of priority, but in order to decide what we can afford. That is not a decision on which economics as a discipline can offer an answer, though obviously if we are prepared to say that improved length and quality of life are the objectives of all our activities, then in principle cost per QALY rules OK over the entire realm of society's resource allocation decisions. Fortunately health economists have enough to occupy themselves with in the terrain they already inhabit, without needing to indulge any megalomaniacal fantasies they may have in that particular direction.

A recent book on the current state of medicine, by a very

well-informed medical scientist, was called *The End of the Age of Optimism*, so it may seem paradoxical that I should be swimming against the tide and arguing for the beginning of a mood of cheerfulness. My reason for so doing is that so far we have hardly begun to use the discipline of health economics for the improvement of the people's health. In a professional sense, this thought frustrates and sometimes even depresses me. But it means that there is great potential there waiting to be tapped, and, after all, we have only been in serious business as a subdiscipline for a couple of decades at most. As a professional group, we have youth and idealism on our side, though I must admit that my colleagues have an unfairly large share of the youth, which I try to compensate for by hogging an unfairly large share of the idealism. I think big gains have been made in the perceived relevance of the discipline of health economics to the problems of health and health care in this country, and I am confident that the contributions of my colleagues will demonstrate the value of what we have to contribute. We are *not* defeatist prophets of gloom and doom, obsessed with death and taxes, but active, and often creative, workers for improvement, concerned to improve the quality of people's lives to the maximum feasible extent. *That* is why I think that health economics is the cheerful face of the dismal science.

2 The Measurement of Inequality in Health

RAYMOND ILLSLEY AND JULIAN LE GRAND

Wherever reliable statistics exist, even in relatively prosperous and egalitarian societies, such as the countries of Scandinavia, they show that persons from poorer social strata and environments have higher death rates than their better-off peers (Kohler and Martin, 1985; WHO, 1986). In the countries of Western and Southern Europe, death rates have fallen over many decades and the expectation has been that the fall would be greatest in those socio-economic groups with the highest death rates, leading ultimately towards an equalisation of rates of death and age at death. In Britain, the National Health Service and the Welfare State were created largely to achieve that objective – along with its correlates of better health and an enhanced quality of life. For reasons of both social equity and of effectiveness in the funding and administration of our health and related social services, it is crucial to know how far equalisation of mortality between individuals and groups has been achieved.

The outcome is disputed. The Black Report (1980), the most comprehensive and informed review of the issue ever attempted, came to the conclusion that the disparity between social classes, defined by reference to occupation, had not decreased since the 1949–52 Census period, and indeed that the mortality of the semi-skilled and unskilled worker had actually deteriorated in comparison with that of the professional classes. The results of the analysis are even more disturbing in that, using the same methods and sources of data, it was apparent that the class gap could not have narrowed since the 1921 Census – and indeed might have widened. Almost the only major exception was a narrowing of the differential in child death rates as the rate itself fell to very low levels; some evidence to the same effect has emerged more recently for post-neo-natal deaths in legitimate births. Data from the 1981 Census and deaths in the years 1979–80 and 1982–3 appear to show a further widening of the gap (OPCS, 1986; Marmot and McDowall, 1986; Townsend, 1987), although major changes in social classification make it difficult to assess the degree of widening.

CLASS-BASED INEQUALITY MEASUREMENT

It is the interpretation of these facts, and not the facts themselves, that is disputed.[1] It is common ground that at each point in history, socio-economic inequality exists, that inequality in death exists and that one is related to the other. The disputed question is whether, over the whole period from 1921 to 1983, with its manifold political, social, economic changes and upheavals, inequality in mortality has narrowed, widened or stayed the same. It is also common ground that no reliable quantified data exist about health status or changes in health status over time, about the differential use of health services over time or about the possible effect of differential use on health or death. Indeed, one reason for analysing death rates over time is to throw some light on these questions.

One problem of interpretation relates to the measurement of social class. The need exists for a measure which summarises the individual's experience of poverty, wealth and standards of living. Over long time periods this is not available and as a proxy indicator individuals are allocated to their occupational category and that category is then grouped with others to form a 'class'. Not only is this group measure a very indirect indication of the individual's experience, but also it is not self-evident that in comparing class I in 1921 with class I in 1981 and in comparing each with its class V counterpart that we are comparing like with like. The measuring rod may change and our results may reflect that change rather than any changes in group health. This point is argued more fully below.

A further problem of interpretation concerns the meaning and measurement of equality. If equality is measured on the basis of differences between social groups (or socio-economic classes), is greater equality achieved if the size of the affluent (healthy) groups increases as a proportion of the population and the poor (unhealthy) groups decline? Or does inequality persist unchanged if the death rates of the extreme classes remain in the same relationship, even though the lowest class may have decreased to a small minority whilst the highest class has multiplied?

Both problems, although for different reasons, involve questions about the number and characteristics of socio-economic classes – the only social indicator available over time which can easily be related to death rates, and hence the indicator used by the Black Report and earlier investigators to measure disparities in death rates between social groups over time. The five occupational classes traditionally used by the Registrar-General are based on the occupations of the population at Census or (for deaths) on death registration certificates. They therefore reflect the occupational structure as it changes. Thus if occupations increase, the class to which they belong increases; and if they decrease or disappear, the class shrinks. We consider that the Black Report underestimated the possible impact of such changes. For the technical reason that the classification itself tends to be modified at each Census to take account of new occupations or changes in the status of existing occupations, there are pitfalls in comparing population figures across the decades. Nevertheless, it is on such figures that the 'widening-gap' claim is based: they are therefore relevant to its further discussion.

Table 2.1 (from Illsley, 1986), using data drawn from the Black Report, shows that, for males aged 15–64, occupational class I increased by 178 per cent, between 1931 and 1971, whilst class V decreased by 35 per cent. Lesser, but still substantial changes occurred in class II and class IV. Thus the low death rates of the upper classes now apply to a larger proportion of the population whilst the highest rates apply to a decreasing segment. This has been a continuous process across recent decades, each new cohort entering the labour market containing a higher ratio of class I to class V workers (Illsley, 1986). Using a definition of equality based on the total population, the maintenance of a stable ratio between class death rates alongside a growing upper segment could be regarded as increasing equality. The Black Report takes a more pessimistic definition by which inequality persists unchanged if relative death rates are maintained, even if the high rates apply to a shrinking lower segment; in this sense, inequality would remain unchanged if class V were reduced to one individual provided his/her risk of death remained unchanged *vis-à-vis* the remaining 55 million.

A further problem arises from the probability that changing relative sizes will be accompanied by changes in the relative status of classes, in recruitment criteria and in the typical characteristics of class members.

TABLE 2.1   *Distribution of economically active men by occupational class for England and Wales, 1931–71*

| Year | Occupational class | | | | | All Classes |
	I	II	III	IV	V	
1931	1.8	12.0	47.8	25.5	12.9	100
1951	2.7	12.8	51.1	23.3	9.7	100
1971	5.0	18.2	50.5	18.0	8.4	100
% change 1931–1971	+178	+52	+6	−29	−35	

Source: adapted from the Black Report (Black, 1980), Table 3.16.

The validity of inter-class comparison over the decades depends upon the assumption that class dividing lines hold the same status significance. How far can today's growing cadre of professional workers be regarded as the social counterpart of yesterday's elite? Equally, how far can today's small and decreasing group of unskilled workers be seen as the equivalent social counterpart of what used to be a substantial segment of the population? To what extent has the growth of class I led to social status dilution? Or the decline in class V caused it to be composed more concentratedly of social and health casualties?

Whilst we cannot reproduce the evidence here, one of the authors (Illsley, 1986) has shown both the very large amounts of inter-class mobility, and the way in which it leads to selective recruitment into classes between generations. Broadly speaking, those who rise from lower classes do so because their environment of upbringing is favourable; this is reflected in their social, physical and intellectual growth and development. Their departure from the lower classes is accompanied by a downward movement from those in the upper classes whose micro-environment has been less favourable. There thus occurs a constant inter-class exchange which serves to reinforce the characteristics of both classes. The net result, in terms of outcome (see Stern, 1983) depends upon the amount and directions of movement and the severity of selection. Provided selectivity remains the same, high social mobility is thus likely to produce greater inter-class inequality. Since the factors which encourage upward social mobility are also favourable to health (and *vice versa*) the continuous stream of inter-class movement reinforces class differences and the class gap in health.

TABLE 2.2   *Percentage distribution of age-at-death, England and Wales, 1921–83*

| Year | Age-at-Death | | | | |
	0–14	15–44	45–64	65+	*All ages*
Males					
1921	27	16	24	32	100
1931	16	14	28	42	100
1951	5	6	26	62	100
1971	4	5	26	65	100
1983	1	4	22	73	100
Females					
1921	22	17	21	40	100
1931	12	15	23	50	100
1951	4	6	18	72	100
1971	3	3	16	78	100
1983	1	2	13	84	100

A third problem arises because occupations cannot be given to persons aged 0 to 14, because the reported previous occupations of retired persons are known to be inaccurate and because, particularly in earlier decades, a large proportion of women were not gainfully employed. Most class-based analyses, including those of the Black Report are restricted to males aged 15 to 64 (or less frequently, married women aged 15 to 64 classified according to their husband's occupation). This means that conclusions about equality derived from class death rates are based on only a fraction of all deaths. Table 2.2 shows that in 1921, 27 per cent of males died before the age of fifteen, and 32 per cent died at sixty-five or later. The equivalent figures for 1983 were 1 per cent and 73 per cent. The change has been even greater for women. This means that the conclusions about increasing inequality in health between classes are founded on 40 per cent of male deaths in 1921 and 25 per cent in 1983 (38 per cent and 15 per cent for females). We must ask: what can be the meaning and validity of conclusions about inequality based on 15 per cent of all deaths? What effect, moreover, is produced by comparing data based on 38 per cent of deaths (1921) with data on 15 per cent (1983)?

Two types of exclusion are involved: young persons and elderly persons and their exclusion will have different impacts on the results. Infant death has been widely used as an indicator of poverty and this is true, but to a lesser extent, of childhood deaths. The exclusion of this category, which over our time period was reduced from 27 per cent of all deaths to 1 per cent, inevitably means an understatement of the reduction of poverty-related disease over time. It is, of course, true that until recent times, the death rates in each occupational class fell at the same rate so that in terms of the widening-gap theory, greater equality had not been achieved. On the other hand, in assessing the impact of either poverty or inequality in a population, it is curious not to include a process which led a quarter of deaths – and the bulk of premature deaths – to be eliminated.

The class gradient in the death rates of the 65+ age group is unknown. The Black Report quoted class death rates for the 65–79 age group derived from the OPCS Longitudinal Study. This shows a much attenuated and irregular class gradient, part of the irregularity being, perhaps, due to bias in the reporting of occupations. If the results were accurate, and taking into account of the size of the group (76 per cent of all deaths), its inclusion could have a major (narrowing) impact on the results.

In the absence of historical data a model can be developed to illustrate one major and misleading result of terminating the analysis at age sixty-four. Since, in the 15–64 age-group, class death rates have widened, the assumption has been that inequality has increased over the period studied. As mentioned earlier, this result is likely to be an artefact of the tool of measurement, i.e. occupational class. However, leaving this aside, another problem arises. Reduction in the general death rate, even if the reduction occurs at the same pace in each class, nevertheless does lead to a differential improvement in the survival of the lower occupational class. This is illustrated in Table 2.3 where two class cohorts are followed across two age periods (e.g. 20–29 and 30–39). Two differing assumptions are made about the level of death rates. The first example assumes class cohorts of equal size at the beginning of the period with death rates twice as high in the upper class as in the lower class. Death rates are increased in the second age group but still keep their two-to-one relationship. In the second example we assume that death rates are halved in each class in each age-period – the relationship of class deaths thus remaining unchanged at a lower level. For both examples we calculate (1) survival rates in each class at each age out of the initial cohort, and (2) the ratio of survival rates in the upper class to survival rates in the lower class.

Under the first set of assumptions, the ratio of class survival rates is 1:1.125 in the first age-group rising to 1.50 in the second age-group. When death rates are halved, the upper/lower class survival ratios are

TABLE 2.3 *Differential chances of survival to age 65*

Example	Class	Age-Group 1					Age-Group 2				
		Population	Death rate %	Survivors	Survival rate %	Ratio of class survival rates	Population	Death rate %	Survivors	Survival rate %	Ratio of class survival rates
A	Upper	1000	10	900	90.0		900	20	720	72.0	
	Lower	1000	20	800	80.0		800	40	480	48.0	
	All	2000	15	1700	85.0	1.125	1700	30	1200	60.0	1.50
B	Upper	1000	5	950	95.0		950	10	855	85.5	
	Lower	1000	10	900	90.0		900	20	720	72.0	
	All	2000	7.5	1850	92.5	1.06	1850	15	1575	78.8	1.19

reduced to 1:1.06 and 1:1.19. Thus although death rates have fallen at the *same* rate in both classes, the lower death rates produce a reduction in inequality in survival. Moreover, the process is cumulative with age, greater equality in the first age-period being re-inforced at the second period. Thus the increase in inequality in survival by age is reduced with each fall in death rates.

These examples demonstrate that the persisting or widening gap in 15–64 class death rates is compatible with increasing equality in survival if the general death rate falls – as indeed it did over the whole of the 62-year study period. There is, therefore, a choice: do we attach more importance to relative death rates in the ages 15–64 or to the relative chances of survival to age 65? The Black Report used death rates – but in discussing the importance of the topic it commented 'The duration of the human lifetime is one of the best means of approximating the lifelong pattern of health and whole populations.' We, too, feel that survival to a late age, or conversely the avoidance of premature death is the more important measure.

This process continues after the age of sixty-four. Hence any attempt to evaluate the nature and direction of events over the last six decades is inevitably incomplete, if it omits the increasing proportion of the population surviving until sixty-five or more. It is difficult to justify a cut-off point of sixty-four even in 1921: with mean age-at-death in England and Wales being sixty for men and sixty-nine for women. When, as in 1983, the mean ages-at-death had become seventy-one and seventy-seven, a cut-off point of sixty-four becomes even harder to support; for it means excluding the successes of social change, leaving judgements about the impact of change based on what remains to be done instead of what has been achieved.

INDIVIDUALLY-BASED INEQUALITY MEASUREMENT

So far we have argued that class-based inequality measurement has certain intrinsic defects that make it difficult, if not impossible, to draw any unambiguous conclusions about trends in inequality in health over time. An alternative method of measurement based on differences between individuals, rather than between groups such as classes, has been developed in the literature on the measurement of inequality in income and wealth (for a selection, see Atkinson, 1980). Although not without problems of its own, use of this methodology avoids many of the difficulties that beset class-based measures, as we shall now try to demonstrate.[2]

The first task is to select an indicator of health that can be attached to individuals, in a way that, for instance, income or wealth holdings can be attached. This immediately distinguishes the approach from methods of measurement we have been discussing so far; for these have relied on indicators only applicable to groups, such as mortality rates. If the focus is on mortality as a measure of health, then an appropriate individual indicator would seem to be length of life, or age-at-death; and it is on this that we shall concentrate in what follows.

The second task is to choose an inequality measure or index. There are a wide variety of such measures, including the variance, the coefficient of variation, the index of dissimilarity, the Gini coefficient, and 'welfare' based measures such as the Atkinson and Kolm indices. With such a profusion of possibilities, it is necessary to have some procedure for choosing between them. The procedure adopted here is to list the set of properties that it would be desirable for an index to possess for the task in hand, and then to choose the index that has as many of these properties as possible.

What are the properties that it would be desirable for an inequality measure defined by age-at-death to possess? We may identify three. First, *population independence*. If we are comparing two distributions with different populations, but with the same proportion of the population dying at any given age, the inequality measure should remain unchanged. The desirability of this property should be readily apparent: if we are comparing changes in distribution over time, we do not want the results to be 'contaminated' by changes in the overall population size.

A second property, generally considered desirable in the income distribution literature, is the *principle of transfers* (Cowell, 1977, pp. 64–71). This is the property that a transfer of income from a rich individual to a poor one should always reduce inequality. Since it is impossible directly to transfer age-at-death from one individual to another in the sense that income can be transferred, we cannot take on this property literally. It is possible to devise a parallel property, however, which we might term the *principle of differences*. Consider two distributions, say at different time periods, with identical size populations and with the same numbers dying at any given age, except for two individuals in each period. In one period, the difference between the ages-at-death of the two exceptional individuals is greater than the differences between the ages-at-death of the two exceptional individuals in the other period. Then measured inequality should be greater in the case of the first period than the second. This principle says, roughly, that the larger the 'distances' between the inhabitants' ages-at-death in a time period, the greater should be that period's measured inequality. As such it seems a relatively mild requirement. However, the introduction of the concept of 'distance' does raise a number of other issues that we should mention at this point.

The first concerns the notion of distance implicit in measures such as the variance, the coefficient of variation and in the index of dissimilarity. These consider only differences in ages-at-death from the mean age-at-death: a limited and apparently rather arbitrary distance concept. Moreover, the first two add a further element of arbitrariness by squaring those differences. On the other hand, the Gini coefficient, for instance, incorporates the difference between *every pair* of ages-at-death, a perhaps more reasonable concept of distance.

However, even this concept has its peculiarities. For any measure based on it is sensitive not simply to the distance between ages-at-death but also to the numbers of individuals whose ages-at-death fall within that distance. This implies that, for instance, the value of the Gini coefficient would be more sensitive to differences in distance that occurred in densely populated parts of the age-at-death distribution (such as the very early and the very late years) than to differences that occurred in relatively sparse parts. Whether this is a desirable or undesirable property will depend on the priorities of the user.

A third property borrowed from the income distribution literature is that of *scale independence*. There it is argued that if everyone's income has changed by the same proportion, there has been no essential change in the distribution and hence there should be no change in the inequality measure. The equivalent in our context is the requirement that if the distribution of age-at-death in one period differs from that in another simply by a scale factor then there should be no difference in measured inequality.

The desirability of scale independence has been challenged, even within the income distribution literature (Kolm, 1976). And, indeed the rationale for concentrating on proportional differences, rather than, say, absolute differences, is not immediately apparent – particularly in the case of length of life or age-at-death. An alternative to scale independence that might be as useful in the health context is *translation independence*. This is the requirement that if one period's age-at-death distribution were the same as another's except for a constant term there should be no difference in measured inequality.

Thus, if, for example, two periods had different mean ages-at-death, but had the same absolute differences between individuals' age-at-death, inequality measures with this property would show no difference between them.

Almost all of the common inequality measures, including the Gini coefficient and the variance, have the first two properties. Of the measures listed earlier, all except the variance possess the third property; only the variance possesses the fourth. Since it is not clear which of the last two properties is most desirable in the health context, it seems sensible to use at least one measure with each property. Among the common measures, this confines us to the variance for translation-independence; the choice is wider for scale-independence, but partly on the grounds of familiarity and partly because of the superiority of the distance concept involved, we shall select the Gini coefficient.

Before we present the results, however, it should be noted that there have been other attempts to apply summary statistics of this kind to the problem of health inequality measurement, notably those of Preston, Haines and Pamuk (1981), Pamuk (1985) and Koskinen (1985). The statistics used include the Gini coefficient, the index of dissimilarity and what Pamuk terms the slope index of inequality. The methodology employed is rather different from that used here, however, and it is as well to be aware of the key differences.

In order to effect the comparison, we concentrate on the use of the Gini coefficient by Preston, Haines and Pamuk (PHP) and on the slope index of inequality by Pamuk; the essential points apply to the other measures used. PHP use mortality data grouped by social class to obtain points with which to construct a Lorenz curve. Specifically, 'classes are first ordered according to their degree of mortality, from low to high. For each of the time periods under consideration (1921–72, for England and Wales), mortality decreases monotonically from social class V to social class I. The X-axis represents the cumulative percentage shares of the total population attained by the ranked social classes and the Y-axis represents the cumulative percentage shares of the total age-standardised deaths. The points thus plotted are connected by a series of straight lines to form the Lorenz curve itself' (p. 248).

The first difference between this procedure and that used in this paper is that PHP use (the cumulative percentage of) total deaths on the Y-axis, whereas we use (the cumulative percentage of) years lived. The latter is, of course, a function of the former; but it is also a function of the number of years associated with each death. The use of number of deaths alone, as PHP do, has some curious aspects. First, it implies that complete equality will be achieved when *x* per cent of the population has *x* per cent of the deaths (the index of dissimilarity, as they use it, has the same implication). Given that the one certain fact of our existence is that it will come to an end, this interpretation of equality will always be achieved if the time period concerned is sufficiently long. The interpretation, and the procedure based on it, makes a little more sense if the time period is only a year; the Lorenz diagonal, and thus complete equality, then corresponds to *x* per cent of the population having *x* per cent of the deaths per year. Even this has its peculiarities, however. For instance, complete equality under this interpretation would be achieved if, for instance, there were the same number of deaths per year in the two halves of the population, but with all the deaths in one half being infant deaths, and all the deaths in the other being at three score years and ten.

The other major difference between the PHP procedure and that described above is the use of social classes as a means of grouping the data so as to construct the inequality measures. This means that the measures take no account of *intra*-group variation, and hence that they will underestimate 'true' inequality. PHP are aware of this problem and endeavour to overcome it by re-doing one of their calculations using a much finer occupational classification, with 182 occupational units. The effect is almost to double the Gini coefficient and *virtually to eliminate the time trend they claim to have observed*; an outcome that illustrates the magnitude of the problem.

This raises the question as to the role of these groupings in the first place. The procedure of using data based on occupational groupings ranked in terms of mortality is complex and, as PHP's own calculations exemplify, the results are sensitive to the classification procedure chosen. This fact alone makes the procedure difficult to use for comparisons over time.

It might be thought that the use of social class does, at least, mean that the procedure enables us to gain some insight into inequality between the classes. However, this would be incorrect. For occupation is only serving as a means of grouping the data; the rankings that result are based purely on mortality and not on status or any other considerations that might determine social class. This can be seen from the fact that, if there was a class-reversal such that, say, social classes I and V 'swapped' their share of age-standardised deaths, the PHP measure would remain unchanged. This is also true of the methodology used here; but it provides no reason for choosing one over the other.

Pamuk's work is more sophisticated. There 143 occupation units are ranked according to the Hope–Goldthorpe classification scale and a weighted least squares procedure is used to estimate a regression line, relating mortality rates to position in the (cumulative) proportionate ranking. The slope of this line is interpreted as a measure of inequality; when estimated using the same data as the Black Report, the slope increases over time, thus supporting its conclusions.

This does appear to overcome the problem of changing class sizes that was noted earlier, and, as such, represents a significant improvement on previous work. However, it does not resolve many of the other problems to which we have drawn attention, notably the omission of any information concerning mortality outside the limited age ranges considered, the omission of *intra*-group variation, and the focus on mortality rates rather than age-at-death. Nor does it go beyond the question of changing size to take account of the changing criteria of recruitment to classes with its associated selectivity. It is still, therefore, a long way from providing us with definitive answers to the question to which it is addressed.

In short, it is not obvious that there are any advantages to adopting these methods of approach, while there are distinct disadvantages to doing so. In any case, whatever their merits or demerits compared to those of the methodology employed in this paper, they are clearly rather different from that methodology. Hence any results obtained from using the methodology are unlikely to duplicate or replicate previous work.

RESULTS: ALL CAUSES

Figures 2.1, 2.2 and 2.3 show the trends in mean age-at-death, the variance and the Gini coefficient for all men and women in Scotland, England and Wales for the 1921–83 period and, to complement the class analysis, the same trends for males aged 15–64 in England and Wales. To facilitate comparison, the figures are drawn on a semi-logarithmic scale. The estimates on which they are based are provided in Table 2.4; the details of the methods of calculation can be found in the Appendix. The following points may be noted:

1. With very few exceptions there is a continuous increase in the mean

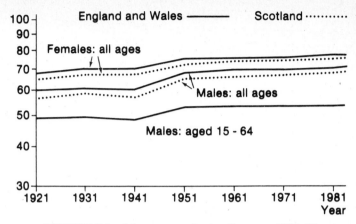

FIGURE 2.1   *Mean age-at-death, all causes, 1921–83*

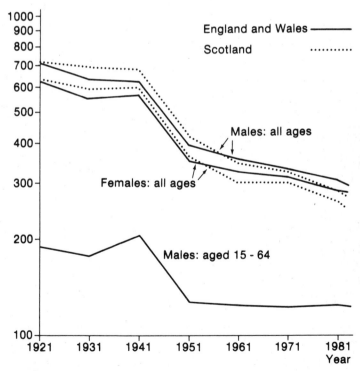

FIGURE 2.2   *Inequality in age-at-death, all causes, 1921–83, variance*

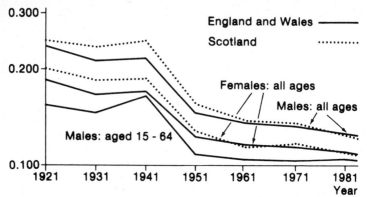

FIGURE   2.3   *Inequality   in   age-at-death,   all   causes,   1921–83,   Gini co-efficient*

age-at-death over the period, regardless of gender, country or type of distribution. The exceptions all concern 1941, when there are falls in the mean for male deaths in England and Wales and Scotland, and for the equivalent for females in England and Wales; the reasons why that year might be exceptional are not hard to find.

2. Again, with the exception of 1941, there is a continuous fall in inequality over the period, *however or wherever it is measured*. Both for Scotland and England and Wales, both for males and females, and both the variance and the Gini coefficient show a continuous decline in all cases. The largest fall occurs between 1941 and 1951, suggesting that, while the immediate effects of war might have been to create greater inequality, its subsequent effects were quite the reverse.

3. In both England and Wales and Scotland there was consistently greater inequality among males than females; but there was a degree of convergence over time – most pronounced in the case of the Gini coefficient.

4. Although there is greater inequality at the beginning of the period in Scotland for both males and females than in England and Wales, by the end of the period the gap had completely disappeared – indeed, according to the variance it had actually reversed.

5. There is generally a lower degree of inequality in the 15–64 male age-group; but that inequality stopped falling in 1951, whence it has remained virtually static.

TABLE 2.4 *Inequality in age-standardised age-at-death: all causes England and Wales*

	Males: all ages*			Females: all ages		
Year	Mean	Variance	Gini	Mean	Variance	Gini
1921	59.98	712.11	0.237	68.87	624.27	0.185
1931	62.64	638.56	0.212	70.63	552.15	0.167
1941	61.79	628.66	0.216	70.31	562.66	0.170
1951	68.40	393.58	0.147	75.59	351.88	0.122
1961	69.11	354.96	0.137	76.19	323.19	0.116
1971	69.49	331.18	0.132	76.25	314.17	0.115
1981	70.26	306.59	0.127	76.84	285.26	0.110
1983	70.40	296.40	0.125	76.84	280.19	0.109

* Estimates for males 15–64 obtainable from the authors.

The first two points are particularly significant. For they show that over the last sixty years for the population as a whole *there has been an almost continuous rise in the mean age-at-death and a fall in its dispersion.* This combination of a simultaneous increase in the length of life of the average individual, and a reduction in the differences between individuals' lengths of life is a major social phenomenon, whose importance should not be underestimated.

However, although these results may be significant in terms of assessing the contribution of changes in mortality to improvements in general social welfare, they do not directly answer the question with which we begun this paper: what has happened to inequality in mortality between different socio-economic groups in the population? Is there any way in which those results – or, more generally, the methodology used to obtain them – can be applied so as to offer some insight into this issue?

Some clues can be obtained from Table 2.2. There it is apparent that much of the fall in the overall dispersion of age-of-death from 1921 to 1983 is likely to be a result of the sharp reduction in the number of deaths in childhood: from 27 per cent for males and 22 per cent for females to 1 per cent for both. Since childhood mortality is heavily – and negatively – correlated with socio-economic status, it seems likely that this reduction has improved the mortality experience of those at the bottom of the social scale relative to those at the top. This point is reinforced if we examine variation in *causes* of death, as we illustrate in the next section.

RESULTS BY CAUSE OF DEATH

Data on cause of death are subject to changing knowledge, changing practices of recording and the many revisions that have taken place in the International Classification of Diseases (ICD). Discussing these limitations, the authors of a recent OPCS Report (1978) recommended that 'long-term comparisons are sometimes best confined to broad and well-recognised disease groups'. Comparisons of this kind for nine main disease groups for 1931, 1951 and 1973 are illustrated in Figure 2.4, drawn from the same report. The authors commented: 'The most striking feature of the comparison is the virtual disappearance of mortality due to infective diseases and to maternal causes, together with the reduction in the relative frequency of deaths due to respiratory, digestive and genito-urinary disease. To complement these decreases there have been increases in mortality due to three cause-groups, circulatory disease, neoplasms and accidents; between them these causes now account for 75 per cent of all deaths.'

These changes are reflected in our results. The variance and Gini coefficient were estimated for six major disease categories: infectious diseases, lung cancers, all other cancers, respiratory diseases, circulatory diseases and injuries due to accidents and poisonings. Between them these accounted for 92 per cent of all male deaths in 1983 and 89 per cent of all female deaths. The results are available from the authors; those for the variance are illustrated in Figures 2.5 and 2.6.

What would otherwise be a steep and continuous decline in the indices for infectious disease was interrupted by a re-classification of the ICD in 1968. Respiratory disease shows a steep and continuous decline reflecting the virtual eradication of TB deaths in the earlier years and at young ages, and the diminished importance of pneumonia and bronchitis in the elderly population of more recent years. The indices for accidents persist around the same level, although their nature varies, owing less to occupational hazards in recent years and more to traffic accidents and violence. The increase in the number of deaths due to malignant neoplasms apparent in Figure 2.3 stems from the increase in lung cancers. The inequality indices for lung cancer initially declined, perhaps reflecting the spread of smoking from the middle to the working class, but have increased again, perhaps because of the recent decline in middle-class habits. Other cancers, an extremely varied cause group, show little change in the inequality

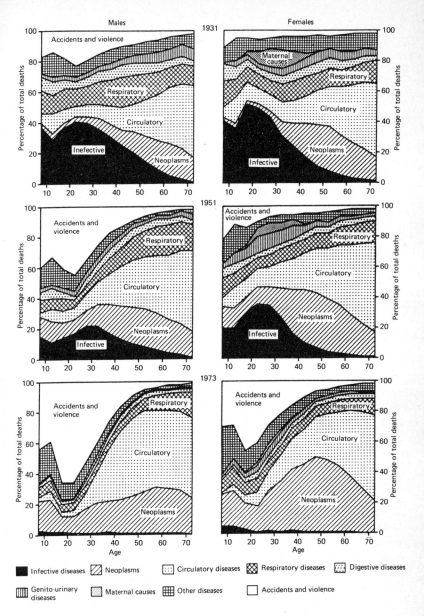

FIGURE 2.4 *Mortality by cause, age and sex, 1931, 1951, 1973*
Source: OPCS (1978).

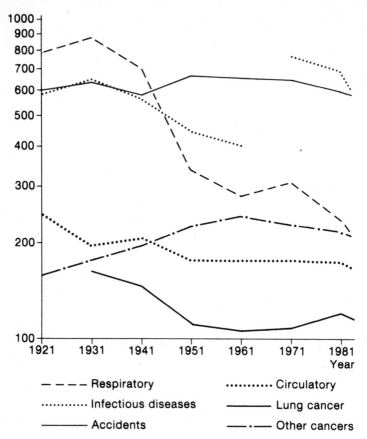

FIGURE 2.5 *Inequality in male age-at-death, selected causes, 1921–83, variance*

indices. Circulatory diseases, over the study period, have become the major cause of death; the inequality indices show stability, but it is a stability derived from the balancing of opposed trends, an increase in death rates under sixty-five and a decrease at later ages.

Now, of the groups for which inequality indices have been calculated, the two disease groups with, historically, the strongest relationship to socio-economic deprivation are infectious diseases and respiratory diseases, and the two with the least are cancers, excluding lung cancer, and circulatory diseases. Figures 2.4, 2.5 and 2.6 show that infectious diseases and respiratory diseases have fallen the most, both in absolute numbers and in the inequality indices, whereas

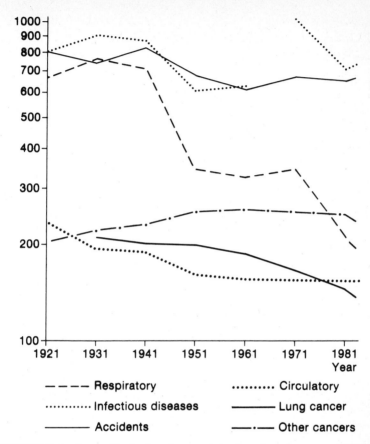

FIGURE 2.6   *Inequality in female age-at-death, selected causes, 1921–83,
variance*

cancers excluding lung cancer and circulatory diseases have fallen the
least – again both in absolute numbers and in the inequality indices.
Hence we would expect the relationship between inequality in overall
mortality and socio-economic deprivation to have weakened over
time. In other words, the reduction in the importance in the diseases
most associated with poverty would suggest that the differences in
mortality between poor and rich had systematically declined over
time: a conclusion that conflicts with the outcome of class-based
analyses.

The argument can be taken further. It is a useful property of the
variance that it can be 'decomposed', so as to permit analysis of

inequality within and between groups of the population (Cowell, 1977, pp. 165–7). Use of the appropriate decomposition formula yields the conclusion that in 1921, 32.8 per cent of the overall variance for men and 30.2 per cent for women arose from infectious diseases and respiratory diseases, whereas by 1983, the corresponding percentages were only 11.5 per cent and 11.4 per cent. Over the same period, the proportion of the overall variance arising from circulatory diseases and neoplasms (including lung cancers) rose from 7 per cent for males and 9.7 per cent for females to 42.4 per cent and 44.7 per cent respectively. Since circulatory diseases and neoplasms are more evenly distributed between the classes than infectious or respiratory diseases, it would be likely that, even if there had been *no* fall in the overall variance, age-at-death would be much more evenly spread between the classes. The fact that, in actuality, the overall variance fell as well, simply reinforces the point.

Now, as pointed out by OPCS, interpretation of the increasing cause groups (neoplasms, circulatory diseases and accidents) need to be handled with caution. Some diseases show absolute increases in age specific death rates over the period, others only relative increases, i.e. they increase as a proportion of all deaths because of the absolute decline in other categories. Some increase (or decrease) only within certain age bands. The precise significance of these changes has yet to be calculated. What seems certain, however, is that the diseases which have decreased in size and in inequality were more strongly related to poverty in the earlier decades than those which have increased to take their place as the major cause of death.

This interpretation could be challenged. In particular, it could be argued that the reduction in inequality consequent upon the virtual elimination of infectious disease as a cause of death has been replaced by the increased relative importance of other diseases, such as circulatory disease and lung cancer, which are themselves class-related. For example, a class reversal occurred during the 1950s in the incidence of coronary heart disease, the death rates for this condition being lower in social class V than in social class I in 1949–53, but higher in 1959–63. The question is whether such changes could have offset the increase in equality caused by the decrease in the traditional lower class diseases. Given that the mean ages-at-death for infectious diseases over the whole period, and those for respiratory diseases in the earlier part of the period, were lower than for circulatory diseases and for all forms of cancer, it seems likely that the switch from the former to the latter as a cause of death among the poor will have raised the average age-at-death relative to that of the better off and hence have reduced inequality. We do acknowledge, however, that this question deserves further examination.

CONCLUSION

Research into inequalities in health has had a long history. One question highly relevant to social policy has recurred many times, that is, have the effects of socio-economic status and experience upon health diminished or increased over time? For lack of better data, health has been measured in terms of death rates and individual social status and experience has been summarised in group membership – occupational class. Our analysis of class-based inequality at death in the first part of our paper suggests that the results obtained are likely to have been misleading because the occupational class measure has its own properties (size, inter-class distance, selection) which contaminate the results and because it involves the exclusion of significant categories of the population from analysis. In general, the properties of the measure have tended towards an artefactual widening of the gap in mortality between classes. It may well be justifiable to claim that in recent history, unemployment and associated changes in the distribution of wealth and welfare provision have brought about increases in health inequality; but the extension of the argument back to 1921 is inherently improbable.

With respect to this last point, we must emphasise that the findings and the argument presented in this paper have been developed to explain the behaviour of class death rates over a sixty-two-year period, encompassing fundamental political, economic, social, medical and technological changes and events. Whilst they have relevance to the events of the last decade, they are not specifically focused upon them and they were finalised before the results of the recent decennial supplement on occupational mortality became known.

In the paper we have also explored the properties of other indices of inequality based on individuals rather than groups. We are clear that these indices do not address the same problems as that addressed by class death rates. In particular they do not pretend directly to measure the efforts of social and economic inequality. The only data fed into the calculations are the ages at death of individuals. The results are various measures of age at death and the distribution of death across the whole span of human lifetime. They record an increasing avoidance of premature death and indeed a changing perception of the age at which deaths might be regarded as premature. Further they show a substantial reduction in inequality in age-at-death; itself a social fact of significance, independently of the relationship to social and economic inequality.

The tool itself is neutral. Explanatory power is likely to be derived from its use in sub-categories of deaths. In the present paper we have only explored cause-of-death categories over time. This suggests that increasing equality in the total population derived largely from changes in two major categories of disease, infectious diseases and respiratory diseases, both of which have always been strongly related to conditions of living, and both of which have declined sharply in their incidence. Further development of the tool depends upon the ability to apply it to a variety of categories, such as country, region and class. An attempt has been made to apply it to the task of international comparisons (Le Grand, 1987); we plan to explore the possibility of applying it to social class itself in future work.

The social class measure attempted to accomplish too much in a single index – basically to summarise social, economic, medical and health history in a few statistics. Our individualistic measures also result in summary statistics. They, too, present only one aspect of the picture – albeit a rather different one. We would not, however, claim that they do more than this. What is needed is a variety of measures, including but not exclusively, those based on occupational class, to produce a more balanced and, it is to be hoped, ultimately more accurate, picture of trends in health inequalities than has hitherto been possible.

APPENDIX

The data are all taken from the relevant issues of the Registrar General's Annual Reports and OPCS Mortality Statistics Series DH2. The data were grouped in age ranges. It was assumed that the average age-at-death in each range was in the middle of the range. The last range (85+ for Scottish data and 80+ for England and Wales data) was open-ended; it was assumed that it 'closed' at 100. Two grouping assumptions were used. One, the upper bound, assumed that deaths were divided equally between the upper and the lower ends of each age range; the other, the lower bound, assumed that all deaths took place in the middle of the range. The mean of the two was taken as the final figure.

Results were calculated for actual and age-standardised distributions for male, female and aggregate (male and female) deaths. Those for age-standardised male and female deaths are presented in Table 2.4; those for actual deaths (male, female and aggregate) and for aggregate age-standardised may be obtained from the authors. The standardisation procedure was to calculate the deaths that would have occurred at each age in a particular year if its age-specific mortality rates had been applied to the age distribution of 1981.

Le Grand and Rabin (1987) present slightly different estimates for the Gini coefficient for most of the years investigated here. They were calculated under different assumptions concerning the closure of the open-ended age-range category, and used a different year for age-standardisation.

NOTES

We are very grateful to Christine Mullings, without whose tireless efforts this paper would never have been finished. Maria Evandrou and Ray Kobs provided indispensible programming assistance. Thanks are also due to Frank Cowell for the use of his inequality analysis package and also to Richard Wilkinson for helpful (if critical) comments. We alone, of course, are responsible for the paper's content.

The research was supported by the Welfare State Programme at the Suntory–Toyota International Centre for Economics and Related Disciplines, London School of Economics, and by The Economic and Social Research Council.

1. For an important recent contribution to the debate, and one that takes issue with several of the points raised here, see Wilkinson (1986).
2. For an earlier application of some of these techniques to the trends in British health inequality, see Le Grand and Rabin (1987); for an application to international comparisons of health inequality, see Le Grand (1986).

REFERENCES

Atkinson, A. B. (ed.) (1980) *Wealth, Income and Inequality*, 2nd edn, Oxford: Oxford University Press.

Black, D. (1980) *Inequalities in Health*, report of a research working group chaired by Sir Douglas Black, London: Department of Health and Social Security.

Cowell, F. A. (1977) *Measuring Inequality*, Oxford: Philip Allan.

Illsley, R. (1986) 'Occupational Class, Selection and the Production of Inequalities in Health', *Quarterly Journal of Social Affairs*, 2, 151–65.

Kohler, L. and Martin, J. (1985) *Inequalities in Health and Health Care*, Goteborg: Nordic School of Public Health.

Kolm, S.-C. (1976) 'Unequal inequalities', *Journal of Economic Theory*, 12, 416–42; 13, 82–111.

Koskinen, S. (1985) 'Time Trends in Case-Specific Mortality in England and Wales – An exploratory study', prepared for the International Union for the Scientific Study of Populations xx General Conference, 5–12 June, Florence, Italy.

Le Grand, J. (1987) 'Inequalities in Health: Some International Comparisons', *European Economic Review*, 31, 182–91.

Le Grand, J. and Rabin, M. (1986) 'Trends in British Health Inequality, 1931–83', in A. J. Culyer and B. Jonsson (eds), *Public and Private Health Services*, Oxford: Basil Blackwell.

Marmot, M. and McDowall, M. (1986) 'Mortality Decline and Widening Social Inequalities', *Lancet*, ii, 274–6.

Office of Population Censuses and Surveys (OPCS) (1978) *Trends in Mortality, 1951–1975*, London: HMSO.

Office of Population Censuses and Surveys (OPCS) (1986) *Occupational Mortality, 1979–80, 1982–83*, London: HMSO.

Pamuk, E. (1985) 'Social Class Inequality in Mortality from 1921–1972 in England and Wales', *Population Studies*, 39, 17–31.

Preston, S. H., Haines, M. R. and Pamuk, E. (1981) 'Effects of Industrialization and Urbanization on Mortality in Developed Countries', in International Union for the Scientific Study of Population, 19th International Population Conference, Manila, 1981, *Selected Papers*, Vol. ii, Liege.

Stern, J. (1983) 'Social Mobility and the Interpretation of Social Class Mortality Differentials', *Journal of Social Policy*, 12, 27–49.

Townsend, P. (1987) 'The Geography of Poverty and Ill-Health', Chapter 3 in this volume.

Wilkinson, R. G. (1986) 'Introduction', in R. G. Wilkinson (ed.), *Class and Health*, London: Tavistock.

World Health Organization (WHO) (1986) *The Health Burden of Social Inequities*, Copenhagen: World Health Organization.

3 The Geography of Poverty and Ill-Health

PETER TOWNSEND

The object of this paper is to review the significance of some recent work on inequalities in health for the development of better health policies both locally and nationally. There are a number of different groups undertaking research within the City of Bristol (for example, the University's Mental Health, Child Health, Geography, Sociology and Botany departments and the School for Advanced Urban Studies; the International Centre for Child Studies, and the City's Environmental Health Department). This paper draws on that work but draws particularly on a recent programme of research into the relationship between 'health and deprivation' by a team in the Department of Social Administration. Some of the results and implications of that research partly undertaken in collaboration with outside bodies – in the North of England and in London as well as in the City of Bristol, will be reported.

TWO TRADITIONS OF RESEARCH INTO INEQUALITIES OF HEALTH

In 1980 the report of a Government appointed Research Working Group on *Inequalities in Health* (The Black Report, 1980) was published. This attracted, and continues to attract, widespread attention not least for its conclusion that material deprivation and ill-health are highly correlated and therefore that health policies should be explicitly widened to include a set of measures to counteract deprivation – including improvements in the income of poor minorities and families with disabled or child dependants, better housing and measures to improve bad working conditions and poor environmental facilities as well as deal with pollution. The Working Group recognised that the correlation needed to be worked through in much greater detail, however, and they listed a range of recommendations for further research. (See ibid., Chapter 7, pp. 199–227, and recommendations nos 1, 2, 4, 6 on pp. 358–60.)

There are two traditions of research in Britain which have enlarged knowledge about the distribution of health and laid a basis for health care institutions. One is the tradition of research describing, and seeking to explain, the widely varying health of people living in different areas. In the nineteenth century a large number of studies of public health reviewed death rates from different diseases in particular localities (for example: Farr, 1841 and 1860; Chadwick, 1842; Engels, 1844). In fact, authority for this kind of work had been sealed with the publication of the first annual report of the Registrar General (1839). Interest in geographical variations gave impetus to the adoption of new public health policies because specific theories about those variations, like John Snow's proof that cholera was caused by impure water at the Broad Street Pump in 1849, could be put forward. In the depression years of the 1930s, such work on area inequalities in health came to play an important part in the nation's realisation of the need for a national health service (see, for example: Orr, 1936; M'Gonigle and Kirby, 1936; Titmuss, 1938).

In the 1970s and 1980s work on area inequalities in health has burgeoned. (For the 1980s see Bradshaw *et al.*, 1980; OPCS, 1981; Howe, 1982; Irving and Rice, 1984; Fox *et al.*, 1984; Townsend, Simpson and Tibbs, 1984; West of Scotland Politics of Health Group, 1984; Ashton, 1984; Thunhurst, 1985a and 1985b; Betts, 1985.) Such research was given fresh impetus by the Report of the Resource Allocation Working Party (DHSS, 1976). From 1971 the geographical framework used in the Census has permitted analysis by groupings based on enumeration districts (numbering 110 000 in that year) as well as by wards. The OPCS sponsored analyses which arranged small areas into socio-economic clusters (see for example, Webber and Craig, 1976). That has borne fruit in subsequent analyses – whereby thirty-six geographic clusters have been derived by grouping wards according to census variables (Webber, 1977; Morgan, 1983; Morgan and Chinn, 1983). However, others have raised doubts about the ultimate uses of such cluster analysis, arguing that they are not good alternatives to measures based on the circumstances of individuals (Fox, Jones and Goldblatt, 1984; and see Mays, 1986, pp. 16–17).

Area studies have therefore posed questions simultaneously both about the objectives of health policies and the distribution of health services. But they cannot yet be said to provide a sophisticated mapping of social structure and organisation in relation to health which represents a highly developed approach to scientific theory.

The second tradition of research has been into health in relation to social class. For Britain the work has covered most of the present century (Stevenson, 1928; Morris, 1975; Brotherston, 1976; Hollingsworth and Rogers, 1981; Stacey, 1977; Hart, 1985) and has been a feature of the Registrar General's Decennial Supplements on Mortality (see for example OPCS, 1978). In 1986 the theme has acquired a new impetus (Scott-Samuel, 1986), despite its depreciation in the latest of the Decennial Supplements (OPCS, 1986).

There have been a substantial number of studies in other countries. They provide what one overseas observer has described as 'undisputed evidence of a strong negative association between socio-economic status and the probability of death' (Koskinen, 1985, p. 1). The results are well-attested and produce rather similar 'gradients' for different countries, whether socio-economic status or class is defined according to occupation (OPCS, 1978; Saull, 1983), education (Kitagawa and Hauser, 1973; Holme *et al.*, 1980; Saull, 1983; Salonen, 1982), income (Holme *et al.*, 1980; Rogers, 1979; Salonen, 1982; Wilkinson, 1986b) or some combination of these (Valkonen, 1982; Holme *et al.*, 1980). The results apply to poorer countries and not only European and North American countries (United Nations, 1983; International Union for the Scientific Study of Population, 1984; for North America, see, for example, Kosa *et al.*, 1969; Antonovsky, 1972; and Kitagawa and Hauser, 1973).

The differentials apply to nearly all causes of disease, though the gradient is much steeper for some diseases than others. For Britain in earlier years the gradient was found to be reversed for a number of specific diseases, but these 'diseases of affluence' have now largely disappeared (The Black Report, p. 70). The same has been demonstrated for Finland (Valkonen, 1982). The diseases which no longer provide the exceptions include non-valvular heart diseases (Marmot *et al.*, 1978; Halliday and Anderson, 1979), peptic ulcer (Susser, 1962) and some malignant neoplasms (Logan, 1982). The microfiche tables provided by OPCS in 1986 (for example Tables GD 28, 31, 34, 35, 38 and 41) allow this development to be updated to the early 1980s (OPCS, 1986).

Strenuous efforts have been, and are being, made to clarify and begin to explain the class gradient. One theme in research has been that upward and downward social mobility depends in part on individual health. Ill people are presumed to descend and healthy people to ascend the occupational class scale. A further presumption is made that the perpetuation of inequalities of health between classes in Britain and in other countries is an artefact produced by the decline of unskilled and partly skilled classes at the foot of the social scale and the enlargement of the more prosperous skilled non-manual and manual classes. This theme has effectively been relegated to one of small importance by the reports on a longitudinal study by Fox and his colleagues (1982, 1985a and b) and research into specific grades of a single occupation like that of Marmot and his colleagues (1978, 1985, 1986) and by detailed analytical reviews of the evidence. 'Although there is evidence that social mobility is affected by ill-health and/or health potential, its contribution to observed class differences in health is probably always small in relation to the overall size of the mortality differentials. At older ages the condition may become almost insignificant' (Wilkinson, 1986a, p. 16).

A very different theme is that, far from over-stating the effects upon health of differences in material living standards, the occupational class measure understates them. In particular, designation by occupational class may conceal a trend towards greater inequalities of health which may be attributed to greater inequalities in economic position or living standards. First, with the decline of certain 'mass' occupations the variation in earnings within single occupations may now be more marked. When taken in conjunction with the spread of home ownership (and the inheritance of housing) to manual families, the variation of living standards within occupations may be greater than in previous decades. Second, there is some variation in earnings for different occupations within a single occupational class. Third, the risk of unemployment in the 1970s and 1980s introduces a further element of likely variation, certainly for manual groups, into occupational class as an indicator of living standards. Fourth, the substantial importance for some groups of employer fringe benefits is not shared by other groups. Finally, the increased number and proportion of female partners holding paid jobs introduces a major element of potential variation into the living standards of families classified to the same occupational category.

As a consequence, it can be concluded that rankings by occupational class 'understate the true impact of socio-economic inequalities on health' (Wilkinson, 1986a, p. 17). Such a conclusion is supported by the analysis of mortality among civil servants by Marmot and his colleagues (1978, 1985). Two other general analyses of trends over several decades have shown that since 1951 the widening class differences in mortality which were first properly described in the Black Report, are not a function of decreased social mobility (Koskinen, 1985; Pamuk, 1985). One of these reviews has also shown that the use of different classifications in drawing up a ranking by occupational class and the changing numbers in occupations made little impact on the trends in mortality differentials (Pamuk, 1985).

FINDINGS FROM CONTEMPORARY RESEARCH

The two traditions of area studies and social class studies are therefore fruitful but not, as I have tried to explain, unproblematic. This can be illustrated from current research research findings. I shall report some of the results from the programme of work within the University of Bristol's Department of Social Administration.

London

As part of a project on Poverty and the London Labour Market, financed initially by the GLC, the relationship between ill health and material deprivation is being investigated. Detailed information from a sample of the adult population in Greater London has been collected and is now being processed. As a basis for subsequent analysis we developed an index of material deprivation and have plotted the results for all 755 wards in Greater London. Figure 3.1 shows the distribution of multiple deprivation.

The index is based on four criteria:

1. percentage of economically active population unemployed;
2. percentage of households lacking a car (an income surrogate);
3. percentage of households not being owner-occupiers (a wealth surrogate);
4. percentage of households experiencing overcrowding.

These indicators of deprivation were combined into a single index using the standardised score (Z-score) technique. Table 3.1 shows the ten wards ranked most and least deprived, together with information about each of the components of the index. Figure 3.2 shows the

42

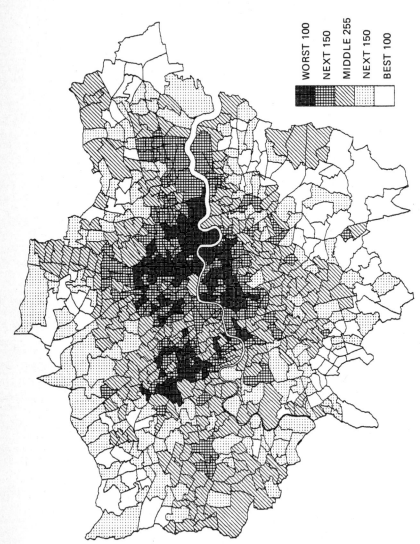

WORST 100

NEXT 150

MIDDLE 255

NEXT 150

BEST 100

FIGURE 3.1 *Wards ranked on multiple deprivation indicator*

TABLE 3.1 *London wards ranked high and low on measure of multiple deprivation (1981)*

Rank	Ward	Borough	Z-score index	Unemployed %	Overcrowded %	Not owning home %	Not owning car %
1	Spitalfields	Tower Hamlets	8.4	21.9	28.3	96.5	79.6
2	St Mary's	Tower Hamlets	6.9	19.5	16.5	95.2	74.0
3	Carlton	Brent	6.5	21.7	10.3	97.6	77.0
4	Golborne	Kensington & Chelsea	6.3	19.1	13.2	93.1	73.7
5	Shadwell	Tower Hamlets	6.3	17.3	14.1	98.1	71.3
6	Blackwall	Tower Hamlets	6.1	21.1	11.4	97.5	68.7
7	Haggerston	Hackney	6.1	18.0	13.2	97.3	72.1
8	St Katharine's	Tower Hamlets	6.1	15.4	15.7	97.1	69.0
9	White City	Hammersmith & Fulham	6.0	17.6	12.4	88.7	74.3
10	Kings Park	Hackney	5.9	19.3	11.5	97.8	68.1
746	Falconwood	Bexley	−8.8	3.2	2.1	2.4	25.4
747	Emerson Park	Havering	−8.8	4.3	1.3	6.0	16.3
748	Crofton	Bromley	−8.9	2.6	1.1	9.8	18.2
749	West Wickham North	Bromley	−9.1	3.1	0.6	10.0	18.5
750	Farnborough	Bromley	−9.4	3.2	1.1	7.8	15.0
751	Biggin Hill	Bromley	−10.0	3.1	2.0	9.9	7.9
752	Woodcote	Sutton	−10.0	4.8	0.7	14.5	6.6
753	Cheam South	Sutton	−10.7	2.8	0.6	8.9	11.0
754	Selsdon	Croydon	−10.8	2.6	0.5	6.7	13.5
755	Cranham West	Havering	−11.0	3.2	0.9	4.1	12.4

Source: Produced with the help of the London Research Centre (formerly GLC, now the London Residuary Body).

44

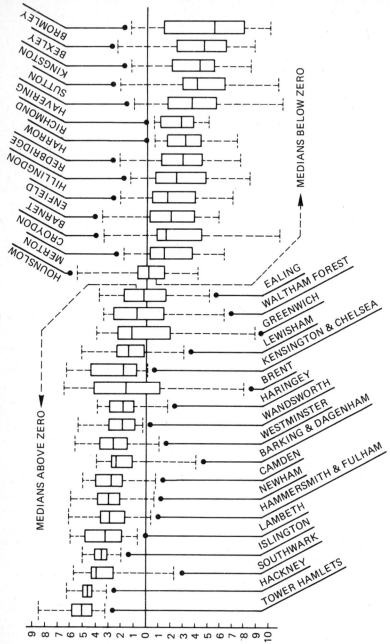

FIGURE 3.2   *Ranking of GLC wards on an index of poverty calculated from four indicators*

'spread' of wards, in terms of multiple deprivation, in each of the London boroughs. There is no overlap, for example, between wards in the richest and the poorest London boroughs.

In the broadest terms the results may not surprise some readers. Conditions in outer London suburbs, especially to the south and east are far better than those in the inner city – particularly in a band of wards running from Hackney and Tower Hamlets through to Lambeth. However, the method of amalgamating different indicators of deprivation allows London conditions to be described much more precisely and lays the basis both for comparison with indicators of health, and for subsequent follow up to determine the exact character and severity of such deprivation. For example, the index helps to demonstrate the polar extremes of material conditions of life within Greater London.

Table 3.2 shows mortality rates for the twenty-five London wards at either extreme of the scale of deprivation. (The data were worked out in collaboration with the London Research Centre, County Hall.) For age-groups under 65 crude mortality rates in the most deprived of the 755 wards were about double those in the least deprived wards. For the over-65s mortality rates were still higher – though less markedly. The correlation between material deprivation and mortality is further described in the interim report on this project (Townsend, 1987), and will be related to the evidence about individuals in the London population in the full report due in 1987–8.

TABLE 3.2 *Mortality rates 1982–4 in twenty-five most deprived and twenty-five least deprived London wards*

Ward	Borough	Crude mortality rates per 1000 population		
		Under 45	45–64	65+
Most deprived				
Spitalfields	Tower Hamlets	0.90	14.16	75.41
St Mary's	Tower Hamlets	1.57	18.92	54.55
Carlton	Brent	1.13	9.80	67.42
Golborne	Kens. & Chelsea	1.66	10.75	73.97
Shadwell	Tower Hamlets	1.70	14.23	77.40
Haggerston	Hackney	0.95	10.85	48.86
Blackwall	Tower Hamlets	0.94	10.75	59.68
St Katharine's	Tower Hamlets	1.68	13.81	66.96
Kings Park	Hackney	0.94	15.28	72.19
White City & Shepherds Bush	H'smith & Fulham	1.40	13.18	67.13

Ward	Borough	Crude mortality rates per 1000 population		
		Under 45	45–64	65+
Ordnance	Newham	1.49	14.84	67.99
Angell	Lambeth	1.83	13.37	67.48
Westdown	Hackney	1.03	10.56	69.92
St Dunstan's	Tower Hamlets	1.28	11.54	64.28
Liddle	Southwark	1.06	10.19	71.30
Harrow Road	Westminster	1.07	9.34	61.14
Eastdown	Hackney	1.07	11.50	48.04
Queen's Park	Westminster	1.67	11.35	61.39
Stonebridge	Brent	1.36	8.00	48.01
Larkhall	Lambeth	1.05	9.57	68.12
Rectory	Hackney	0.85	6.89	46.14
Avondale	Kens. & Chelsea	1.19	9.52	48.29
Weavers	Tower Hamlets	1.37	11.81	59.42
Vassal	Lambeth	1.15	10.45	93.39
Westbourne	Westminster	1.40	10.50	78.54
Mean of 25 wards		1.27	11.59	63.78
Least deprived				
Cranham West	Havering	0.35	7.02	55.91
Selsdon	Croydon	0.73	6.86	53.62
Cheam South	Sutton	0.43	6.21	106.02
Woodcote	Sutton	1.07	7.87	40.72
Biggin Hill	Bromley	0.61	8.06	50.34
Farnborough	Bromley	1.14	6.04	57.75
West Wickham North	Bromley	0.66	4.74	45.24
Crofton	Bromley	0.78	7.77	46.92
Emerson Park	Havering	0.62	5.48	54.58
Falconwood	Bexley	0.74	6.30	50.75
Malden Manor	Kingston	0.00	6.03	54.35
Ickenham	Hillingdon	0.85	7.14	52.69
Petts Wood and Knoll	Bromley	0.48	6.10	46.13
West Wickham South	Bromley	0.70	5.95	46.84
Upminster	Havering	0.52	7.00	50.92
Shortlands	Bromley	0.74	5.90	48.29
Woodcote and Coulsdon W.	Croydon	0.75	9.07	92.80
North Cheam	Sutton	0.15	6.92	46.51
Worcester Pk S.	Sutton	0.38	7.38	41.10
Monkhams	Redbridge	0.64	6.09	52.45
B'don & Penhill	Bexley	0.48	5.87	49.91
Pinner West	Harrow	0.35	6.30	42.60
Headstone North	Harrow	0.72	5.55	46.20
Tolworth East	Kingston	0.40	7.12	48.70
Ardleigh Green	Havering	0.81	4.84	47.44
Mean of 25 wards		0.62	6.56	55.52

Note: These are not age-standardised rates.
Source: London Research Centre.

The Northern Region of England

A second project was much larger in scope. In conjunction with the Statistics Branch of the Northern Regional Health Authority and financed by the Northern RHA a statistical analysis of the relationship between material deprivation and health has been completed for all 678 wards in the region (Townsend, Phillimore and Beattie, 1986). An index of material deprivation identical with that used in London was applied, but the analysis was not restricted to comparisons with mortality. An overall health index was developed to match that for material deprivation, and equal weight was assigned to each of the three components. Again, the 'Z-score' technique was used to deal with the problem of ranking on a combined measure of the three elements:

1. *mortality*: Standardised Mortality Ratios (SMRs) for persons (i.e. both sexes together) averaged over three years, 1981–3;
2. *disablement*: the proportion of all residents in private households aged 16 and over who classed themselves as permanently sick or disabled at the 1981 Census;
3. *delayed development*: the proportion of live births below 2800 gms, based on births over three years, 1982–4.

The full results are now available (Townsend, Phillimore and Beattie, 1986). They confirm the observed relationship between material deprivation and health but also develop certain aspects of that relationship for the North of England. First, a high correlation was found between mortality and other health variables, contrary to the impression sometimes conveyed in the continuing discussion of the merits of the Resource Allocation Working Party (RAWP) formula. The correlation (as measured by Spearman rank correlation coefficients) between mortality and permanent sickness or disability is particularly strong, but is also significant between each of these and low birthweight.

Second, as Table 3.3 illustrates, not only is the correlation between different indicators of material deprivation quite strong, but the correlation between overall ill-health and overall deprivation is very strong. Figure 3.3 illustrates the correlation in the form of a graph. Multiple deprivation in Tyne and Wear and in Cleveland is very marked. Among the most deprived 25 wards in the North of England as many as 13 are in Tyne and Wear and another 10 are in Cleveland.

Third, the four indicators of material deprivation each make a significant contribution towards explaining overall ill-health within the

TABLE 3.3 *The twenty-five wards with the greatest overall deprivation in the Northern Region (as defined and ranked by overall deprivation index)*

Rank	Ward	District	Urban or non-urban	Population	Unemployed 1981		Households with no car 1981		Households not owner-occupied 1981		Overcrowded households (over one person/room) 1981		Manual-class households 1981		Overall Health Rank
					%	Rank	%	Rank	%	Rank	%	Rank	%	Rank	
1	Palliser	Middlesbrough	U	5803	30.9	(6)	76.1	(12)	92.2	(23)	13.4	(1)	94.1	(1)	41
2	Thorntree	Middlesbrough	U	10410	36.7	(2)	76.6	(9)	95.9	(9)	8.3	(22)	93.3	(4)	40
3	West City	Newcastle	U	9267	29.8	(7)	84.3	(1)	97.1	(3)	7.9	(26)	86.6	(29)	2
4	Owton	Hartlepool	U	6296	29.7	(8)	73.2	(18)	95.2	(11)	8.4	(21)	91.5	(10)	14
5	Walker	Newcastle	U	11055	23.2	(49)	81.6	(2)	93.3	(16)	8.6	(17)	85.3	(42)	87
6	Church Lane	Langbaurgh	U	4612	28.4	(16)	68.2	(47)	91.7	(25)	8.9	(12)	85.1	(45)	25
7	Felling	Gateshead	U	9928	22.1	(62)	72.3	(21)	88.0	(33)	10.8	(4)	78.6	(124)	34
8	Town End Farm	Sunderland	U	11686	26.7	(21)	69.2	(40)	92.7	(20)	8.6	(18)	83.0	(71)	136
9	Monkchester	Newcastle	U	9289	21.1	(71)	78.3	(6)	88.7	(32)	8.9	(13)	85.8	(34)	63
10	St Hilda's	Middlesbrough	U	3844	32.9	(4)	78.2	(7)	66.8	(179)	9.4	(10)	84.6	(51)	11
11	Hardwick	Stockton	U	6015	25.9	(26)	69.5	(34)	96.4	(6)	7.8	(27)	91.5	(11)	52
12	Scotswood	Newcastle	U	10667	26.5	(23)	73.7	(15)	68.2	(157)	12.3	(2)	71.2	(227)	24
13	Woodhouse Close	Wear Valley	U	5505	23.5	(48)	67.0	(54)	86.7	(39)	10.9	(3)	78.8	(123)	5
14	Grangetown	Langbaurgh	U	4685	32.6	(5)	69.0	(43)	80.8	(65)	8.6	(19)	91.8	(8)	32
15	South Hylton	Sunderland	U	11664	27.2	(18)	67.4	(51)	86.8	(38)	8.8	(15)	81.3	(88)	99
16	Southwick	Sunderland	U	11285	25.1	(34)	69.7	(32)	83.0	(52)	9.6	(7)	83.2	(68)	109
17	Park End	Middlesbrough	U	6614	29.0	(11)	64.6	(61)	84.2	(48)	9.1	(11)	85.6	(36)	56
18	Thornley Close	Sunderland	U	12343	26.3	(24)	72.0	(23)	97.3	(2)	5.7	(73)	85.3	(41)	71
19	Riverside	North Tyneside	U	9614	25.6	(29)	76.3	(11)	84.6	(47)	6.5	(50)	82.3	(81)	39
20	Beechwood	Middlesbrough	U	5498	27.7	(17)	69.4	(37)	88.8	(31)	6.7	(42)	86.0	(32)	57
21	South Bank	Langbaurgh	U	6308	34.1	(3)	69.1	(41)	59.6	(244)	10.5	(5)	87.8	(21)	12
22	Pelaw	Durham	NU	2953	22.6	(55)	72.3	(20)	89.4	(29)	7.1	(35)	77.2	(141)	72
23	High Fell	Gateshead	U	9563	17.0	(137)	69.7	(33)	94.7	(13)	8.8	(14)	84.2	(55)	191
24	Castletown	Sunderland	U	10678	22.8	(51)	67.1	(53)	93.2	(19)	7.3	(29)	89.1	(16)	78
25	Bede	Gateshead	U	9235	22.7	(52)	77.2	(8)	84.6	(46)	6.6	(44)	82.3	(79)	4

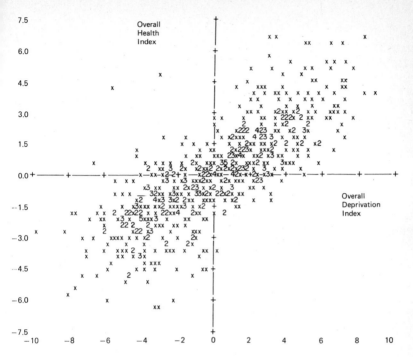

FIGURE 3.3 *Deprivation compared with health*
Note: Each X represents one of the 678 wards; a number instead of an X indicates that more than one ward is situated at that point.

Region. Using regression analysis the four indicators when combined were found to 'explain' 65 per cent of the variation among the wards in health, as measured by the three indicators of death, permanent sickness and delayed development. In Cleveland and Tyne and Wear the figure was found to rise to around 80 per cent.

Fourth, the correlation between material deprivation and ill health remains remarkably consistent for different sexes, age-groups, urban and rural areas and when deaths are grouped by cause. Table 3.4 shows the results of placing the 678 wards in five quintiles or ranks and comparing them on different component criteria of ill-health and deprivation. Figure 3.4 illustrates the step-wise gradient for each of the component indicators.

By grouping wards, the three most common causes of death in Britain today: all cancers combined (neoplasms); circulatory system diseases (which include heart attacks and strokes), and respiratory system diseases could be traced in relation to the overall measures of

TABLE 3.4 *Health and deprivation for ward groupings based on ranking of wards by overall health index*

	Worst health decile (68 wards)	Best health decile (68 wards)	Ratio Worst/ Best	Worst health Quintile (136 wards)	Next Quintile (136 wards)	Middle Quintile (134 wards)	Next Quintile (136 wards)	Best health Quintile (136 wards)
Persons 0–64 SMR (Actual number of deaths)	156.4 (4604)	69.8 (868)	2.2	142.6 (9231)	120.5 (6947)	107.3 (5419)	98.9 (4204)	79.9 (2341)
Residents 16+ permanently sick (%)	3.9	1.2	3.3	3.6	2.8	2.3	1.8	1.3
Live births under 2800 gms (%)	18.7	8.4	2.2	17.9	15.1	14.1	12.7	10.1
Unemployed persons 16–59/64 (%)	22.8	5.9	3.9	20.2	15.6	11.4	9.1	6.3
Households not owner-occupied (%)	76.4	27.1	2.8	72.9	60.5	50.1	35.7	24.9
Households with no car (%)	67.4	23.4	2.9	64.3	55.4	45.5	35.9	23.6
Households with more persons than rooms (%)	6.5	1.4	4.6	5.9	4.2	3.2	2.2	1.5
Households with head in manual class (%)	80.6	37.8	2.1	77.9	71.8	63.0	52.0	40.8
Households without exclusive use of bath and WC (%)	3.4	2.4	1.4	3.4	4.3	3.2	3.0	2.0
Households with single parent family (%)	7.9	3.1	2.5	7.2	5.6	4.8	3.9	3.3
Unemployed persons 16–24 (%)	29.3	11.3	2.6	26.9	21.8	17.8	15.2	11.8
17-year-olds not in full time education (%)	83.9	47.6	1.8	82.7	77.0	71.1	62.2	49.3
Population	354617	156814		787575	697455	628403	545082	375567

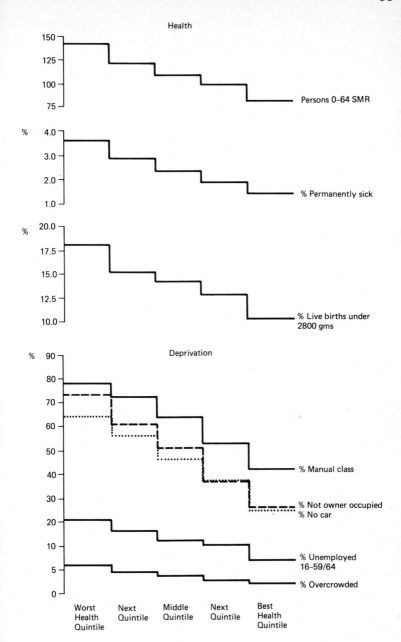

FIGURE 3.4   *The structure of inequality in the Northern Region: wards ranked on overall health index.*

health as well as the component indicators. Within cancers it proved feasible to trace lung cancers, breast cancer and cancers of the digestive organs, which between them account for around two out of every three cancer deaths. Finally, it was possible to trace SMRs for accidents, poisoning and violence, together with a crude rate for suicides and self-inflicted injury.

With the sole exception of breast cancer, where the SMRs are close to or slightly better than the England and Wales average across the spectrum of wards, there proved to be considerable inequality between the two extremes of the ranked wards, and the familiar step-wise gradient of variation could be observed from one quintile band of wards to the next. Thus, the same consistent configuration was apparent. Inequality was widest with respiratory deaths, where the SMRs for both sexes in the 10 per cent of wards with worst health are more than five times higher than in the 10 per cent of wards with best health; but the ratio is still as high as 4:1 in the case of lung cancer for both sexes, and close to 4:1 for female deaths from circulatory causes. Leaving aside breast cancer, the only ratio of less than 2:1 is found for female deaths due to accidents (see Table 3.4).

Bristol

A preliminary project of a similar kind was completed for the City of Bristol in 1984 (Townsend, Simpson and Tibbs, 1984 and 1985) following collaboration between members of Avon County Council Planning Department, Bristol and Weston District Health Authority and the University of Bristol. A slightly larger number of deprivation indicators were utilised:

1. households with fewer rooms than persons;
2. households lacking a car;
3. economically active persons seeking work;
4. children receiving school meals free; and
5. households having their electricity disconnected during the previous twelve months.

The twenty-eight wards of the city were ranked according to these indicators, and subsequently indicators of the health of their populations were examined.

Table 3.5 compares the health of wards ranked from least to most deprived. It can be seen that the ratio of still births and infant deaths,

TABLE 3.5   *Indicators of health in Bristol wards, ranked by their level of material and social deprivation*

Rank	Ward	Stillbirths and infant deaths per 1000 1977–81	Deaths per 10 000 adults aged 15–64 1977–80	Percentage low birth weight (under 2800 g)	Deaths per 10 000 aged 65+ 1977–80
1	Westbury-on-Trym	14	22	4	527
2=	St George East	18	25	6	510
2=	Durdham	11	27	4	502
4	Stapleton	14	44	4	(958)
5	Bishopston	11	38	7	563
6	Stockwood	14	23	7	468
7	Brislington	22	36	5	653
8	Bedminster	29	39	10	599
9	Henbury	19	34	7	437
10	Knowle	19	33	5	498
11	Clifton	26	40	7	666
12	Hillfields	23	29	8	493
13	Southville	10	45	5	616
14=	Horfield	11	48	8	741
14=	Redland	17	43	4	670
16	St George West	22	43	8	625
17	Eastville	22	31	8	494
18=	Somerset	30	41	6	632
18=	Avon	37	47	10	807
20	Cabot	23	43	8	590
21	Windmill Hill	22	48	9	661
22=	Hengrove	25	45	9	782
22=	Southmead	26	41	9	606
24	Bishopsworth	26	38	9	594
25	St Philip & Jacob	20	57	8	764
26	District	26	39	9	547
27	Easton	26	58	13	757
28	St Paul's	29	57	11	626
Bristol		21.4	38.8	7.7	620

and of deaths of adults aged 15–64, is around or more than 2:1. The City's Environmental Health Department issued a preliminary research report in 1986 which adds to this material (Chief Environmental Health Officer, 1986). Unfortunately some of the mortality data have been found in that report to have been wrongly coded for wards with boundaries which have been re-drawn and additional analysis must await re-coding. Once it is completed there will be mortality data for a larger span of years and a group of most deprived can be compared with a group of least deprived wards by cause of death. Regressions can also be applied to begin to expose features of the distribution of health which cannot easily be explained by applying available knowledge about material deprivation.

An example of a candidate for explanation is provided in Table 3.6. Drawn from the 1984 report this table demonstrates the broad correspondence found between wards when they were ranked according to separate indicators of both health and deprivation. At the

Table 3.6   *Cumulative rank on four indicators of material and social
deprivation of six wards with 'best' and six wards with 'worst' health in
Bristol*

Wards ranked by health	Cumulative rank on four indicators	
	Health[a]	Material and social deprivation[b]
St George East	13	15
Westbury-on-Trym	15	7
Stockwood	19	23
Durdham	26	11
Knowle	27	45
Henbury	30	36
Windmill Hill	77	84
St Philip & Jacob	77	98
Hengrove	86	92
St Paul's	94	110
Easton	100	104
Avon	103	66

Note: [a] Stillbirths and infant deaths per 1000 (1977–81); deaths per 10 000 adults aged 15–64 (1977–81); deaths per 10 000 adults aged 15+ (1977–80); percentage of births under 2800 grammes.
   [b] Fewer rooms than persons in household; households without car; unemployed; children receiving free school meals.

foot is the ward of Avon – which on a cumulative score was ranked lowest for health but not very low for material deprivation. This finding was not in fact given particular attention in the 1984 report but attracted public notice subsequently, and deserves some discussion here, because it illustrates the potentialities of this method of small areas analysis which relates ill-health and deprivation.

ENVIRONMENTAL POLLUTION AND DEPRIVATION

One facet of material deprivation for which national statistics on a small area basis are very difficult if not impossible in theory to produce is level of environmental pollution. Neither that nor poor environmental facilities are covered by the national indicators of deprivation which are available for analysis. However, in correlating measures of ill-health and deprivation, environmental pollution is clearly one of the causal elements of ill-health which may account for some of the unexplained variation between populations living in different areas. This is the theoretical possibility which must inspire much future work.

Avonmouth in the North West of Bristol is the site of one of the world's largest primary smelting works. Substantial quantities of zinc, lead and cadmium (see Coy, 1984) are emitted into the atmosphere mostly as small particles which are carried up to twenty kilometres and more north-east of Avonmouth by the prevailing south-westerly winds – though other areas experience some fall out. There is evidence of substantial airborne pollution. Botanists from the University and elsewhere have collected oak and elm leaves from many different sites, and have placed moss bags on poles to check deposits covering hundreds of square miles. This work, much of it carried out in the early 1970s, showed ratios of deposits in Avonmouth, compared with outlying areas, of 60:1 for cadmium, 36:1 for lead, 17:1 for iron, 12:1 for copper and 8:1 for zinc. 'The maps all illustrate', they reported, 'a pronounced epicentre corresponding to the emission source at Avonmouth' (Little and Martin, 1972 and 1974). Certainly there is no shortage of people living in these areas who testify to the problems of clean washing hanging in gardens which is quickly covered by smuts, or vegetables which fail to grow or develop diseases, and ailments which are attributed to such pollution. The question is whether proof of past or present effects on health can be accumulated which justifies further preventive measures on the part of industry, local authorities, health authorities and government.

The city environmental health department has carefully explained its diligent monitoring activities. The Chief Environmental Health Officer, for example, has carefully emphasised that the results of monitoring of heavy materials show 'quite plainly that all the levels found, including that around Avonmouth in which is situated the largest primary zinc lead smelter in the word, are a fraction of the European limits' recommended as the safety limits within which operations should be permitted (Cooper, 1985, p. 81).

This reassurance has been reiterated in a more recent publication. In its first research report on inequalities of health in Bristol the city environmental health department argued that evidence of raised lead levels in Avon ward did not mean that these levels were harmful to health and went on to point out that pollutant concentrations around the time of sudden infant deaths were 'nowhere near the maximum values permitted by the EEC' (Chief Environmental Health Officer 1986, p. 6). But a large range of research data were not referred to in that report and clearly this problem has to be resolved more by

systematically checking possible causes of local variation in mortality
and morbidity at all ages than continuing only to monitor pollution
levels. The claim by the environmental health department in its
conclusion to the 1986 report that 'no evidence has been found to date
which links pollution with inequalities of health' is specious because
that evidence was not examined.

Recent research has in any case thrown considerable doubt on the
concept of a safety level or threshold for some pollutants. There is for
example the problem of assuming that human beings absorb similar
quantities of some metals from natural sources. In Britain the recent
work of environmental chemists provides a good example. The zinc
deficiency in modern diets, believed to be related to conditions such as
anorexia nervosa, is attributed to three modern agricultural practices:
(i) the use of phosphate fertilisers which render zinc less readily taken
up by growing plants; (ii) the failure to maintain the organic content of
many soils; (iii) the failure to re-cycle zinc (as well as other
nutritionally essential trace elements) to soils. (Bryce-Smith, 1986,
p. 118). For this reason different people will experience very different
health effects from the same additional quantity of some pollutant
which their bodies are expected to absorb. The toxic effects of even
low levels of lead have also been shown to have more serious effects
than formerly believed. Elevated traces of lead and cadmium and zinc
deficiency seem to be correlated with serious malformation, poor
foetal development and low birthweight. 'Of all environmental
pollutants so far identified, the neurotoxin lead is evidently the most
serious and widespread in its subtle and insidious impact on man.
There now appears to be no observable threshold for its toxic effects
on the development and function of the child's brain . . . adverse
mental effects . . . and blood pressure' (Bryce-Smith, 1986, pp. 118–
22).

In addition to this evidence of the varying capacity of individuals to
absorb the same quantities of pollutants without ill-effects to their
health, there is the additional problem of local variations in the
distribution, magnification and processes of absorption of pollutants.
Valuable evidence is being collected by zoologists, biologists and
botanists for 'biological indicators' like earthworms, fruit flies, ants,
slugs and snails. Woodlice are the latest addition because they are able
to store a range of metals to very high concentrations. Recent work by
the University of Bristol's Botany Department not only maps via the
measurement of woodlice the familiar 'epi-centre' characteristic of
Avonmouth (see Figure 3.5) but the paradoxical variations within each

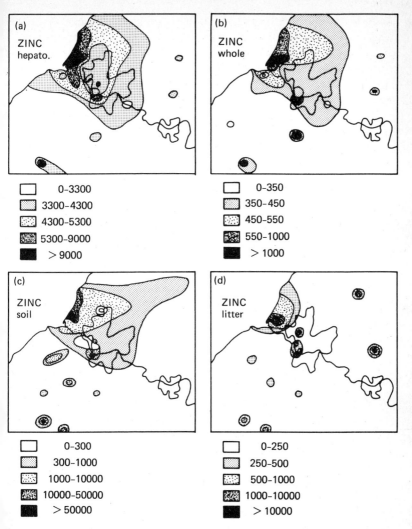

FIGURE 3.5 *Distribution of concentrations of zinc in (a) the hepopatopancreas; (b) whole specimens of* Porcellio scaber; *(c) soil; and (d) leaf litter in Avon and North Somerset (μgg⁻¹)*

area because of differences in soil and leaf litter, concentrations due to historical and modern waste material dumps and emissions on and near motorways and other roads from heavy traffic (Hopkin, Hardisty and Martin, 1986).

It seems important to review medical research into conditions where environmental stress and industrial pollution are suspected causal agents and to commission an integrated programme of research into raised levels of morbidity and mortality in areas like Avonmouth. Important examples are Harrop-Griffiths (1975–7) who has researched conditions in south-east Wales, on the other side of the Severn Estuary.

There are scientists who, in the light of such evidence, believe there is a good case for imposing stronger controls on the emissions from plants such as Avonmouth in the public interest, without waiting for the results of further studies.

SOCIAL CLASS AND HEALTH

The relationship between social class and health represents a second tradition of research. It has become more rather than less significant in the late 1980s because of the need to explain Britain's higher than average mortality in Europe (see for example Catford and Ford, 1984) as well as widening inequality of mortality rates.

It is important that the tradition be reaffirmed. The latest *Decennial Supplement on Occupational Mortality* (OPCS, 1986) does not really build on that tradition. There are a number of regrettable features of the *Supplement*. Reservations are expressed about the concept of social class (p. 17) but these are neither adequately explained nor discussed. Reservations are also expressed about the 'serious bias' in the calculation of SMRs for social classes (pp. 17 and 44) but these are found to apply principally to a category of labourers and unskilled workers not elsewhere classified in social class V – only part of a category representing as little as 6 per cent of the male population. No effort was made to correct for such bias and nonetheless to produce reliable, if revised, tables in the main commentary.

In view of the reservations about the smaller class V it is particularly regrettable that advantage was not taken of presentations combining classes IV and V, making up between a fifth and a quarter of the population, and comparing them with classes I and II (like those for example in Black, 1980, and Fox and Adelstein, 1978).

The unwillingness to present data for several decades is also regrettable in view of the admission that the effects of re-classifying occupations on comparisons between the mortality data for 1979–83 and those for 1970–2 'are generally small' (OPCS, 1986, p. 45). There is a further technical point which illustrates the negative attitude in the report towards social inequality. If the *technical* difficulties of operationalising class so that trends in unequal mortality can be traced are substantial why was an alternative not developed, for example, using deciles or quintiles? Data for the 1980s and far earlier decades could have been reconstructed.

Has this new-found uneasiness about 'social class' as a concept and in technical terms anything to do with the expressed opposition of government ministers (for example, Sir Keith Joseph in a book on *Equality* co-authored with J. Sumption) to the serious treatment of the concept; or the Government's savage cuts in the compilations of social statistics (including the range of work of OPCS) and even its doubts about the necessity of the census itself; or the shift of resources in Britain towards the extremes of the social scale?

It is difficult not to interpret the *Decennial Supplement* of 1986 as an equivocal document, pouring cold water on analyses of social class in the printed commentary in part one and yet allowing the results of those analyses to be found (with great difficulty and only by having to transpose some data) within the large number of 22 000 tables on microfiche in part two. To put off all but the hardiest specialists the total cost of the Report is £55.20 and the means of extracting useful data really depend not just on having access to a microfiche display unit, but one with a printer as well. The equivocation about social class is nicely symbolised on p. 43. A table of estimates of social class SMRs is published prominently but a note to the table states that 'these data are subject to serious bias and do not represent usable estimates of mortality by social class'. If they are unusable why print them? Perhaps because, deep down, the Registrar General's staff know they are a vital part of the analysis.

What do the mortality data reveal? Even allowing for 'bias' in the classification they demonstrate that the trend picked out by the Working Group under Sir Douglas Black has continued. The mortality experience of classes I and II has continued to improve, relative to classes IV and V, as Table 3.7 shows. The latest direct age-standardised mortality rates for men and for married women are given in Table 3.8, where the class differences are clearly discernible. There have been only slight improvements in the mortality rates at different ages for men and women in the manual classes, and rather more substantial improvements in classes I and II. This is a matter of the foremost importance in the management of national policy and of the National Health Service in particular.

A recent event adds piquancy to this discussion. The primary author

TABLE 3.7 *Mortality of men by occupational class (1931–81) (standardised mortality ratios)*

Occupational class	1930–32	1949–53 (a)	1959–63 unadjusted	1959–63 adjusted (b)	1970–72 unadjusted	1970–72 adjusted (b)	1979–80 82–83 unadjusted	1979–80 82–83 adjusted (c)
I Professional	90	86	76	75	77	75	66	70
II Managerial and administrative	94	92	81	—	81	—	76	—
III$_N$ Skilled non-manual	97	101	100	—	104	—	94	—
III$_M$ Skilled manual				—		—	106	—
IV Partly skilled	102	104	103	—	114	—	116	—
V Unskilled	111	118	143	127	137	121	165	(124)

Notes: All but the final column of this table is drawn from Black (1980); (a) corrected figures as published in Registrar General's *Decennial Supplement, England and Wales, 1961: Occupational Mortality Tables*, London: HMSO, 1971, p. 22; (b) occupations in 1959–63 and 1970–2 have been re-classified according to the 1950 classification; (c) the figure of 70 is given in OPCS, 1986, p. 45 after allowing for occupational re-classification between 1970 and 1980. 'Changes in the other classes due to the new classification are minimal.' The figure of 124 is drawn from the Longitudinal Survey for men dying between 1971 and 1981 and is given in OPCS, 1986, p. 45. Pending secondary research it will give a close 'adjusted' figure, but from internal evidence it is unlikely to be less.

TABLE 3.8 *Mortality of men aged 20–64 and married women aged 20–59, direct age standardised mean annual death rates (per 1000 population), 1979–80, 1982–83*

Men

Social class	Britain		Northern Region	
	Per 1000	Numbers of deaths	Per 1000	Numbers of deaths
I	3.75	(10808)	4.02	(530)
II	4.25	(56535)	4.64	(2886)
III$_N$	5.29	(33370)	5.97	(1900)
III$_M$	5.97	(116218)	6.44	(8411)
IV	6.51	(69415)	7.70	(5360)
V	9.44	(36574)	10.55	(3186)
Armed forces	9.60	(1902)	10.67	(54)
Unoccupied	8.06	(10526)	6.93	(581)

Married Women

	Per 1000	Numbers of deaths	Per 1000	Numbers of deaths
I	1.45	(3532)	1.30	(161)
II	1.81	(17518)	1.98	(1097)
III$_N$	2.04	(8420)	2.16	(756)
III$_M$	2.29	(32609)	2.36	(2408)
IV	3.04	(17958)	3.67	(1650)
V	3.99	(7194)	4.50	(726)
Armed forces	1.12	(526)	1.49	(10)
Unoccupied	0.90	(2319)	0.91	(1577)

Note: Married women classified on husband's occupation. Note that the number of deaths given for married women in the Northern Region are in fact deaths of all women.
Source: OPCS, 1986, Table GD 19 and GD 27.

of the 1986 occupational mortality report was M. E. McDowall. He has now published a further paper jointly with M. G. Marmot in the *Lancet* (1986), based on the statistical data collected by OPCS showing that 'the relative disadvantage of manual compared with non-manual classes has increased for four major groups of causes of death'. It seems odd that the analysis was not included in the official report, and odd too that a further breakdown between skilled and other manual groups was not attempted.

Many specialists will be examining the OPCS data in greater detail. Two final comments should be made. Occupational status has been a convenient surrogate for social class. Now that many women have been employed for long periods of married life, and have themselves

TABLE 3.9   *Changes in extent of poverty 1960–1983 (Britain)*

Income in relation to supplementary benefit standard	1960[a]	1975	1979	1981	1983
	Number in thousands				
Below SB standard	1260	1840	2090	2610	2700
Receiving SB[b]	2670	3710	3980	4840	6130
At or up to 40 per cent above SB standard	3510	6990	5500	7210	7550
Total	1440	12540	11570	14660	16380
	Percentage				
Below SB standard	2.3	3.5	4.0	4.9	5.0
Receiving SB[b]	4.9	7.0	7.6	9.1	11.4
At or up to 40 per cent above SB standard	6.4	13.2	10.4	13.5	14.1
Total	14.2	23.7	22.0	27.5	30.5

Notes: [a] The 1969 data are for the UK and are on a household rather than an income unit basis. It should be noted that the estimates are based on national assistance scales, not supplementary benefit scales.

[b] Drawn separately from supplementary benefit sample enquiry with people drawing benefit for less than 3 months excluded. Thus people unemployed or sick or disabled for less than 3 months are counted as having the incomes they had last in employment.

Sources: For 1960, B. Abel-Smith and P. Townsend, *The Poor and the Poorest*, London: Bell, 1965, pp. 40 and 44. The data are drawn from the FES of that year. For subsequent years, DHSS analyses of the FES. The most recent of these, covering 1983 and revised estimates for 1979 and 1981, was placed in the House of Commons Library on 27 July 1986.

contributed to family incomes, and now that more people have the chance of inheriting wealth, especially a house, male occupational status is no longer as powerful a guide to the family's economic position or living standards as once it was. Means therefore have to be found (as the Black Working Group argued) to augment occupational status as a basis of identifying social class, perhaps by using objective supporting measures of income or perhaps by combining men's and women's occupations in some form of weighted 'family' class. However, the authors of the latest *Decennial Supplement* on occupational mortality should reflect that social class is not disappearing or becoming impossible to measure; it merely needs to be measured, even roughly, by alternative or additional means from those adopted traditionally.

The second observation concerns income. The social distribution in Britain of income and wealth seems to have become more polarised in recent years. Certainly this would be indicated by statistical data on earnings, taxation, household incomes, and employment published by different government departments. Table 3.9 provides an example of the evidence. The growth of unemployment, together with the relative increase in the number of prematurely retired people, disabled people and one parent families, and the fall in low wage-levels, have contributed to the growth in numbers of people experiencing hardship. Current statistical studies of inequality in health by area and by class reflect some of the outcomes of that development. Much more work needs to be done on the relationship between the level of life-time resources (both income and wealth) and ill-health, mortality and development. There are relatively few studies. A Canadian study in the Hamilton Region, using sophisticated techniques, found that median family income explained nearly half the mortality variation among the census tracts of the study area (Liaw, Hayes and McAuley, 1986). In Britain the work of Wilkinson (1986a and 1986b, and see also Carr-Hill, 1985) require replication and expansion elsewhere.

CONCLUSION

In this paper two traditions of research in Britain into inequalities of health have been described. One is the tradition of area studies, and the other of social class. Both have gathered momentum in the late 1970s and early 1980s.

Three sets of findings from research at the University of Bristol are described to illustrate work on the relationship between material deprivation and ill-health (as a means of bringing together the two traditions). Data were collected for 755 wards in Greater London, 678 wards in the North of England, and 28 wards in the City of Bristol. Different indicators of material deprivation for these wards were found to be highly correlated with each other. Three indicators of ill-health in these wards – mortality, permanent sickness and delayed development – were also found to be highly correlated with each other (contrary to the suppositions of some social scientists in recent discussion). As a third step in each of these analyses material deprivation and ill-health, each defined in terms of an overall index – on the basis (in London and the North of England) of four and three indicators respectively – were found to be themselves highly correlated. In regressions the four deprivation indicators were found to 'explain' 65 per cent of the variation of health in the 678 wards of the North of England. These findings have major implications for policy and support the analysis put forward in the Black Report (1980).

The implications of the method of analysis for policy are also illustrated for Bristol, by showing that environmental pollution is likely to be a contributory causal agent of ill-health in the ward of Avon (now Avonmouth).

Finally, the need to relate social class analysis to small area analysis is discussed, and the latest OPCS report on occupational mortality is reviewed. Despite official reservations about social class analysis its importance as an agent of scientific discovery is reaffirmed. The latest national data show that inequalities between occupational classes have continued to widen, and this is attributed to the development of social polarisation, with an increasing percentage of the population having relatively depressed or poor living standards.

REFERENCES

Antonovsky, A. (1972) 'Social Class, Life Expectancy and Overall Mortality', in E. G. Jaco (ed.) *Patients, Physicians and Illness*, New York: Free Press.

Ashton, J. (1984) *Health in Mersey – A Review*, Department of Community Health, University of Liverpool.

Betts, G. (1984) *Health in Glyndon, Report of a Survey of Health in the Glyndon Ward, Greenwich*, London: Greenwich Resource Centre.

Black Report (1980) *Inequalities in Health*, report of a research working group chaired by Sir Douglas Black, London: DHSS.

Bradshaw, J., Edwards, H., Staden, F. and Weale, J. (1980) 'Area Variations in Infant Mortality 1975–77', *Journal of Epidemiology and Community Health*.

Brotherston, J. (1976) 'Inequality: Is it Inevitable?' in C. O. Carter and J. Peel (eds), *Equalities and Inequalities in Health*, London: Academic Press.

Bryce-Smith, D. (1986) 'Environmental Chemical Influences on Behaviour and Mentation', the John Jeyes lecture, *Chemical Society Reviews*, 15, 93–123.

Carr-Hill, R. A. (1985) 'Health and Income: A Longitudinal Study of Four Hundred Families', *Quarterly Journal of Social Affairs* 4, 295–307.

Catford, J. C. and Ford, S. (1984) 'On the State of the Public Ill-Health: Premature Mortality in the United Kingdom and Europe', *British Medical Journal*, 289, 1668–70.

Chadwick, E. (1842) *Report on the Sanitary Conditions of the Labouring Population of Great Britain*.

Chief Environmental Health Officer (1986) 'Inequalities of Health in the City of Bristol', report to the Special Public Protection Committee, 23 April 1986, Bristol: Environmental Health Department.

Cooper, P. (1985) 'The Environmental Health Function in Relation to Inequalities of Health', in Bristol City Council, *Inequalities of Health in the City of Bristol*, transcript of conference held at the City Hall, 6 February 1985, Bristol City Council, Bristol.

Coy, C. M. (1984) 'Control of Dust and Fumes at a Primary Zinc and Lead Smelter', *Chemistry in Britain*, May, 418–20.

Denham, C. (1980) 'The Geography of the Census, 1971 and 1981', *Population Trends*, 6–12.

DHSS (1976) *Report of the Resource Allocation Working Party*, London: DHSS.

Engels, F. (1844) *The Condition of the Working Class in England*, Oxford: Blackwell, 1958.

Farr, W. (1841) *Registrar General's Fifth Annual Report*, London: HMSO.

Farr, W. (1860) 'On the Construction of Life Tables, Illustrated by a New Life Table of the Healthy Districts of England', *Journal of the Institute of Actuaries*, IX, July.

Fox, A. J. and Adelstein, A. M. (1978) 'Occupational Mortality: Work or Way of Life?', *Journal of Epidemiology and Community Health*, 32, 73–8.

Fox, A. J. and Goldblatt, P. O. (1980) 'Socio-Demographic Mortality Differentials from the OPCS Longitudinal Study 1971–75', Series LS No. 1, London: HMSO.

Fox, A. J., Goldblatt, P. O. and Jones D. R. (1985) 'Social Class Mortality Differentials: Artefact, Selection or Life Circumstances?' *Journal of Epidemiology and Community Health*, 39, 1–8.

Fox, A. J. and Leon, D. A. (1985) 'Disadvantage and Mortality: New Evidence from the OPCS Longitudinal Study', Social Statistics Research Unit Working Paper, London: City University.

Fox, A. J., Jones, D. R. and Goldblatt, P. O. (1984) 'Approaches to Studying the Effect of Socio-Economic Circumstances on Geographic Differences in Mortality in England and Wales', *British Medical Bulletin*, 4, 309–14.

Halliday, M. L. and Anderson, T. (1979) 'The Sex Differential in Ischaemic Heart Disease: Trends by Social Class 1931–1971', *Journal of Epidemiology and Community Health*, 33, 74–7.

Harrop-Griffiths, H. (1975) 'The Sub-Clinical Effects of Environmental Stress', in D. D. Hemphill (ed.), *Trace Substances in Environmental Health – IX, A Symposium*, Columbia: University of Missouri.

Harrop-Griffiths, H. (1977) 'Environmental Stress and Aspirin', *Proceedings of the Royal Society of Medicine*, 70, Supplement 7, 22–3.

Hart, N. (1985) *Sociology of Health and Medicine*, London: Causeway Press.

Hollingsworth, J. and Rogers, D. (1981) 'Inequalities in Levels of Health in England and Wales, 1891–1971', *Journal of Health and Social Behaviour*, vol. 22.

Holme, I., Helgeland, A., Hierman, I., Leren, P. and Lund-Larsen, P. G. (1980) 'Four Year Mortality by Some Socio-Economic Indicators: The Oslo Study', *Journal of Epidemiology and Community Health*, 30, 48–52.

Hopkin, S. P., Hardisty, G. N. and Martin, M. H. (1976) 'The Woodlouse Porcellio Scaber as a Biological Indicator of Zinc, Cadmium, Lead and Copper Pollution', *Environmental Pollution*, Series B, 11, 271–90.

Howe, G. M. (1982) 'London and Glasgow: A Spatial Analysis of Mortality

Experience in Contrasting Metropolitan Centres', *Scottish Geographical Magazine*, 119–27.

International Union for the Scientific Study of Population (1984) *Methodologies for the Collection and Analysis of Mortality*, proceedings of the meeting held in Dakar, Senegal, 1981.

Irving, D. and Rice, P. (1984) *Information for Health Services Planning for the 1981 Census*, London: King's Fund Centre.

Kitagawa, E. M. and Hauser, P. M. (1973) *Differential Mortality in the United States*, Cambridge, Mass.: Harvard University Press.

Koskinen, S. (1985) 'Time Trends in Cause-Specific Mortality by Occupational Class in England and Wales', paper given to the IUSSP Conference, Florence, Italy; Department of Sociology: University of Helsinki.

Kosa, J., Antonovsky, A. and Zola, I. K. (eds) (1969) *Poverty and Health, A Sociological Analysis*, Cambridge, Mass.: Harvard University Press.

Liaw, K. L., Hayes, M. V. and McAuley, R. G. (1986) 'Analysis of Local Mortality Variation', Research Report No. 161, Faculty of Social Sciences, McMaster University, Ontario, Canada.

Little, P. and Martin, M. H. (1972) 'A Survey of Zinc, Lead and Cadmium in Soil and Natural Vegetation around a Smelting Complex', *Environmental Pollution*, 3, 241–54.

Little, P. and Martin, M. H. (1974) 'Biological Monitoring of Heavy Metal Pollution', *Environmental Pollution*, 6, 1–9.

Logan, W. P. (1982) *Cancer Mortality by Occupation and Social Class*, OPCS Studies of Medical and Population Subjects No. 44, London: HMSO.

Marmot, M. G. and McDowall, M. E. (1986) 'Mortality Decline and Widening Social Inequalities', *Lancet*, ii, 274–6.

Marmot, M. G., Rose, G., Shipley, M. and Hamilton, P. J. S. (1978) 'Employment Grade and Coronary Heart Disease in British Civil Servants', *Journal of Epidemiology and Community Health*, 32, 244–9.

Mays, N. (1986) 'SMRs, Social Deprivation or What?', Social Medicine and Health Services Research Unit, London, St Thomas Campus of United Medical Schools of Guys and St Thomas Hospitals.

M'Gonigle, G. E. N. and Kirby, J. (1936) *Poverty and Public Health*, London: Gollancz.

Morgan, M. (1983) 'Measuring Social Inequality: Occupational Classification and their Alternatives', *Community Medicine*, 5, 116–24.

Morgan, M. and Chinn, S. (1983) 'ACORN Group, Social Class and Child Health', *Journal of Epidemiology and Child Health*, 37, 196–203.

Morris, J. N. (1975) *Uses of Epidemiology*, Edinburgh: Longmans.

OPCS (1978) *Occupational Mortality: Registrar-General's Decennial Supplement, England and Wales, 1970–72*, Series DS No. 1, London: HMSO.

OPCS (1986) *Occupational Mortality Decennial Supplement, 1979–80, 1982–3, Great Britain*, Series DS No. 6, London: HMSO.

Orr, J. B. (1936) *Food, Health and Income*, London.

Pamuk, E. R. (1985) 'Social Class Inequality in Mortality from 1921 to 1972 in England and Wales', *Population Studies*, 39, 17–31.

Registrar General (1839) *First Annual Report of the Registrar General of*

Births, Deaths and Marriages in England (1837–1838), London: HMSO.
Rogers, G. B. (1979) 'Income and Inequality as Determinants of Mortality: An International Cross Section Analysis', *Population Studies*, 33, 343–51.
Saull, H. (1983) *Occupational Mortality in 1971–75*, Central Statistical Office of Finland, studies No. 54, Helsinki.
Salonen, J. T. (1982) 'Socio-Economic Status and Risk of Cancer, Cerebral Stroke and Death Due to Coronary Heart Disease and any Disease: a Longitudinal Study in Eastern Finland', *Journal of Epidemiology and Community Health*, 36, 294–7.
Scott-Samuel, A. (1984) 'Need for Primary Health Care: An Objective Indicator', *British Medical Journal*, 288, 457–8.
Scott-Samuel, S. (1986) 'Social Inequalities in Health: Back on the Agenda', *Lancet*, 1084–5.
Stacey, M. (1977) 'Concepts of Health and Illness: a Working Paper on the Concepts and their Relevance for Research', in *Health and Health Policy – Priorities for Research*, the report of an advisory panel to the Research Initiatives Board, London, Social Science Research Council, May.
Stevenson, T. M. C. (1928) 'The Vital Statistics of Wealth and Poverty', *Journal of the Royal Statistical Society*, XCI.
Susser, M. (1962) 'Civilisation and Peptic Ulcer', *Lancet*, i, 115–19.
Thunhurst, C. P. (1985a) *Poverty and Health in the City of Sheffield*, Environmental Health Department, City of Sheffield.
Thunhurst, C. P. (1985b) 'The Analysis of Small Area Statistics and Planning for Health', *The Statistician*, 34.
Titmuss, R. M. (1938) *Poverty and Population*, London: Macmillan.
Townsend, P., Simpson, D. and Tibbs, N. (1984) *Inequalities of Health in the City of Bristol*, Department of Social Administration, University of Bristol.
Townsend, P. with Corrigan, P. and Kowarzik, U. (1987) *Poverty and Labour in London: An Interim Report of a Centenary Survey*, London: Low Pay Unit.
Townsend, P., Phillimore, P. and Beattie, A. (1986) *Inequalities in Health in the Northern Region: An Interim Report*, Newcastle and Bristol: Northern Regional Health Authority and Department of Social Administration, University of Bristol.
United Nations, WHO CICRED (1983) *Socio-Economic Differential Mortality in Industrialised Societies, Vol 3*, proceedings of meeting in Rome 24–7 May 1983.
Valkonen, T. (1982) 'Socio-economic Mortality Differentials in Finland', Department of Sociology, University of Helsinki, Working Paper No. 28.
Webber, R. (1977) 'The Classification of Residential Neighbourhoods: An Introduction to the Classification of Wards and Parishes', PRAG Technical Report TP23, London: Centre for Environmental Studies.
Webber, R. and Craig, J. (1976) 'Which Local Authorities are Alike?', *Population Trends*, 5, 13–19.
West of Scotland Politics of Health Group (1984) *Glasgow, Health of a City*.
Wilkinson, R. G. (1986a) 'Socio-Economic Differences in Mortality: Interpreting the Data on their Size and Trends' and Wilkinson, R. G. (1986b) 'Income and Mortality', both in Wilkinson, R. G. (ed.) *Class and Health: Research and Longitudinal Data*, London: Tavistock.

4 Distributive Justice with Special Reference to Geographical Inequality and Health Care

GAVIN MOONEY AND
ALISTAIR McGUIRE

INTRODUCTION

The National Health Service (NHS), as originally envisaged in 1948, was to provide the best possible medical care for everyone. The stock of ill-health was to be gradually eroded by the quality and comprehensiveness of the services provided. The demand for health care, insofar as it was a function of ill-health, would decrease and in turn the quantity of resources consumed by the health service would diminish.

Clearly this did not happen – partly because of the view of health care as a right and the growth of medical technology (see Aaron, 1981) – but partly also because of changing expectations encompassed, for example, in the realisation that needs were relative and not absolute. The recent injection of greater realism regarding such expectations has meant more emphasis on planning and evaluation to improve efficiency in the NHS. Beyond this, however, there remains the important issue of what the objective function of the NHS is: in particular, can we determine how equity fits into the goals of health care?

In this paper we address this question by considering what is meant by equity and also by looking at the implementation of policy in the NHS as it relates to equity. More fundamentally, however, we attempt to show that economics is relevant to the determination of policy and is not just a set of tools used to implement policy.

The paper discusses equity in health care from an economic perspective. In particular, it considers why the objective of equity exists and in what ways – in terms of territorial equity – it is being pursued in the NHS. Depending upon the rationale adopted for explaining equity in health care, different objectives and policies may be pursued. It will be pointed out that the definitions of objectives, in so far as they relate to issues of equity, are all couched in terms of equality. This in itself leads to difficulties as the question is then raised: equality of what? We suggest that the objective pursued is based upon horizontal equality of opportunity. In other words the aim is to ensure that those in similar positions to one another (in terms of their health care needs) have equal access to health services. The goal is then equal access for equal need. As we shall see, this appears to have been the objective most frequently found in policy documents. We shall, however, suggest that the implementation of policy in the pursuit of this objective is difficult to sustain, not least because of the individualistic nature of the goal. Thus policy implementation corrupts the objective such that a standard of equal inputs for equal needs becomes sought at an aggregate, territorial level.

With this as our underlying theme, the next section discusses different possible theories of justice. The section after that outlines policy implementation in the NHS with regard to equity. Finally, some possible rationales for equity as an objective of the NHS which have been suggested by economists are considered. This final section is particularly important in that it indicates that economics *is* concerned with these more difficult questions, for example those related to objectives, and is not merely a tool-kit to be applied to specific problems.

WHAT IS JUSTICE?

We do not intend to attempt to give any uniquely correct answer to this age-old question. Rather, we highlight briefly different theories of justice and consider a few possible definitions of equity in health care.

Following Veatch (1981), we may examine four theories of justice. First, there is the entitlement theory which is based on the premiss that if people have acquired what they possess in a just fashion, then they are entitled to those possessions. Thereafter individuals are entitled to use these endowments in whatever way they can. Given the nature of health and disease it is difficult to argue for the use of entitlement theory in considerations of health, although it might arguably be used in health care, in terms of entitlement to access.

Veatch then discusses a second theory of justice – traditional utilitarianism, which essentially advocates the pursuit of the greatest happiness for the greatest number. In the way that this is normally interpreted by economists – and conventional economics is founded on utilitarianism – it is not a theory of justice at all, but the criterion for economic efficiency: i.e. the maximisation of social benefit subject to resource availability (often, or normally, irrespective of the distributional consequences). In this narrow sense utilitarianism is not a theory of justice at all, in that it counts each person for one and none for more than one.

Thirdly, Veatch considers the 'maximin theory'. This is most commonly associated with Rawls's theory of justice (Rawls, 1972). Rawls assumes that rational individuals acting behind a veil of ignorance (i.e., they do not know what their own position in society will be) would choose to arrange social and economic inequalities in such a way that they are to the greatest benefit of the least advantaged (i.e. *max*imising the *min*imum position). While this may well have some appeal in the context of health care, there is a possible danger that it could lead to the impoverishment of a society who poured scarce health care resources into what might in practice be 'hopeless' cases.

However, such principles, according to Rawls, are only to be applied to 'primary social goods' among which health care is not listed. An alternative (proposed by Daniels (1985) among others) is to consider the health service, and thereby health care, as being among the basic institutions involved in providing, in Rawls's theory, fair equality of opportunity. That would in the context of health care get us, through Rawls, to an equity goal founded upon equal opportunity for equal need in the use of health care.

Lastly, Veatch considers an egalitarian theory which enjoins equality of welfare among individuals. In the context of health care this would presumably be interpreted as equal health which even if standardised by age and sex would not appear as an acceptable, practical goal for at least two reasons. First, it might mean a very low level of equal health, since to raise the level of health of some even by a small amount could prove very expensive. Second, for resources to be deployed to achieve this end would require much better knowledge than presently exists of the effectiveness of different forms of health care.

In this brief review of the main approaches to distributive justice, it will be noted that, widespread as these approaches are, they are all based on individualistic considerations. In other words, while they are rightly concerned with problems of social choice, they are founded upon individual interests.

HEALTH CARE, EQUITY AND EQUALITY

While the rationale for health care policies may well be concerned with equity, their implementation has been dominated by considerations of equality. Yet it is possible to have equitable inequalities and inequitable equalities. Bearing this in mind, it is also true that various definitions and objectives for equality in the NHS have been proposed (see Mooney, 1986). Amongst the most prominent are equality of

1. expenditure *per capita*;
2. inputs *per capita*;
3. inputs for equal need;
4. access for equal need;
5. utilisation for equal need;
6. marginal met need; and
7. health.

It should be noted that it is difficult, in some cases impossible, to reconcile these objectives with one another. Thus in the context of territorial equity, equality of inputs *per capita* may differ from equality of expenditure *per capita* if the inputs (land, labour, capital) vary in price in different regions. (For example, land is more expensive in Central London than it is in Yorkshire.) More importantly perhaps, neither of definitions (1) and (2) acknowledges that individuals may differ in terms of their health status and/or need for care. This is recognised in some of the other definitions listed, but raises the interesting question of whether equality should be addressed at an individual or more aggregate level.

The difference between (3) and (4) is simply that to achieve equal access (defined as equal *opportunity* to use health care resources) may require differential levels of inputs. For example, all other things being equal, higher levels of resources might be allocated to more sparsely populated areas. Utilisation (5) refers to actual consumption rather than to access, where the opportunity to consume may or may not be realised.

An objective of equal health would raise problems in defining and comparing health levels as well as being, as we noted before, exceedingly expensive to obtain. But equalising marginal met need may be possible. If it could be assumed that all regions ranked their health care needs in the same order and that each ordering was rationally based on the principles of cost-benefit analysis (i.e. doing those things first in which the ratio of benefit to cost was highest), then one definition of equality could be that the need that it was just possible to meet (i.e. the 'marginal met need') should be the same in all regions.

In principle it is possible to choose any of the definitions and indeed to combine them to differing degrees. Thus equal access for equal need might be a preferred definition, but one qualified in the sense that in some situations it might be deemed too expensive or too inefficient to be implemented. For example, providing equal access for equal need to coronory care units for the people living in particularly remote parts of the country such as the Islands of Mull or Colonsay might not be acceptable.

It is of course pertinent to ask whether we can determine from policy statements what the equity goal of the NHS is. Certainly from its beginning, the emphasis appears to have been upon access (Ministry of Health, 1944). The clearest recent outline of the objectives of the NHS is given in the report by the Royal Commission on the NHS (1979) which listed seven distinctive objectives as follows:

> to encourage and assist individuals to remain healthy;
> to provide equality of entitlement to health services;
> to provide a broad range of services of a high standard;
> to provide equality of access to these services;
> to provide a service free at the time of use;
> to satisfy the reasonable expectations of its users;
> and to remain a national service responsive to local needs.

Having listed these objectives the report did state that they lacked precision and indeed that some must be viewed as being unattainable. Furthermore they suggested that they were neither comprehensive nor immune to amendment, but that in the absence of detailed and publicly declared principles they should be considered as a starting point for any discussion on the objectives of the NHS.

As we can see the principle of equity tends to have been related to that of equality, and specifically to equality of entitlement to health care and equality of access to these services. Again we may ask whether these objectives are consistent. One means of reconciling them is to pursue policies based upon equal access for equal need, that is to pursue policies of horizontal equality of opportunity. And indeed this is the objective which appears in policy documents. At this point it may be worth mentioning that the main concern of the Black Report (Black, 1980) was with inequalities in health, although there is no evidence of government policy adopting this as an objective.

Thus in considering equity at a territorial level we may examine the report of the Resource Allocation Working Party (RAWP) (DHSS, 1976) whose terms of reference were to 'review the arrangements for distributing NHS capital and revenue to RHAs, AHAs and Districts respectively with a view to establishing a method of securing, as soon as practicable, a pattern of distribution responsive objectively, equitably and efficiently to relative need and to make recommendations' (ibid., p. 5). This report is currently under review and further developments should be reported by the end of 1986. The original report took as 'the underlying objective of their terms of reference as being to secure, through resource allocation, that there would eventually be equal opportunity of access to health care for people at equal risk' (ibid., p. 7), which is consistent with the objectives outlined by the Royal Commission.

RAWP recommended that a specific needs-based formula should be used in allocating resources to regions. Thus in allocating health care resources the DHSS estimates relative need using a population-based formula but adjusted to take account of the age and sex composition (since for example, the old tend to have more need for health care than the middle aged) and sickness. Further adjustments are made for patient cross-boundary flows, medical education and capital investment.

In practice this process is followed for seven different categories of service, in part because need estimates vary from one service to another but also because costs vary between services. These categories are as follows (with the estimated national percentages of revenue expenditure on each service in brackets):

Non-psychiatric inpatient services	(55.9)
All day and outpatient services	(13.4)
Mental illness inpatient services	(8.8)
Mental handicap inpatient services	(3.5)

Community services	(12.2)
Ambulance services	(5.7)
Administration of family practitioner services	(0.5)
TOTAL	100.0

The avowed intent of these formulas is to provide 'equal access for equal need' across the different regions, although in practice the extent to which they get beyond 'equal inputs for equal need' is very limited. The problem is that it is easier to reconcile expenditure with inputs than with access. Largely this is because it is easier to define and measure inputs than it is to measure access. A further problem is that of measuring differential health and consequently relative needs in the different regions. In practice since no better measure exists this is done using Standardised Mortality Ratios. These ratios compare the number of deaths actually occurring in a region with those that would be expected if the national mortality ratios, adjusted by age and sex, were applicable to the population of that region. Note also that no generally acceptable measures of health status are available which allow comparison of individual health.

It is important to realise that government policies are not concerned with trying to equalise health status either across regions or individuals. Not only is there a problem in measuring health, there is also a problem in determining the effect of health care upon health. In other words it is difficult to assess the proper level of inputs to be directed to the particular health need.

The point is that equity, as associated with government distributive policies, is not about equality of output with regard to health care. Ostensibly, it is concerned with equality of opportunity. Yet in reality, given the problem of reconciling expenditure with opportunity, in this case of access, the policy is largely concerned with equality of inputs, albeit weighted by some proxy of need. The benefits to be derived by a region (or an individual for that matter) from a given volume of inputs or expenditure obviously depend upon the characteristics of that region, hence the attempt to measure and define needs. How inputs relate to equality of opportunity – that is equal access for equal need – is less than clear. In this respect equality statements become ambiguous. This ambiguity is heightened by the fact that there is little attempt to attach equity considerations, i.e. notions of distributive justice, to these statements.

SOME ECONOMISTS' VIEWS

For some there may be doubts over the legitimacy of the economists' concern with such questions. Consequently this section attempts to show that economists are not merely concerned with efficiency considerations but have also attempted to suggest various possible rationales for the concern with equity in the NHS. Lees (1962) saw the decisive step in setting up the NHS as the abandonment of prices. His conclusion most relevant to any discussion of equity is that 'the basic purpose of the NHS is to enforce equality of consumption of medical care'. This is, he says, 'the only logically necessary, intellectually defensible purpose of the NHS', in which 'a single . . . set of preferences is formulated at the centre and then applied uniformly to all who use the NHS'. Lees thus saw equity as taking the form of equality of *consumption* of health care.

In his explanation of the NHS, Culyer (1976) emphasised what is termed the caring externality in terms of *health status*: the fact that most of us care about the state of health of our fellow citizens. He states: 'Individuals are affected by others' health status for the simple reason that most of them care . . . the state of health of others is itself an objective of interest to all.' That is, there is an effect which is associated with an individual's health status, and consequently that individual's consumption of health care in so far as this relates to his health status, which has an effect on the welfare of other individuals. That is, there is an external effect on other individuals' welfare.

Titmuss (1973) extended his well-known analysis of voluntary blood donation to the NHS as a whole. If each individual acted on the basis of the negligible contribution his blood donation would make to the total, there would be little, if any, voluntary donation. Consequently, according to Titmuss, such donations are to be explained in terms of some Kantian sense of duty.

On the basis of a similar argument, he suggests that 'the most unsordid act of British social policy in the twentieth century has allowed and encouraged sentiments of altruism, reciprocity and social duty to express themselves; to be made explicit and identifiable in measurable patterns of behaviour by all social groups and classes'. Titmuss thus saw the NHS as promoting not just health but also altruism.

There is in fact a close similarity between the duty embodied in Titmuss's explanation of equity in health care and the notion of commitment as expressed by another economist Sen (1976–7). Indeed, central to the debate on equity is the distinction which Sen draws between the concept of sympathy and that of commitment. Sympathising for another means that as that other individual's welfare increases (decreases) so does one's own; i.e. there is a positive (negative) externality. As Sen states: 'behaviour based on sympathy is in an important sense egoistic, for one is oneself pleased at others' pleasure and pained at others' pain, and the pursuit of one's own utility may thus be helped by sympathetic action'. Commitment is defined 'in terms of a person choosing an act that he believes will yield a lower level of personal welfare to him than an alternative that is also available to him'. This definition can be extended to include situations where a choice does increase an individual's anticipated personal welfare but where this is not the reason for the choice.

If this concept of commitment is accepted it creates problems for conventional economics which is based primarily on the notion that personal choice and personal welfare have a common identity and that each individual seeks to maximise his utility (personal welfare). Thus as Sen states 'the basic link between choice behaviour and welfare achievements in the traditional models [of economics] is severed as soon as commitment is admitted as an ingredient of choice'.

Sen does not consider health care explicitly. His concern is with the impact on economic analysis more generally of the introduction or acceptance of commitment. As indicated above, the key distinction that Sen makes between sympathy and commitment is that the conscious choice of the latter means either a reduction in anticipated utility or, if not, that it could have resulted in a reduction in utility had there not been an increase in utility as a result of some other characteristic of the choice. It is this feature of utility loss which is important to the discussion in this paper.

Surprisingly Sen offers no explicit explanation of why individuals choose commitment. It is clearly a conscious choice otherwise Sen would not have defined it as commitment. This conscious choice element is crucial in another sense in that the notion of sympathy in the form of externalities is already present in many economic models and even where it is not, can be built in without too great difficulties. But, as Sen states 'commitment does involve, in a very real sense *counterpreferential choice*, destroying the crucial assumptions [on which conventional economics stands] that a chosen alternative must be better than (or at least as good as) the others for the person choosing it' (our emphasis added).

All of these economic models of individual behaviour may be

extended to provide explanations for the pursuit of equity in the NHS. The Lees model implies that equity should be seen in terms of equality of consumption. The Culyer model explains the rationale for equity in the NHS in terms of a caring externality where the dimension of caring is founded upon health status. Titmuss emphasises a Kantian sense of duty with altruism as a commodity in its own right. Sen, on the other hand, emphasises commitment with the implication that people make choices in the interests of equity even if they personally suffer (lose in terms of personal welfare) as a result.

We now turn to discuss one final economic model in more detail – largely because this model is consistent with concern for equality of access for equal need. This model is based upon work undertaken by Margolis (1982) who has attempted to build a 'new' paradigm which allows a fuller economic analysis of social policy than previously. He postulates the idea of self-interested man and group interested man *within the same individual* (i.e. each individual has two different utility functions, or aspects of personal welfare, between which he allocates his resources). Any allocation to himself results in selfish welfare gain. 'Group' welfare is obtained from any allocation to the group (in which the individual is included but given equal weight with all others).

Particularly relevant in Margolis's argument is his 'value ratio', the ratio of marginal group utility to marginal selfish utility to the individual. This is defined in terms of the individual's *values*, not his resources. There is thus 'no necessary connection between the value ratio and [the individual's] own participation in the provision of goods either to himself or to society at large' (p. 38). Second, the marginal utility of the group is *as perceived by the individual*, but is unaffected by the individual's allocation (it is negligible *vis-à-vis* total group resources) to the group.

To prevent the exploitation of the relatively unselfish (more group-interested members of the group) Margolis incorporates 'participation altruism' (i.e. relatively unselfish members have a propensity to limit their willingness to *act* with regard to group-interest to the extent that they have already done so). The utility the individual gets from contributing to the group is in terms of participating, of 'doing his fair share'. The individual then attempts to maximise his utility by allocating his resources between selfish utility and group participation utility.

The approach is based on 'intuitive perceptions of what it is that gives a human being the psychological sense of having done his or her "fair share"' (p. 36). It is this which gives the 'FS model' its name.

This model can be extended to equity in health care. A literal interpretation of the approach would require each individual to array all the options open to him for the spending of his group resources and then allocate them in the way which would provide the group (of which he is an equal member) with the highest expected utility. But given the costs to the individual of such rigorous appraisal he will settle for something more akin to satisficing. That is, he will not seek the best alternative in the feasible set, but will limit himself to what seems satisfactory. 'Rules of thumb' may therefore play an important role in his choice of allocation. The less the information readily available to the individual and the more costly the search for it, the more likely will he opt for some cultural norm, particularly as these search costs will fall on his selfish allocation.

There are features of health care – uncertainty, irrationality, unpredictability, ignorance and externalities – which make it a particularly strong candidate for group interest, or in the terms of the model, for the marginal group utility to be relatively high. This in turn means that the equilibrium between selfish and group participation occurs at a higher level of allocation to the group than would otherwise be the case.

Given the FS concept, one of the central concerns is whether individuals' group interests are sufficiently similar to prevent those with less group interest 'exploiting' those with greater group interest. When this is linked to the implications of uncertainty, irrationality, ignorance, unpredictability and individuals' *awareness* of these factors – both in terms of maintaining and indeed fostering group interest and making allocations of resources to group interest efficient – there is a case for public ownership, that is for coercion. Put crudely, the model's rationale for the NHS is as follows: individuals are all motivated to do their fair share for the group interests in health care; this cannot be attained through any insurance system since insurance is motivated wholly by selfish utility. To individuals, the search costs would be too high to use group interest resources efficiently in health care. Therefore an organisation (the NHS) should be set up to establish how most efficiently to organise group resources.

For equity more specifically, under the FS approach the individual seeks to ensure that *he* is in equilibrium regarding his allocation both selfishly and to the group. He obtains outcome utility in the former, and process utility in the latter. That is, personal welfare is maintained in terms of the insurance coverage provided for the individual by the NHS but also by his participation in the process of providing health care for the group. Given that both forms of utility are present and that the group contains the individual as an equal, then it is enough for the individual simply to care about providing access to health care. Whether other individuals out of selfish interest then utilise the group resources is not relevant to the individual. Given commonality of group interest this will point to equality of access for equal need for members of the group, leaving the selfish interest of different individuals to determine the value placed on health and health care and hence individuals' consumption. 'Caring' is present but it is not concerned with health or health care directly; it is simply caring about caring.

In terms of the FS model, such actions as smoking and excessive drinking impinge on the group utility of others. If the randomness of ill-health is seriously disturbed by self utility indulgences, then group utility will also be affected since the previous equilibrium will be altered. We thus have an explanation of this concern in terms of the threat to the commonality of group interest.

CONCLUSION

In his presidential address (Chapter 1 of this book), Alan Williams suggested that much of the suspicion about health economics and health economists arises from the belief that we see the output of health care largely in terms of allowing people to work better and/or more. What this paper has tried to show is that economics and economists are concerned with much wider perspectives.

The paper has highlighted that the stated objectives of the NHS about equity have not been subject to thorough analysis. Equity has been defined with regard to equality – specifically equality of access for equal need – while policy implementation has largely been based upon the pursuit of equal inputs for equal need. To a large extent this is because it is easier to reconcile expenditure levels with inputs. To the extent that expenditure is allocated through the regions there is some concern with territorial equity. Thus concern with equity is pursued through equality of input levels at an aggregate regional level. As such, questions may be raised with respect to the relationship between policy and the concepts of distributive justice in health care.

The paper also gave a brief overview of the work which has been undertaken by economists on *why* equity in health care matters. Admittedly we have not got very far on this subject – but that is not through lack of concern. Moreover if the behavioural paradigm favoured by this paper to explain the welfare associated with participation is accepted, then this would suggest that policy on equality should in practice (and not just in principle) be more concerned with equality of access than is currently the case. Finally we would hope that this paper would help to stimulate more debate about the nature of equity and equality in health care. Such a debate is much needed.

REFERENCES

Aaron, H. (1981) 'Economic aspects of the role of government in health care', in J. van der Gaag and M. Perlman (eds), *Health, Economics and Health Economics*, Amsterdam: North Holland.

Arrow, K. J. (1963) 'Uncertainty and the Welfare Economics of Medical Care', *American Economic Review*, 53, 5, 941–73.

Black, D. (1880) *Inequalities in Health*, report of a research working group chaired by Sir Douglas Black, London: HMSO.

Campbell, A. V. (1978) *Medicine, Health and Justice*, Edinburgh: Churchill Livingstone.

Culyer, A. J. (1971) 'The Nature of the Commodity "Health Care" and its Efficient Allocation', *Oxford Economic Papers*, 23, 189–211.

Culyer, A. J., Maynard, A. K. and Williams, A. (1981) 'Alternative systems of health care provisions: an essay on motes and beams', in M. Olsen (ed.), *A New Approach to the Economics of Health Care*, Washington and London: American Enterprise Institute.

Daniels, N. (1985) *Just Health Care*, Cambridge: Cambridge University Press.

Department of Health and Social Security (1976) *Report of the Resource Allocation Working Party*, London: HMSO.

Evans, R. G. (1985) *Strained Mercy, The Economics of Canadian Health Care*, Toronto: Butterworth.

Harsanyi, J. C. (1982) 'Mortality and the Theory of Rational Behaviour', in A. Sen and B. Williams (eds), *Utilitarianism and Beyond*, Cambridge: Cambridge University Press.

Lees, D. S. (1962) 'The Logic of the British National Health Service', *Journal of Law and Economics*, 5, 111–18.

Margolis, H. (1982) *Selfishness, Altruism and Rationality, A Theory of Social Choice*, Cambridge: Cambridge University Press.

Maynard, A. K. and Ludbrook, A. (1982) 'Inequality, the National Health Service and Health Policy', *Journal of Public Policy*, 2, 97–116.

Mooney, G. H. (1986), *Economics, Medicine and Health Care*, Brighton: Wheatsheaf.

Ministry of Health (1944) *A National Health Service*, Cmnd 6502, London: HMSO.

Rawls, J. (1972) *A Theory of Justice*, Oxford: Oxford University Press.

Royal Commission on the National Health Service (1979) *Report*, London: HMSO.

Sen, A. K. (1976–7) 'Rational Fools: A Critique of the Behavioural Foundations of Economic Theory', *Philosophy and Public Affairs*, 6, 317–44.

Titmuss, R. M. (1973) *The Gift Relationship*, Harmondsworth: Penguin.

Veatch, R. M. (1981) *A Theory of Medical Ethics*, New York: Basic Books.

5 Transforming the Geography of Health Care: Spatial Inequality and Health Care in Contemporary England

JOHN MOHAN

The removal of spatial and social inequalities in, and barriers to, access to health care, was a fundamental aim of the NHS. There remains considerable debate over the efficacy of the NHS, notably because of the persistent class inequality in health status (Townsend and Davidson, 1982), but the issue of spatial inequality in service provision is still very much on the agenda. This begs a number of important questions: equality in resource distribution, access to care, and health outcomes are by no means synonymous, and there remains confusion about the relationships between efficiency, equity and equality. Moreover, even if these important issues are disregarded, debate on the geographical distribution of health care resources is often limited to repetitions of the inverse care law (Hart, 1971) or to the identification of simple contrasts between the overprovided south and the deprived north of England. Such categorisations are useful starting points but they do not capture the variability that exists in the geography of health care. Furthermore, the individual elements of the health care system – acute and primary, public and private – must all be analysed together as parts of an integrated whole. In this paper the emphasis is on the uneven impact of current and possible future policies on the distribution of health care resources. Three main issues are explored.

The first theme is that of scale. Even if the government can defend their record on the NHS in aggregate terms (record numbers of patients being treated, for instance), it is apparent that minimal growth in expenditure on the Hospital and Community Health Services (HCHS) is necessitating major resource transfers at the subregional level. Consequently, national policy decisions are having massively-differentiated spatial effects. The costs of this are being borne by those localities which are losing resources, not just in terms of access to care but also in terms of job losses.

Secondly, the geography of health care is not just about the distribution of resources on the HCHS, because for most people primary care is the principal point of contact with the NHS. Indeed there is some evidence that poor primary care is associated strongly with high levels of hospital utilisation that are not explicable solely with reference to supply factors. Thus spatial variations in the quantity and quality of GP services are of considerable significance. Evidence is presented which demonstrates such variations at several spatial scales. The likely impacts of alternative policies are also examined.

Thirdly, the recent expansion of private health care – whether acute care or nursing homes for the elderly – has been welcomed by the government on the grounds that the private sector provides additional resources for health care, which is desirable since the government's resources are necessarily finite. However, the private sector's growth has been uneven, in both spatial and social terms. This has implications not just for who benefits from private health care, but, more generally, for the future health care system: is the private sector a valuable supplement to the NHS's limited budget or does it offend the basic principles of the NHS? Finally, the paper concludes by arguing that there is much more to the geography of health care than has been realised, and the likely future geography of health care is discussed.

RESOURCE ALLOCATION IN A PERIOD OF EXPENDITURE RESTRAINT: THE POLITICAL GEOGRAPHY OF RATIONALISATION

Recognition of the problems of spatial inequality in health care provision in England can be traced at least to the late nineteenth century (House of Lords, 1890). The uneven development of hospital provision, both between and within regions (Nuffield Provincial

Hospitals Trust, 1946; Political and Economic Planning, 1937), was to prove an enormous constraint on NHS planning, because of the fixed location of hospitals *vis-à-vis* the changing distribution of the population. The national Hospital Plan (Ministry of Health, 1962) proposed to eliminate regional inequalities in bed provision by varying the rate of capital investment in each RHB area. However, public expenditure restraint, continued debate about the 'optimum' size of hospitals, and apparent indecision in closing hospitals, all hindered the plan's implementation. The Resource Allocation Working Party (RAWP) scheme marked an advance on the Hospital Plan inasmuch as it took seriously the problem of assessing relative need for health care resources. The criticisms of RAWP are well-known and are not repeated here (see DHSS, 1976; Eyles *et al.*, 1982; Radical Statistics Health Group, 1977). In the early years of the application of RAWP, equalisation was taking place by differential growth; all RHAs were receiving growth in funds but some grew faster than others. However, with the cushion of an expanded Parliamentary majority after the 1983 election, the Conservatives were able to abandon the commitment to differential growth. What has happened since looks more like differential cuts, and this section of the paper examines the response by health authorities to their current financial position.

The starting point is that long-term revenue forecasts suggest overall growth in expenditure on the HCHS in England of around 1 per cent per annum. Within this, the Thames RHAs are losing some 0.5 per cent per annum because they are still well above their revenue targets (House of Commons, 1986). Moreover, a consensus seems to be emerging that around 2 per cent annual growth in resources is necessary to keep pace with the pressures generated due to demographic change, rising expectations and the costs of introducing new technology. There has been debate about whether 2 per cent growth should be in resources or in services delivered, with government ministers arguing that there remains sufficient fat on the carcass of the Thames RHAs, for example, to sustain a rapid cost improvement programme. It is obvious, however, that such a programme is having to be implemented quickly in order that the Thames RHAs can stand still, and some of the local effects of this are explored below. Whatever the merits of the 'growth in services or resources' debate, there is no doubt that the effect of current policies in England has been to slow down the rate at which RHAs are moving towards their revenue targets, and this recently led the House of Commons Social Services Committee to conclude that in the present financial climate, 'it may be unrealistic to expect the original RAWP process to go much further' (House of Commons, 1984).

The second problem with RAWP is the way it is applied subregionally. There are four interrelated difficulties. First, a common criticism of RAWP is that it takes very little or no account of the impact of social deprivation on utilisation of health services. The existence of high concentrations of the deprived in the inner city is held by some commentators to generate higher demands on health services there, and this justifies the allocation of additional funds to such areas (Jarman, 1983; Woods, 1982). Second, RAWP is a technical exercise which is conducted on the HCHS budget without regard to the provision of family practitioner or local authority services. For reasons discussed below the former are usually poor in the inner city, especially, though not uniquely, in London (Acheson, 1981; Jarman, 1981), while the latter are vulnerable to attempts to limit public expenditure through ratecapping. Health care resource allocation must see these as three elements of an interacting system. Third, there is the problem of cross-boundary flows and the funding health authorities receive for these; a number of technical problems have been identified by Bevan *et al.* (1985). The effect of these is that health authorities are adequately funded for providing regional and sub-regional specialities, but facilities for local people are not adequately resourced. Hence the acute specialities are invariably protected but small, local community-based hospital facilities are very vulnerable to expenditure reductions. Fourth, the pace of change is even more critical at DHA level because of the enormous variations that exist in distance from revenue targets at this scale: in N.E. Thames, for instance, Islington is 25 per cent above target while Southend is 19 per cent below target. To attempt to equalise that over a ten-year planning cycle is enormously difficult, if not the height of folly.

Thus there are several reasons why the application of RAWP at a time of minimal expenditure growth in the service is posing severe problems for DHAs. Nor are these confined to London; because of population losses from inner city districts many other DHAs are deemed to be overfunded. A good example is Newcastle DHA which, although it is in a RAWP-gaining RHA, has had to make cuts in its budget totalling £3.5m this year (Newcastle Health Concern, 1986). Finally, even health authorities in RAWP-gaining localities are being forced to consider cost containment measures because of the stress in central government policy on the need to generate resources through greater efficiency. Some of the local effects of this are now examined.

The Response: Overcapacity and Restructuring

There are several courses being taken by DHAs in these straitened circumstances. Firstly, DHAs can draw on their financial reserves and postpone capital projects. Neither of these involve cutting into existing services but both are fraught with danger: using up reserves obviously puts the DHA at the mercy of unforeseen contingencies; postponing capital projects may be courting disaster since certain DHAs have apparently been ordered by central government to make savings on other parts of their budget on pain of being refused government approval for capital developments (London Health Emergency, 1986).

Secondly, and far more common, is the *ad hoc* rationalisation of services that is now a feature of the London hospitals scene. For technical reasons explained above, the regional and sub-regional speciality services are usually insulated from expenditure cuts, but there are also political factors: the professional dominance of the medical profession comes into play. The process of 'shroud-waving', as consultants in the hi-tech specialities raise the grim spectre of patients dying for lack of renal dialysis or cardiac surgery, has the effect of protecting the major acute specialities. The result has been a progressive withdrawal of services from all but the main acute hospitals. Acute hospitals in London lost 6400 beds between 1980 and 1986; 32 hospitals were wholly or partly closed in this time period (ALA, 1986); a further 26 total or partial closures have been approved (GLC, 1985). This has particularly affected single-speciality units, small acute hospitals, and casualty departments. Temporary closures of wards and hospitals, and the introduction of five-day wards, have become commonplace. The strategic plans of the Thames regions suggest major reductions in hospital capacity over the next decade in most inner London DHAs; in some authorities acute hospital capacity will be reduced by up to 50 per cent (S.W. Thames RHA, 1985).

Thirdly, expenditure can be restrained by controlling access to hospital treatment. Many DHAs have considered or have actually introduced emergency-only admissions. Controlling the type of operations performed is also a possibility. For example, surgeons in the cardiology and neurosurgery department at City and Hackney DHA have been instructed to reduce the number of operations performed from 600 to the quota of 450 (London Health Emergency, 1986). The most dramatic and best-publicised example of this was the media campaign mounted in May 1986 by a group of eleven prominent surgeons at major London teaching hospitals, the aim of which was to demonstrate the effect of financial cuts on the quality and quantity of service they could provide. This achieved its short-term aim, of persuading government to allocate some additional resources to the capital, but whether it will be successful in the longer term remains to be seen (see below). Finally, the emphasis on increased patient throughput, cited by government as evidence of record levels of efficiency, is imposing massive financial pressure on DHAs as increased throughput threatens their ability to contain expenditure. As a unit administrator commented, he would not wish to see increases in throughput because 'we are heading for a £1.5m overspend next year and *we don't want to see a lot of patients being treated*' (quoted in the *Health and Social Service Journal*, 27 February 1986). Increased throughput is cash-demanding, not cash-releasing.

Fourthly, DHAs may attempt to release resources by cost improvement programmes, chief among which is the restraint of the wages bill. Central government have encouraged this by underfunding pay settlements, by imposing manpower ceilings, and by directing that any increases in staff ought to be in front-line troops (medical and nursing personnel in particular), rather than in support services. In addition, DHAs are seeking savings through intensification of working practices (e.g. reducing overlaps between nursing shifts), non-replacement of staff, and privatisation of ancillary services. The marginal impact of the latter – savings of £41m on an annual budget for support services of £3000m – have been bought at the expense of the wages and terms and conditions of service of the worst-paid workers in the NHS. Some 4250 cases of redundancy or early retirement are expected this year (House of Commons, 1986, p. xix). Restraint of NHS manpower costs has again had a geographically differentiated impact. Regionally, the Thames RHAs have borne the brunt of the reductions; subregionally, the impact of privatisation, for example, has been hardest in inner city areas, devastated by deindustrialisation, where the NHS has hitherto been a major source of stable employment. Table 5.1 shows employment change in DHAs in London from 1982–5; note that these factors do not allow the effects of privatisation to be separated from those of hospital closures. Though some displaced ancillary workers will have found employment with private contractors, this will have been associated with a weakening of their labour market position due to the poorer wages and conditions offered by contractors (Coyle, 1985; Leedham, 1985).

Finally, health authorities are operating on overtly commercial lines

TABLE 5.1   *Nursing and ancillary employment change in Greater London DHAS, 1982–5*

DHA	Nursing				Ancillary			
	1982	1985	Change	%	1982	1985	Change	%
Barnet	3220	2930	−290	−9.0	1340	1080	−260	−19.4
Harrow	1430	1390	−40	−2.8	670	470	−200	−29.8
Hillingdon	2120	2020	−100	−4.7	830	720	−110	−13.2
Hounslow/Spelthorne	2210	1950	−260	−11.7	970	510	−460	−47.4
Ealing	1770	1850	80	4.5	750	470	−280	−37.3
Brent	2120	2040	−80	−3.7	870	750	−120	−13.8
Barking/Havering	3290	3340	50	1.5	1320	1080	−240	−18.2
Enfield	1430	1530	100	7.0	620	510	−110	−17.7
Haringey	1380	1310	−70	−5.1	650	450	−200	−30.8
Redbridge	1550	1620	70	4.5	590	480	−110	−18.6
Waltham F.	2780	2550	−230	−8.3	1300	930	−370	−28.5
Bexley	1660	1580	−80	−4.8	700	570	−130	−18.6
Greenwich	2310	2180	−130	−5.6	1310	1000	−310	−23.7
Bromley	2380	2200	−180	−7.6	1000	480	−520	−52.0
Croydon	2540	2500	−40	−1.6	1130	860	−270	−23.9
Kingston/Esher	1650	1640	−10	−0.6	700	570	−130	−18.6
Rich/Twick/Roe	1470	1470	0	0	570	340	−230	−40.3
Merton/Sutton	2960	2840	−120	−4.0	1220	810	−410	−33.6
Paddington	2140	2150	10	0.5	980	780	−200	−20.4
Hammersmith/Fulham	1630	1660	30	1.8	770	670	−100	−13.0
Victoria	2830	2730	−100	−3.5	1260	840	−420	−33.3
Hampstead	2220	2180	−40	−1.8	1220	960	−260	−21.3
Bloomsbury	3850	3330	−80	−13.5	2100	1610	−490	−23.3
Islington	1680	1590	−90	−5.3	850	670	−180	−21.2
City/Hackney	2870	2730	−140	−4.9	1450	1160	−290	−20.0
Newham	1330	1290	−40	−3.0	660	470	−190	−28.8
Tower Hamlets	2400	2330	−70	−2.9	1100	870	−230	−20.9
W. Lambeth	2600	2570	−30	−1.1	1460	1200	−260	−17.8
Camberwell	2180	2210	30	1.4	1130	780	−350	−31.0
Lewisham/N. Southwark	3710	3540	−170	−4.6	1560	1440	−120	−7.7
Wandsworth	3310	3090	−220	−6.6	1480	1090	−390	−26.4
Total	71020	68340	−2680	−3.8	32560	24620	−7940	−24.4

Note: All data refers to whole-time equivalent staff

in order to raise money. A prime example is the disposal of 'surplus' buildings and land. Proceeds from sales are retained by the DHAs concerned, even though variable property prices build in a further dimension to geographical inequality in the NHS. Prime sites – disused urban hospitals and the grounds of psychiatric hospitals – could be a financial lifeline to hard-pressed authorities: what price the 'Epsom cluster', 570 acres of land used by psychiatric hospitals, only minutes from the M25? Not only is this policy a classic case of selling the furniture to pay the rent, it could also affect the rational planning of services, if authorities push through hospital closures for the sake of realising the value of the property.

There are several other ways in which health authorities are seeking to raise funds. These include greater reliance on voluntary and charitable sources of funds – witness the 'saving' of Tadworth Court Children's Hospital with finance from the Spastics Society – and also the overtly commercial approaches being taken by certain DHAs. For example, in Nottingham the DHA are utilising spare laundry capacity by taking in washing on a commercial basis; Central Manchester DHA have considered leasing sites within hospitals to commercial concerns such as hairdressers; and it is reported that Camberwell DHA may resort to charging businessmen for health screening in order to raise funds. On one level, this could be seen as the sensible use of resources, but it is no accident that health authorities are in this position; it reflects systematic government underfunding (House of Commons, 1986). There is a symbolic significance, also, in the penetration of the profit motive into the public hospital – a site from which commercial considerations ought to be banished. It is also obvious that raising funds from commercial or charitable funds will build in still greater geographical inequality in the service, due to regional and local variations in economic development. For evidence of this one has only to look at the wartime Hospital Surveys (Nuffield Provincial Hospitals Trust, 1946) which clearly illustrate the uneven development associated with a part-state, part-private health care system.

The effect of these policies on access to health care at the local scale depends not just on the resources available to health authorities but also on the balance between local authority, family practitioner, and hospital services. The most obvious effect is the concentration of hospital services onto fewer sites. This was the central feature of the 1962 Hospital Plan (Ministry of Health, 1962) but the significant difference is that hospital services are now being progressively withdrawn in an *ad hoc* fashion even though not all the new hospitals promised by the Plan have been provided. As Harrison (1983) reminds us, 'transport is the third element of the health care system' and so the impact of this concentration of resources on accessibility may be more or less serious depending on access to transport, which is geographically differentiated by the nature of transport systems and by the spatial segregation of social classes since car ownership is obviously related to income. For those without private transport, current proposals to deregulate bus services will not necessarily improve the situation, because the scope for cross-subsidisation of routes will be much reduced as private operators snap up profitable routes but do not take on potentially unprofitable ones.

A related effect is that hospitals chosen for closure are often specialist units. Casualty departments are a case in point, with N.E. Thames RHA operating a policy of one department per DHA. However, a number of specialist hospitals have also closed, depriving patients of specialist facilities. There are arguments for closure on efficiency grounds but there is no doubt that these closures have generated substantial resentment from the affected communities.

A third consequence of rationalisation results from the balance between hospital and family practitioner services. The poor quality of the latter in inner London (see Jarman, 1981) means that residents tend to use casualty departments as an alternative source of primary care, imposing yet greater burdens on the hard-pressed acute sector.

Finally, these expenditure policies severely restrict the ability of health authorities to develop services for priority groups. For example, City and Hackney DHA's *Operational Plan* actually *proposes* a shortfall of 39 beds and 49 day places for the mentally distressed, and a shortfall of 14 beds and 58 day places below the *minimum* requirements for the elderly mentally infirm. The DHA lacks the funds to support compensating increases in community care, as does the local council (London Health Emergency, 1986). The laudable principles of community care are likely to fail, therefore, for lack of adequate funds (House of Commons, 1985).

PRIMARY CARE: SPATIAL INEQUALITIES UNDIMINISHED?

The 1979 Royal Commission concluded that the NHS was failing to provide adequate primary care in inner city areas. This was endorsed by the Jarman and Acheson reports, both of which showed the problems of inner city general practice with reference to individual FPCs in London (Acheson, 1981; Jarman, 1981). However, the general conclusions of these reports must be qualified: the picture they present of a contrast between the deprived inner city and the well-off suburbs is an overgeneralisation. Moreover, any attempt to examine spatial inequalities in GP services must consider inequalities in the nature of services provided: practice quality is an essential component of access to services. Without disaggregating the scale of our analyses and without considering service quality, we risk being left with yet another appeal to the 'inverse care law' (Hart, 1971). Here I want to

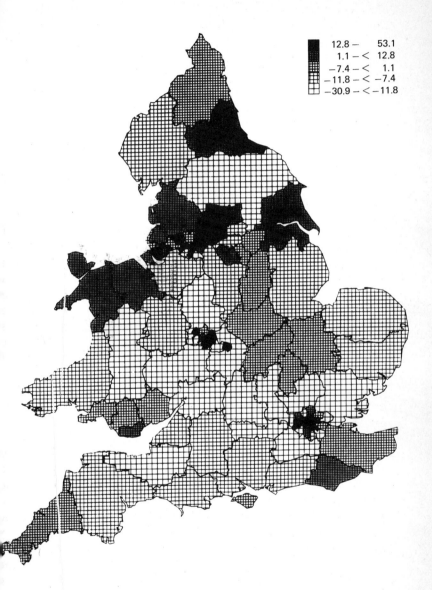

12.8 —   53.1
 1.1 — < 12.8
−7.4 — <   1.1
−11.8 — < −7.4
−30.9 — < −11.8

FIGURE 5.1   *Underprivileged area (UPA) score for FPCs in England and*
Wales, 1981

put forward evidence which begins to question the conventional wisdom about the geography of GP services. I go on to consider the implications of the recent Green Paper for the geography of primary care.

Taking 'need' for health care first of all, and allowing for the technical and conceptual problems in assessing need, it can be shown, using the composite index derived by Jarman (1983), that need for health care seems to be higher in the inner London DHAs than in outer London. On the 'Jarman 8' composite index, the inner urban Family Practitioner Committee (FPC) areas clearly come out as areas with particularly high need (Figure 5.1). The inner London DHAs are among the highest need areas nationally but even Waltham Forest ranks fortieth.

Turning to levels of service provision, at the RHA level, variations in list size are small: in 1984 average list size for RHAs varied from 1947 in the South Western RHA to 2155 in Trent (*Regional Trends*, 1985, Table 4.13). For FPCs in England and Wales it is possible to extract the number of responsible General Medical Practitioners per 10 000 population from the FPC Performance Indicators. The range here in 1984 was from 5.86 GPs/10 000 people, in Kensington, Chelsea and Westminster, to 4.1 in Rotherham FPC. Note that, although these figures indicate respective population/GP figures of 1707 and 2439, this is not equivalent to list size. At a more local scale, Powell (1986) notes the contrast between inner and outer London DHAs on several indicators of service provision, with the inner areas in general being better off. Powell demonstrated negative correlations between census-based need indicators and provision indicators, so that high needs were generally matched with high levels of provision. However, there were important spatial variations in service provision relative to average levels of provision which did not fit the idea of a simple inner city/outer city dichotomy, and these variations were not constant across all health services. The generalisation that inner cities are in all cases worse off than their suburban counterparts should therefore be taken with a pinch of salt.

Indicators of service quality also show considerable spatial variations. There are problems with deriving an appropriate index but in general the proportion of GPs practising single-handed is a reasonable indicator since group practice is usually regarded as more desirable. While Inner and Outer London exhibited a quite different pattern of practice, individual DHAs *within* each area very considerably. Haringey closely resembles an Outer London DHA but

TABLE 5.2   *General practitioner provision and practice structure: selected DHAs in N.E. Thames RHA, 1981*

	Population per GP	% GPs practising single-handed	% GPs practising from health centres
Inner London			
Bloomsbury	994	38.1	21.6
Hampstead	2096	43.6	10.9
Haringey	1570	22.5	7.0
Newham	1972	21.7	10.4
Average for Inner DHAs	1562	28.9	15.5
Outer London			
Barking/Havering	2263	29.6	6.4
Enfield	1824	13.5	12.8
Redbridge	1904	25.4	23.7
Waltham Forest	2104	41.0	22.5
Average for Outer DHAs	1915	22.1	14.0

Source: Powell, 1986.

the percentage of GPs practising single-handed in Waltham Forest (41 per cent) was second only to Hampstead (Table 5.2).

So the generalisation that there is a contrast between the poorly-provided inner city, and the well-off suburbs, cannot be sustained: even at DHA level, there are departures from this expectation. Within DHAs there are also major variations in provision. Table 5.3 shows average list size, the proportion of GPs aged over 65, and the proportion of GPs practising single-handed, for MPCs within the Waltham Forest DHA. On these indicators of practice structure, Chingford has the highest proportions of elderly and of single-handed GPs. However, Leyton has a low proportion aged over 65 and has no GPs practising from health centres. It is clear, then, that variations at

TABLE 5.3   *General practitioner provision indices for MPC areas in Waltham Forest DHA, 1981*

MPC Area	List size	% Practising single-handed	% Aged over 65*
Leyton	2188	38	8
Walthamstow	2126	30	19
Chingford	1887	65	32
Waltham Forest DHA	2010	41	17

* Estimate, based on no. of GPs qualified for over 40 years.
Source: Powell, 1986.

this spatial scale are at least as great as those between DHAs, though we cannot accurately compare these variations with variations in need at MPC scale, as we lack reliable population figures for MPCs.

The geography of primary care is complex: it is much more than the simple question of the distribution of GPs in relation to population. In addition, we need to consider the distribution of groups in need for care and also variations in the quality of GP services. These are topics which have been hotly debated and upon which no consensus exists. Moreover, variability is likely to be greatest at the local (e.g. MPC area) scale.

All this has implications for resource allocation. There have been welcome signs of a move away from the average list size as a criterion on which to judge whether or not a MPC area needs additional GPs. Jarman (1983) has recommended the use of the composite Under Privileged Area (UPA) score, though this has been criticised for being based on GP perceptions, using an arbitrary list of variables, and compositing indicators in an additive manner for no obvious reason (see Scott-Samuel, 1984 and Thunhurst, 1985). Whatever the relative merits of the Jarman and Scott-Samuel schemes, future policy will have to attempt to incorporate some consideration of need and, for all their limitations, census data are the best we have at present. However, merely allocating more money to areas in need will be inadequate without monitoring service quality and performance.

In this context the recent Green Paper has some positive features. It recommends, among other things, controls on GP retirement age; increased building allowances, and possibly salaried practice, in inner cities; abolishing the minimum practice allowance and giving more incentives to take on NHS patients by moving towards a capitation-fee system; some quality control, by using a system of peer group reference; and incentives for GPs to provide certain services (e.g. doing their own deputising). In principle, all of these are to be welcomed as a step towards improving the quality of GP services in the inner city (and indeed nationally), but whether implementing them will be politically feasible remains to be seen.

Finally, there is a need for much research on these lines. Although attention has been focused here on the inner city, especially London, there are other areas (e.g. postwar council estates) where service provision has not kept up with need. A national study of regional and local variations in the GP service is essential. This should be linked to an examination of the relatonships between the distribution of services and that of groups in need. Finally, the GP service should not be looked at in isolation. Ideally, an examination, on a small-area basis, of the relationships between social deprivation, the distribution and use of GP services, and the provision and utilisation of hospital services, is required. At present the GP and hospital services are considered and planned in isolation, but they have to be seen as part of an integrated health care system.

THE PRIVATE SECTOR: HARBINGER OF A TWO-TIER SYSTEM?

The historical development and the geography of private health care are now reasonably well-known and so discussion is limited to four points, to which relatively little attention has been given. Firstly, the private sector boom has at least as much to do with the visible hand of government as with the hidden hand of the market. Second, the private sector is not undifferentiated. Third, private sector expansion seems to have tailed off, especially in the acute sector, raising the question of how far it can continue. Finally, there is the question of the relationships between the private sector and central government, and between the private sector and the NHS.

The first point can be dealt with quickly. The recent expansion in private health care reflects both the inadvertent and deliberate consequences of government decisions. Inadvertent, because the Labour Party's attempt at eliminating private practice from NHS hospitals created a climate in which developers could invest in private hospitals with confidence; and deliberate, because the Conservatives have introduced various policies designed to facilitate expansion. These have included relaxations of controls on private hospital developments, permitting NHS consultants to carry out more private work, allowing health authorities to enter contractual arrangements with profit-making hospitals, and limited tax concessions to the beneficiaries of company-paid private insurance schemes. However, the private sector is not as independent as it would like to claim, as the repeated private sector criticisms of government policy clearly show: there have been demands for tax relief on insurance premiums and for greater state regulation of hospital development. Private sector growth, then, is not a simple reflection of the free play of market forces: it has been both inadvertently and deliberately stimulated by government decisions.

Secondly, the private acute sector is not undifferentiated. Three types of organisation are identifiable: charitable and religious concerns; commercial British organisations; and multinational hospital chains. In the postwar years, private health care was associated almost exclusively with charitable and religious hospitals. However, these facilities are being slowly squeezed out by competition, mainly because they lack the resources to compete with commercial hospitals. British commercial concerns were slow to enter the market; the main stimuli to their doing so were the 1976 paybed legislation and the realisation that this would provoke an invasion of American capital. However, in the absence of a tradition of commercial involvement in private health care, British investors have been slow to expand their activities. Due to their lower levels of capitalisation and limited resources their activities have been on a smaller scale than multinational corporations, and they have generally avoided areas, such as central London, where competition is most severe. Finally the entry of multinational, particularly American, capital, has been the most distinctive feature of the market in recent years. This has led to the construction of a number of high technology luxury hospitals. The American perception of the ailing public health care system in Britain, as opposed to other West European states such as France, was undoubtedly instrumental in their decision to invest in Britain.

Thus three types of organisation may be identified in the private acute sector, and we may also identify three geographies. Firstly, central London is unique in terms of the size of the private sector (over 25 per cent of all private acute hospital beds in the UK are located there), the prominence of foreign capital, the scale of the individual hospitals, and the high technology nature of the workload. This exceptional concentration, especially around Harley Street, results from the national and international market, and it also reflects the proximity of teaching hospitals, the deliberate policies of exclusion practised by local landowners, and the priority given to medical land uses by the local council, Westminster. Although small in extent, Harley Street is a distinctive area of economic specialisation in much the same way as the City or other zones of functional specialisation in London.

Secondly, the geography of private acute hospitals in the rest of the country primarily reflects geographical variations in insurance coverage. At regional level this ranges from 3 per cent (Northern) to 14 per cent in the Outer Metropolitan Area. More locally coverage may be as high as 18 per cent in parts of Buckinghamshire and Berkshire

(Mohan, 1984). There are also substantial social variations in insurance coverage (OPCS, 1985). These social and spatial variations are reflected in the distribution of acute private hospital beds: N.W. and N.E. Thames RHAs respectively have 41 and 34 such beds per 100 000 population compared to 2 beds in the Northern region. As well as insurance markets, the distribution of these beds reflects the ability of local communities to raise funds, and the details of the location of individual hospitals reflect the influence of NHS consultants: sites as close as possible to major NHS hospitals are highly prized (Mohan, 1984), which has exposed private hospitals to the charge of locational parasitism.

The third, and numerically the largest, component of the private sector is the private nursing homes industry, providing some 32 000 beds in over 1000 institutions. Their distribution broadly reflects that of popular areas of retirement migration along the South Coast (Law and Warnes, 1984) – the Costa Geriatrica. All the RHAs along the South Coast have around 100 beds per 100 000 population in institutions without operating theatres – in other words, nursing homes (see Figure 5.2). There are exceptional concentrations of such facilities in DHAs such as Brighton (1228 beds), Eastbourne (1001), Hastings (896), Worthing (818) and East Dorset (1096) (*Hansard*, 15 April 1985). When one compares these figures with the total number of non-psychiatric NHS hospital beds in each of those DHAs (e.g. Hastings 771, Worthing 1082) it is obvious that we can speak of a dual health care system in some localities since the private sector is as large as, if not larger than, the NHS. Again, the recent boom in these facilities can partly be attributed to government policy, namely restrictions on local authority expenditure and changes to DHSS benefit regulations. Amendments to the latter, introduced in 1980, allow the DHSS to 'pay out extra allowances sufficient to cover fees in private homes for people presenting in need of care' (Godber, 1984, p. 1473). It is merely necessary to demonstrate that no places are available in a local authority home, and strict control of local authority expenditure naturally creates intense pressure on such places. This indirectly plays into the hands of the private sector for, as the Social Services Committee recently observed, health and local authorities may be 'deliberately directing the elderly in need of residential care into the private sector *where the non-cash-limited funds of supplementary benefit can foot the bill*' (House of Commons, 1984, xxviii, emphasis added). Government policies are thus fuelling an unplanned boom in the private sector with associated problems of cost

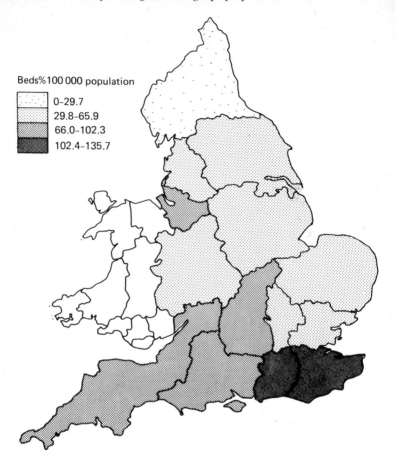

Beds%100 000 population

- 0–29.7
- 29.8–65.9
- 66.0–102.3
- 102.4–135.7

FIGURE 5.2   *Private hospital beds in institutions without operating theatres,*
1983
Source: DHSS information.

control and monitoring of standards (see Phillips and Vincent, 1986a, b).

We can, then, legitimately talk of three private sectors and the character of the private health care industry is spatially differentiated. However there are indications that its expansion, especially in the acute sector, may have peaked. It seems unlikely that insurance coverage will expand much beyond its present level of approximately 8 per cent. In recent years the numbers of individual subscriptions has fallen although the expansion of company-paid policies has continued.

The provident associations are expanding their promotional activities in those areas where insurance coverage is lowest. Precisely because of high levels of unemployment and relatively low disposable incomes, these regions are unlikely to be able to sustain much further growth. Hospital overcapacity is the other problem. It has been estimated that one third of all private beds are empty, and overcapacity problems are apparently occurring in London, West Yorkshire and the West Midlands. The pace of development activity has slowed dramatically in the past two years. Some charitable or religious hospitals have succumbed to competition; one indigenous commercial concern, Sloane Hospitals, was absorbed by AMI in 1984, and the closure of the Nightingale BUPA Hospital in London was recently announced.

While it is an exaggeration to speak of a crisis in the private sector, several criticisms of the government have been voiced as a result of these problems: these share the view that the government ought to do more to guarantee the private sector's expansion. There are technical and political reasons why greater intervention seems unlikely at present (Mohan, 1986a), though one possibility would be greater cooperation with the NHS. For example, it has been argued that private sector work load should be considered in the RAWP calculations. Williams *et al.* (1984) show that some 20 per cent of all elective surgery is carried out privately in some regions, such as S.W. Thames, and they therefore argue that the population of such areas are proportionally better served by the NHS. Their policy prescription would involve reducing the resources made available to health authorities for elective surgery by the proportion of work carried out privately. The technical problem here concerns the rate of change; it would be impossible to remove overnight 20 per cent of S.W. Thames RHA's elective surgery budget without major disruptions to services and cuts in jobs. The political problem, however, is much more serious. Incorporating the private sector in RAWP would imply acceptance that at least part of the nation's health services should be provided privately, thus opening up the possibility of a two-tier health system.

This option seems unlikely to be taken up at present. Much more likely is an expansion of contractual arrangements between the NHS and the private sector. This might even involve preventing DHAs from building new facilities, if suitable spare capacity was available in the private sector. Several initiatives in South East England suggest that the boundary between public and private sectors is becoming more blurred. These have included reliance on charities for funds to keep hospitals open, an expansion of contractual arrangements, and even proposals to rely on commercial funding of the planning of services (Mohan, 1986b). As well as this we are seeing health authorities overtly relying on commercial tactics for fundraising, for instance by leasing sites for shops within hospitals. If the NHS is not to be demolished yet, it seems nevertheless that the basic principle of the NHS – a service provided free at the point of use and funded from direct taxation – is being progressively eroded. The broader implications of this are taken up in the concluding section.

THE FUTURE GEOGRAPHY OF HEALTH CARE?

I want to make three points in conclusion. The first is that spatial inequalities in health care provision are complex and deserving of rather more research attention than has hitherto been the case. Secondly, I speculate on the likely future geography of health care. Finally, I consider the more general implications of the issues discussed here.

First of all there is much more to geographical work on health care than merely describing spatial patterns of service provision. The explanation of these patterns is of course very much a transdisciplinary effort, necessitating the borrowing of ideas from other disciplines such as politics and sociology. However the question of geographical differentiation is of the first importance. Geography genuinely matters: it is not just a passive element in social change but an active agent therein, and three examples will make the point. The crisis in London's hospital services, for example, is a classic illustration of what Harvey (1982, pp. 398–405) calls the 'territoriality of social infrastructures'. By definition, these are fixed in space and thus they are effectively devalued by geographical shifts in employment (and so population). This can lead to the formulation of territorially-based coalitions concerned with defending existing patterns of services, though the danger of this is that health authorities fall into the trap of a debate about the special claims of *their* services, rather than a more general questioning of the reasons why the NHS budget is limited. This point was graphically expressed by Widgery (1979) in his argument that health authorities had 'fallen for the trap of an interregional scrap' when debating the RAWP proposals, while the recent Parliamentary debate and public concern about London's hospitals was perhaps an even better illustration. Although additional resources have been allocated in the short term, in the longer term this concern will only have postponed the crisis, rather than averting it.

Secondly, the uneven geographical development of private health care is itself posing problems as there are too many beds chasing too few patients in certain localities, forcing the private sector to seek new markets elsewhere and also, ironically, provoking criticisms of central government's attitude to private health care. Finally, the task health authorities have to do, the resources available to them, and their political composition, may vary enormously: contrast a typical inner London DHA (high concentrations of deprived populations; poor primary care; losing resources under RAWP; and strong Labour representation on the DHA) with one on the South Coast (high concentrations of the elderly; a very large private sector; strong Conservative representation; and gaining resources under RAWP). Clearly the nature of the tasks to be carried out, and the way this is done, will vary greatly. Geography, then, is important and there are a number of research questions to be answered. These include: the impact of current policies on health care provision, at various scales; the relationships between social deprivation, need for health care, and patterns of service provision and utilisation; geographical variations in the 'performance' of the NHS between DHAs; and the changing balance between public and private health care in different localities.

How these issues are to be researched is a further issue. There is a case for looking at the aggregate patterns of change using what Sayer (1984) describes as an extensive research strategy. The aim here would be to produce an overall map of the geography of health care, and seeking to highlight general patterns and regularities, and local anomalies. A national atlas of the health service would be a useful way to convey the results of such a study. *Explaining* the variations identified would be a different matter. This would involve an intensive research strategy, necessitating in-depth investigations of the processes producing the patterns revealed.

What of the future geography of health care? Assuming the continuation of current policies, the first feature will be continued rationalisation of acute hospital capacity in inner urban areas, though the government's reaction to the crisis in the London teaching hospitals does suggest that they are prepared to allocate additional resources in exceptional cases, to head off suggestions that they lack commitment to the NHS. The review of RAWP currently being undertaken may help the inner cities if it leads to the inclusion of a deprivation factor in the formula. Secondly, we can expect continued expansion in privately-owned, publicly-funded nursing homes for the elderly and limited growth in the private acute sector. There is likely to be a greater degree of commercialisation and probably an expansion of contractual arrangements with the NHS, especially in those areas where NHS waiting lists are high and private sector overcapacity exists. Thirdly, privatisation of ancillary services will be stressed especially in those localities where relatively little has yet been privatised, though this will be uneven because not all areas offer large potential profits to contractors (especially rural DHAs), and because of resistance by DHAs and by NHS unions. Fourthly, we can expect to see decentralised psychiatric care, some redistribution of primary care services, if the current Green Paper is implemented, and possibly increasing voluntary and charitable provision. As yet there is no firm evidence that the government will introduce greater competition into health care provision via the American-style Health Maintenance Organisation (HMO) concept. This would be most likely to benefit well-off suburban areas characterised by middle class young families, but it would do relatively little for the deprived inner city areas or for groups (e.g., the elderly) likely to place high demands on them.

Finally, the issues discussed here are not simply questions of geographical distribution: they reflect political choices about national expenditure priorities. Discussion of the geography of health care cannot be abstracted from three crucial points: Britain's poor record on health care spending as a proportion of GNP; the changing balance of public expenditures between, say, defence and the NHS (Lee *et al.*, 1983); and the systematic underfunding of the HCHS, to the tune of £1.3 billion over the past five years (House of Commons, 1986). The net effect of all this has been to place value for money at the top of the agenda for the NHS, which is valid enough, but it is transforming the nature of debates about the service, which are now all about performance, efficiency and patient throughput. These changes, moreover, are having a differentiated geographical impact. They are forcing difficult, if not impossible, choices on certain health authorities in London (and elsewhere), as well as transforming the balance between public and private health care in certain localities. Economics may be about choices, but the nature of choices made *nationally* can have a massively differentiated effect *locally*. In this respect the study of spatial variations in health care provision is crucial both to complete understanding of how the health care system works, and to a reorientation of geography towards what Smith (1977) calls the study of 'who gets what, where and how'.

ACKNOWLEDGEMENT

The research on which this paper is based is funded by an ESRC Postdoctoral Fellowship, grant no: A23320036. I would also like to thank David Smith and John Eyles for their comments.

REFERENCES

Acheson, D. (1981) *Primary Health Care in Inner London: Report of a Study Group*, London: DHSS.

ALA (1986) *London's Health Service in Crisis*, London: Association of London Authorities.

Bevan, G. and Brazier, J. (1985) 'Subregional RAWP – Hobson's Choice?', *Health and Social Services Journal*, 95 (4963), 1064–5.

Bevan, G., Beech, R. and Craig, M. (1985) 'Alternatives to RAWP' *Health and Social Services Journal*, 95 (4964), 1098–99.

Coyle, A. (1985) 'Going Private: The Implications of Privatization for Women's Work', *Feminist Review*, 21, 5–23.

DHSS (1976) *Sharing Resources for Health in England*, London: DHSS.

Eyles, J., Smith, D. and Woods, K. (1982) 'Spatial Resource Allocation and State Practice: The Case of NHS Planning in London', *Regional Studies*, 16, 239–52.

GLC (1985) *A Critical Guide to NHS Resource Allocation in London*, London: GLC.

Godber, C. (1984) 'Private Rest Homes: Answers Needed', *British Medical Journal*, 288, 1473–4.

Griffith, B., Rayner, G. and Mohan, J. (1985) *Commercial Medicine in London*, London: GLC.

Harrison, P. (1983) *Inside the Inner City*, Harmondsworth: Penguin.

Hart, J. T. (1971) 'The Inverse Care Law', *Lancet*, i, 405–12.

Harvey, D. (1982) *The Limits to Capital*, Oxford: Basil Blackwell.

House of Commons (1984) *Fourth Report of the Social Services Committee: Public Expenditure on the Social Services*, London: House of Commons.

House of Commons (1985) *Sixth Report from the Social Services Committee: Public Expenditure on the Social Services*, London: House of Commons.

House of Commons (1986) *Fourth Report from the Social Services Committee, Session 1985–6: Public Expenditure on the Social Services*, London: House of Commons.

House of Lords (1890) *Report of the Select Committee on Metropolitan Hospital Accommodation*, London: House of Lords.

Jarman, B. (1981) *A Survey of Primary Care in London*, Occasional Paper 16, Royal College of General Practitioners, London.

Jarman, B. (1983) 'Identification of Underprivileged Areas', *British Medical Journal*, 286, 1705–9.

Law, C. M. and Warnes, A. (1984) 'The Elderly Population of Great Britain: Locational Trends and Policy Implications *Trans. Inst. Br. Geogr.*, NS 9(1), 37–59.

Lee, P. *et al*. (1983) 'Banishing dark divisive clouds: Welfare and the Conservative Government, 1979–83', *Critical Social Policy*, 8, 6–44.

Leedham, W. (1986) *The Privatisation of NHS Ancillary Services* (WEA Studies for Trade Unionists, vol. 12, no. 45) London: Workers' Educational Association.

London Health Emergency (1986) *Downhill All The Way: The Crisis in London's Health Service*, London: London Health Emergency.

Ministry of Health (1962) *A Hospital Plan for England and Wales*, London: Ministry of Health.

Mohan, J. F. (1984) 'Geographical Aspects of Private Hospital Developments in Britain', *Area*, 16(3), 191–9.

Mohan, J. (1986a) 'Private Medical Care and the British Conservative Government: What Price Independence?', *Journal of Social Policy*, 15(4), 337–60.

Mohan, J. (1986b) 'Commercial Medicine and the NHS in South East England: The Shape of Things to Come?' in Eyles, J. (ed.) *Health Care and the City*, Occasional Paper 28, Department of Geography, Queen Mary College, London.

Newcastle Health Concern (1986) *Cause for Concern: the State of Newcastle's NHS*, North East Trade Union Studies Information Unit, Newcastle.

Nuffield Provincial Hospitals Trust (1946) *The Hospital Surveys: the Domesday Book of the Hospital Service*, Nuffield Provincial Hospitals Trust, London.

OPCS (1985) *General Household Survey, 1983*, London: OPCS.

Phillips, D. R. and Vincent, J. A. (1986a) 'Private Residential Accommodation for the Elderly: Geographical Aspects of Developments in Devon', *Trans. Inst. Br. Geogr.*, 11(2), 155–73.

Phillips, D. R. and Vincent, J. A. (1986b) 'Petit Bourgeois Care: Private Residential Care for the Elderly', *Policy and Politics*, 14(2), 189–208.

Political and Economic Planning (1937) *Report on the British Health Service*, London: PEP.

Powell, M. (1986) 'Primary Health Care in London: Needs, Resources and Equity', in Eyles, J. (ed.) *Health Care and the City*, Occasional Paper 28, Geography Department, Queen Mary College, London.

Radical Statistics Health Group (1977) *RAW(P) Deals: A Critique of the Resource Allocation Working Party*, London: Radical Statistics Health Group.

Sayer, A. (1984) *Method in Social Science: A Realist Approach*, London: Hutchinson.

Scott-Samuel, A. (1984) 'Need for Primary Health Care: An Objective Indicator', *British Medical Journal*.

Smith, D. M. (1977) *Human Geography: A Welfare Approach*, London: Edward Arnold.

Thunhurst, C. (1985) 'The Analysis of Small Area Statistics and Planning for Health', *The Statistician*, 34, 93–106.

Townsend, P. and Davidson, N. (1982) *Inequalities in Health*, Harmondsworth: Penguin.

Widgery, D. (1979) *Health in Danger*, London: Macmillan.

Williams, B. T., Nicholl, J. P., Thomas, K. J. and Knowelden, J. (1984) 'Contribution of the Private Sector to Elective Surgery in England', *Lancet*, ii, 88–92.

Woods, K. J. (1982) 'Social Deprivation and Resource Allocation in the Thames Regional Health Authorities' in D. M. Smith *et al.*, *Contemporary Perspectives on Health and Health Care*, Occasional Paper 20, Geography Department, Queen Mary College, London.

6 Suicide, Selection and Unemployment

HUGH GRAVELLE

1. INTRODUCTION

The suggestion that increases in unemployment lead to increases in suicides is perhaps the most dramatic example of the argument that there are important social costs of unemployment in addition to the loss of output which could have been produced by the unemployed workers. In this paper I propose to discuss and illustrate the problems which can arise when attempts are made to investigate the relationship between unemployment and suicidal behaviour.

The discussion will be structured by reference to an economic model of suicide which is developed in the next part of this section. The difficulties which can hamper empirical investigations are then outlined. Particular attention will be paid to the selection effect. The implications of selection for the interpretations of the results of some recent British studies will be examined in Section 2. It will be argued that time series studies using aggregate population level data are less likely to suffer from selection effect bias. In Section 3 the preliminary results from a time series analysis of male suicide rates in Great Britain from 1923 to 1981 are presented and discussed in the light of the model of Section 1 and the arguments in Section 2. Section 4 contains some concluding and cautionary remarks.

Since much of the paper derives from the simple models of suicide and selection presented in this section, it may be useful to briefly set out the advantages of such formal modelling. First, the assumptions which underlie arguments are made explicit, so that differences in conclusions can be explained and sensibly discussed. Second, a formal theoretical model guides empirical work by providing explicit hypotheses to test against the data. The appropriate estimating equations may be much more complicated than would be suggested by a casual, informal, account of the determinants of suicidal behaviour. Third, the available data are often incomplete, or otherwise imperfect, and a theoretical model indicates how this should influence the interpretation of empirical results from various types of data. For example, the observation that the unemployed are more suicide prone, or that individuals who commit suicide are more likely to have been unemployed, or that population unemployment and suicide rates are positively correlated, might appear to be clear confirmations of the proposition that increased unemployment leads to increased suicides. As shown in section 2, in the absence of information on predisposing characteristics, these empirical findings could merely be reflections of the selection effect. A formal model will provide some indications of the possible biases arising from missing data or show what assumptions are necessary for such biases not to arise.

A Simple Suicide Model

At time t an individual will decide whether or not to commit suicide by comparing the utility associated with these alternatives. During period t an individual who does not commit suicide will have the expected utility $J_t^0(c_t^0, z_t^0)$. In this notation c_t^0 is a (large dimensional) vector of variables describing the individual's circumstances in the period. It would include such things as health status, employment status, education level, housing conditions, consumption pattern, wealth or income levels, the weather and environmental variables. The individual's tastes or preferences are indicated by the vector z_t^0. It is assumed that the preference parameters are not observable.

If the individual does not commit suicide in period t, he can also expect to enjoy utility in future periods $t + 1, t + 2$, etc. Let $J_t^2(c_t^2, z_t^2)$ denote the expected discounted value at time t of the sum of all future utilities. The individual's circumstances in all future periods, as anticipated at t, are indicated by c_t^2 and z_t^2 describes future tastes.

If the individual does commit suicide at t, his utility is just $J_t^1(c_t^1, z_t^1)$. This utility function is not intended to imply that dead individuals have preferences, nor that live individuals would like being dead. J_t^1 is merely a numerical representation of the individual's preferences (whilst he is alive) over the state of affairs arising if he commits suicide. Thus individuals with a greater distaste for suicide *per se* (perhaps because of religious beliefs) would have, for a given c_t^1, a lower level of J_t^1. Similarly, the circumstances after suicide, denoted by c_t^1, might include the wealth left to heirs.

An individual will commit suicide in period t if, and only if,

$$J_t^0(c_t^0, z_t^0) + J_t^2(c_t^2, z_t^2) < J_t^1(c_t^1, z_t^1) \tag{6.1}$$

Let $Z_t(c_t)$ be the set of taste vectors $z_t = (z_t^0, z_t^1, z_t^2)$ which satisfy (6.1) for given circumstances $c_t = (c_t^0, c_t^1, c_t^2)$. The taste parameter vector z_t is not observable, but we assume that it has a known joint probability distribution. The probability that the individual with circumstances c_t commits suicide is

$$Pr \ [\text{suicide: } c_t] = Pr \ [z_t \varepsilon Z_t(c_t)] = \pi(c_t) \tag{6.2}$$

As a simple example, suppose that there are no unobservable taste parameters in J_t^0 or J_t^2 and $J_t^1 = g(c_t^1) - z_t^1$. The unobservable parameter z_t^1 measures distaste for suicide. Suppose that z_t^1 has a known probability distribution function $F(z_t^1)$. Rearranging (6.1), suicide occurs if, and only if,

$$z_t^1 < J_t^0(c_t^0) - g(c_t^1) + J_t^2(c_t^2) \tag{6.3}$$

and this event has probability

$$\pi(c_t) = F(J_t^0(c_t^0) - g(c_t^1) + J_t^2(c_t^2)) \tag{6.4}$$

Changes in circumstances which reduce J_t^0 or J_t^2 or increase $g(.)$ will reduce suicide probabilities. Other things being equal, one would expect that suicide probability will increase with age because the sum of future utilities (J_t^2) will decrease with age. An increase in current wealth will raise J_t^0 and may also increase g if the individual is concerned about the well-being of his heirs. It is plausible that additional wealth is more highly valued by the individual if it accrues to him rather than his heirs. Hence, wealthier individuals will have lower suicide probabilities.

Unemployment and Suicide Propensity

The suggestion that higher unemployment rates lead to higher suicide rates must be made rather more precise if it is to be tested using the model of individual suicide propensity outlined above. The causal mechanism may be *direct* or *indirect* and can take a number of forms. There may be a direct effect because:

1. *being* unemployed in a period has psychological costs in that period and possibly in future periods as well. Thus J_t^0, and possibly also J_t^2, are reduced;
2. *becoming* unemployed may impose psychological costs of adjusting to a new lifestyle and so J_t^0 may be reduced;
3. *expectations* of future employment status may be influenced by current unemployment rates. Suppose being, or becoming, unemployed has psychological costs. If an increase in the current unemployment rate causes individuals to place a higher probability on being, or becoming, unemployed in future periods, then J_t^2 will be reduced.

Unemployment may have an indirect or precipitating effect on suicide, even if it has no direct effect, because it causes changes in circumstances which do affect the probability of suicide. The most obvious example is that unemployment leads to a reduced income and thus to a lower J_t^0. There may also be psychological costs of adjusting to a lower income. Higher current unemployment rates may also lead to revised expectations of future employment status and thus of future incomes.

It is important to be specific about the route or routes by which increases in unemployment lead to increases in suicide rates for two reasons. First, testing the different hypotheses will require different information. For example, the direct or indirect effects of being, or becoming, unemployed will manifest themselves only amongst the unemployed.[1] If the data available does not enable employment status to be distinguished, then, given the relative sizes of the unemployed and employed groups, these type (1) and (2) effects may be obscured. The expectation effect (3), by contrast, will be present in both employed and unemployed groups and could be tested on an undifferentiated sample. The various hypotheses will also require different types of data about a given sample. For example, the adjustment cost effect (2) will require information on previous employment status, whereas the type (1) effect will not. Although it is typically the case that there is insufficient information to distinguish the various hypotheses or models, it is still essential to make them explicit if the results obtained are to be properly interpreted. As we will see in Section 3, theoretical modelling can indicate the likely bias when certain kinds of information are missing.

The second reason for distinguishing amongst the hypotheses is that they can have very different policy implications. An increase in unemployment will have larger social costs in the form of suicides if it has direct, as well as indirect, effects. If there are indirect and direct effects, then the social costs of a given unemployment rate can be reduced by, for example, increasing the incomes of the unemployed.

Estimation problems: Multi-Collinearity, Omitted Variables and Simultaneity

The list of explanatory variables c_t in equation (6.2) which influence suicide decisions is potentially enormous. It will include not only future and current values of such things as income, prices, employment status, housing conditions etc., but also their past values. This is because the value of some current variables (for example, health or wealth) will depend on what has happened in the past or because forecasts of future variables depend on current and past values. The explanatory variables are often highly correlated. Thus, the unemployed are more likely to have low incomes, health-harming consumption patterns and poor housing. It may be difficult because of this multi-collinearity to disentangle their separate, *ceteris paribus*, effects on suicide probabilities.

With many potentially correlated explanatory variables, the problem of omitted variable bias can be acute. If we omit an explanatory variable (perhaps because of lack of data) which is correlated with some of the included variables, the coefficients on those included variables will be biased, because they will also reflect some of the effect of the omitted variable on suicide probabilities. Thus, omitting income, but including employment status, is likely to result in the effect of unemployment being overestimated.

The suicide – no suicide decision is not the only kind of decision made by individuals. The utility levels J_t^0, J_t^1, J_t^2 used in the evaluation (6.1) of the suicide decision will be generated by other maximising choices. If the individual does not commit suicide he would have utility $J_t^0 + J_t^2$. This sum is maximised by optimal choices for the current period and by optimal contingent plans for future periods. The optimal decisions and plans will depend both on preferences and on the constraints on current and future choices. For example, optimal consumption in the current period will depend on tastes and on such things as current wealth and health, current and expected future prices, current and expected interest rates and on many other variables.

Suppose that we try to estimate $\pi(c_t)$, and include current consumption as an explanatory variable, along with wealth, health, prices, interest rates and other variables (including unemployment). Preferences, indicated by the taste parameters, will in general influence both the suicide decision and the level of current consumption. Simultaneous equation bias will be present if the c_t vector in (6.2) contains variables whose values can be influenced by the individual. As a result, the estimated effects of these endogenous variables will be biased because they also reflect the unobservable taste variables. The solution is either to use an estimation technique, such as two stage least squares, which allows for the simultaneity, or to estimate a reduced form version of (6.2), with c_t being restricted to exogenous or predetermined variables outside the control of the individual.[2]

Selection Effects

A problem which has aroused concern in the recent literature on suicide and unemployment is the selection effect (see, for example, Moser, Fox and Jones (1984), Platt (1984, 1985b)). Suppose that an individual's employment status is determined, in part, by certain characteristics (such as age, education level or psychological traits). Thus the unemployed are not just a random sample of the population, but are a biased selection. Suppose also that suicide propensities are influenced by the characteristics which select for employment status. If the selecting characteristics cannot be controlled for, the comparison of suicide rates for employed and unemployed is likely to overestimate the effect of unemployment on suicide. In this case, the selection effect is merely an example of omitted variable bias: the included variable (employment status) is picking up part of the effect of an omitted variable with which it is correlated (the characteristics affecting employment status).

If data are available on the characteristic (for example, age) affecting selection and suicide propensity, omitted variable bias will not arise, but multi-collinearity will be present, since employment status and the selecting characteristic will be correlated. It may not be possible to disentangle the separate effects of age and employment status on suicide propensity.

It has been tacitly assumed so far that employment status, or unemployment probability, is exogenous, i.e. not influenced by the individual's decisions. This may not be so. The probability of unemployment for an individual will depend on exogenous variables (such as demand conditions and his age) but it can be influenced by his decisions. The individual can decide how much time is to be devoted to searching for a job if unemployed, the wage at which a job offer would be accepted and the types of jobs considered. It does not need to be assumed that unemployment is voluntary, merely that, if job opportunities do arise, the individual can choose to accept or reject them. There will be self-selection for unemployment in the sense that the individual's decisions influence his unemployment probability. These decisions will be affected by preferences or tastes which also influence the suicide probability. Hence, self-selection for unemployment can induce simultaneous equation bias.

A Simple Model of Selection

We start the detailed examination of the implications of selection effects for different types of studies by setting up a model of selection. First we adopt a highly simplified, linear, version of the suicide probability model (6.2).[3]

$$\pi_{isjt} = \alpha_{0s} + \alpha_{1s}x_{ijt} + \alpha_{2s}u_{ijt} + \alpha_{3s}q_{jt} \qquad (6.5)$$

where π_{isjt} is the probability that individual i, with employment status s, in area j commits suicide in period t. The suicide propensity depends on the individual's characteristic (x_{ijt}), the *ex ante* unemployment probability for i in j at time $t(u_{ijt})$ and on a characteristic of the area at time $t(q_{jt})$. The index subscript s on the parameters denotes the employment status of the individual at time t, with $s = u$ or e depending on whether he is unemployed or employed.

This formulation shows two of the direct ways in which unemployment can affect suicide probability. First, for given personal and area characteristics and unemployment probability, the increase in suicide probability if the individual is unemployed rather than employed is

$$\pi_{iujt} - \pi_{iejt} = (a_{0u} - a_{0e}) + (a_{1u} - a_{1e})x_{ijt}$$
$$+ (a_{2u} - a_{2e})u_{ijt} + (a_{3u} - a_{3e})q_{jt} \qquad (6.6)$$

This is the direct effect of being unemployed rather than unemployed. Second, the fact that the unemployment probability enters (6.5) indicates that the individual's suicide propensity may be affected by the anticipation or risk of unemployment. This effect arises for both employed and unemployed, but its magnitude a_{2s} may differ if, say an increase in the unemployment rate leads to a greater reduction in expected future utility for the unemployed than the employed $(a_{2u} > a_{2e})$.

It is obviously possible to include many more variables in (6.5), but this would merely complicate the analysis without greatly altering the main conclusions to be drawn. (Section 3 shows how a fuller version of (6.5) can be constructed.)

We next assume that employment status is influenced (selected) by the personal characteristic x_{ijt}. The probability that i is unemployed in period t is

$$u_{ijt} = \beta_0 w_{jt} + \beta_1 x_{ijt} \qquad (6.7)$$

where w_{jt} is some variable which measures (negatively) the demand for labour in j at t. Increases in demand reduce w_{jt} and raise the probability that i is unemployed $(\beta_0 > 0)$. An increase in x_{ijt} raises the unemployment probability $(\beta_1 > 0)$ *and* the suicide probability $(a_{1s} > 0)$, so that there is a selection effect.

2. EMPIRICAL STUDIES AND SELECTION

It is possible to avoid, or at least mitigate the multi-collinearity, omitted variable and simultaneity problems, whether caused by selection effects or otherwise, if sufficiently detailed data are available. Unfortunately this is rarely the case and studies based on different types of data (individual or aggregate, cross-section or time series) will have different strengths and weaknesses. These attributes will now be examined using the simple model of selection effects and illustrated by reference to the literature. Since Platt (1984, 1985a) provides a masterly survey of the large literature on suicide and unemployment, I will limit myself to discussions of the results of some recent British studies.

Panel Data Studies

Suicide is a rare event,[4] so that in any study based on the general population, a large sample is required to test hypotheses concerning the unemployment–suicide relationship. Because of the expense of collecting data from a large panel of individuals through time, the analyst is generally forced to use data from panels which were designed for other purposes. The only British panel study which is large enough to have accumulated sufficient person-years of data is the OPCS Longitudinal Study (Fox and Goldblatt, 1982; Moser, Fox and Jones, 1984). It is based on a 1 per cent sample of individuals enumerated in England and Wales in the 1971 census. Over the period 1971–81 the suicide standardised mortality rates of men aged 15–64 who were seeking work in 1971, was found to be significantly greater than 100, even after standardisation for social class. The suicide SMR for the wives of these men was also above 100, but the excess was not statistically significant.

The LS contains a large number of individuals, but the information on them is limited to their decennial census records and to birth, death and cancer registrations. Useful as this data is, it suffers from a number of serious drawbacks for the investigation of the relationship between suicide and unemployment. The census does not provide information on income, wealth or duration of unemployment. The ten-year interval between observations means that it will give a very fragmentary picture of employment status over time. Finally, it does not contain any information on predisposing character traits or psychiatric characteristics so that selection bias is difficult to eradicate.[5]

The implications of selection for the interpretation of the LS findings is discussed in Moser, Fox and Jones (1984) and in Fox and Goldblatt (1982, ch. 11). The model of selection used is rather different to that outlined earlier in this section (6.5) and (6.7). The LS authors define ill-health selection for the seeking-work category as occurring if the prevalence of sickness amongst those entering the category is greater than in the population as a whole, *and* is greater than the average prevalence over all the individuals in the seeking-work category, i.e. new entrants and those already in the category.

This type of selection has two main implications. First, a comparison of the health of the seeking-work group with that of the general population will overestimate the effect of employment status on health. Second, the health of the group seeking work in 1971 will improve over time as the sickest new members die and the rest recover

Moser, Fox and Jones use the second of these implications to test for the selection bias resulting from the first. They do not find any indication that the SMR for all causes of death, or for suicide, for the seeking-work group has declined over the 1971–81 period, once allowance is made for social class.

The lack of support for an ill-health selection effect could be due to the fairly short follow up period and the relatively small size of the seeking-work group (3.6 per cent of males aged 15–64). The mortality rate for the employed group shows a tendency to rise over time. This is evidence for good-health selection into the employed group, but does not necessarily imply ill-health selection into the seeking-work group, because the seeking-work group does not include those who were permanently sick and out of the labour force, or those intending to seek work, but sick. Selection effects are present in the LS, but it is not clear how much of the higher mortality of the seeking work group is due to selection bias.

Matched Controls

One way round the need for a large sample of the general population is by matched controls. Each individual in a sample of suicides is matched with one or more individuals who have not committed suicide, but who have the same characteristics (age, sex, area of residence, marital status, psychiatric diagnosis etc.). The unemployment rate amongst the two groups is then compared. If the matching is exact the expected value of the difference in unemployment rates will be:[6]

$$\sum_i (\pi_{iujt} - \pi_{iejt})u_{ijt} (1 - u_{ijt}) [\pi_{ijt} (1 - \pi_{ijt})]^{-1} (1/n) \qquad (6.8)$$

where n is the number of suicides in the sample, π_{isjt}, u_{ijt} are defined by (6.5) and (6.7) and $\pi_{ijt} = (1 - u_{ijt})\pi_{iejt} + u_{ijt}\pi_{iujt}$. The difference in unemployment rates permits inferences about the effect of employment status on suicide propensity, even if there is a selection effect. If the suicide sample is homogenous with respect to the non-employment status variables, so that the u_{ijt} and π_{isjt} are the same for all i in the suicide and matching control groups, then it is possible to estimate the direct effect of employment status ($\pi_{iujt} - \pi_{iejt}$) (6.6) at particular values of the variables (x,u,q) which affect suicide propensity. Usually matched controls will not permit quantification of the effect of unemployment on the suicide propensity of the general population because the suicide sample is not homonogeneous. Hence, even if the relative frequency of the characteristics of the suicide sample (other than employment status) was identical with that of the total population, it will be impossible to estimate $\pi_{iujt} - \pi_{iejt}$ for each separate type of individual from the difference in unemployment rates (6.8).

Cross-Section Studies

In a number of recent papers Platt has examined the relationship between parasuicide[7] and unemployment across different areas in Edinburgh (Platt, 1984, 1985a, 1985b; Platt and Kreitman, 1984). The parasuicide rate for the unemployed was as much as nine times as great as for the employed. Parasuicide rates for both groups increased with the area unemployment rate, although the difference between the groups' parasuicide rates declined with unemployment. The population parasuicide rate (i.e., over both employed and unemployed) was also positively linked to unemployment, though when a measure of poverty was included the association between parasuicide and unemployment rates was no longer significant.

Status-specific propensities

What are the implications of selection for the results of this kind of cross-sectional analysis? Suppose that the true parasuicide model is described by (6.5), (6.7). The expected value of the parasuicide rate in area j at time t for individuals with employment status s will be:

$$m_{sjt} = \alpha_{0s} + \alpha_{1s}x_{sjt} + \alpha_{2s}u_{sjt} + \alpha_{3s}q_{jt} \qquad (6.9$$

where x_{sjt} is the expected value of x_{ijt} for individuals of employment status s and u_{sjt} is the expected value of u_{ijt} for individuals with the (*e post*) employment status s. To simplify the analysis, suppose that x_{ijt} is either 1 or 0, so that it can be regarded as an indicator variable for the possession of an attribute which raises the suicide or parasuicide (π_{isj} and unemployment (u_{ijt}) probabilities. The probability that an individual drawn at random from area j at time t has the predisposing attribute is λ_{jt}. With this simplification we get:[8]

$$x_{ujt} = (\beta_0 w_{jt} + \beta_1)\lambda_{jt} (\beta_0 w_{jt} + \beta_1 \lambda_{jt})^{-1} \qquad (6.10a)$$

$$x_{ejt} = (1 - \beta_0 w_{jt} - \beta_1)\lambda_{jt} (1 - \beta_0 w_{jt} - \beta_1 \lambda_{jt})^{-1} \qquad (6.10b)$$

$$u_{sjt} = \beta_0 w_{jt} + \beta_1 x_{sjt} \qquad (6.11)$$

Substitution of (6.10) and (6.11) in (6.9) gives the true model for the employment status specific parasuicide rate. In the absence of data on predisposing attributes, area specific effects (q_{jt}) and the selection parameter β_1, the equation actually estimated will be:

$$m_{sjt} = a_{0s} + a_{1s}u_{jt} \qquad (6.12)$$

The implications of selection for the interpretation of the a_{1s} coefficients on area unemployment (u_{jt}) can be shown by considering a series of special cases.

Case (i): $\beta_1 = 0$. With $\beta_1 = 0$ there is no selection effect: $x_{ujt} = x_{ejt} = \lambda_{jt}$, and $u_{ujt} = u_{ejt} = u_{jt} = \beta_0 w_{jt}$. Then, provided that neither λ_{jt} nor q_{jt} are correlated with w_{jt}, there will be no omitted variable bias and a_{1s} will be an unbiased estimate of a_{2s}. Some, but not all, of the effect of unemployment is correctly identified in this case.[9]

Case (ii): $\beta_1 > 0$, $a_{2s} = 0$. Now there is selection, but only being unemployed affects parasuicide ($a_{0u} > a_{0e}$, $a_{1u} \neq a_{1e}$, $a_{3u} \neq a_{3e}$). Anticipation of unemployment (proxied by u_{sjt}) has no effect. The area unemployment rate ($u_{jt} = \beta_0 w_{jt} + \beta_1 \lambda_{jt}$) varies with the demand variable w_{jt} and the area population characteristic λ_{jt}. Suppose (case (iia)) that $\lambda_{jt} = \lambda$ for all areas, so that unemployment variations are solely due to demand and each area has the same proportion of individuals possessing the predisposing attribute. Making the appropriate substitutions in (6.9) and differentiating with respect to w_{jt} gives

$$dm_{ujt}/dw_{jt} = -a_{1u}\beta_0\beta_1\lambda(1 - \lambda)u_{jt}^{-2} \qquad (6.13a)$$

$$dm_{ejt}/dw_{jt} = -a_{1e}\beta_0\beta_1\lambda(1 - \lambda)(1 - u_{jt})^{-2} \qquad (6.13b)$$

Since $a_{1s} > 0$, $\beta_1 > 0$ and $\beta_0 > 0$ it is clear that an increase in w_{jt} (which increases unemployment) will *lower* the parasuicide rate in both groups. As the demand for labour falls (w_{jt} increases) more individuals are unemployed. The proportion of individuals possessing the predisposing characteristic who switch from employment to unemployment will, on average, be smaller than for the group already unemployed, but greater than for the group who remain employed. Both x_{ejt} and x_{ujt} will fall and, hence, so will the parasuicide rate in both groups.

If case (iia) is the true model, estimation of (6.10) would lead to seriously misleading conclusions. There would appear to be a negative effect of anticipated unemployment on parasuicide which, in fact, is due to the positive effect of being unemployed. Platt's finding that $a_{1s}>0$ appears to rule out case (iia) unless u_{jt} is correlated with the area environmental variable q_{jt}.

Consider next case (iib), in which demand conditions are identical ($w_{jt} = w_t$ all j), so that variations in unemployment rates are due solely to the proportion of the area population with the unemployment and parasuicide predisposing attribute (λ_{jt}). Differentiating (6.9) with respect to λ_{jt} gives

$$dm_{ujt}/d\lambda_{jt} = a_{1u}x_{ujt}\beta_0 w_t(u_{jt}\lambda_{jt})^{-1} \qquad (6.14a)$$

$$dm_{ejt}/d\lambda_{jt} = a_{1e}x_{ejt}(1 - \beta_0 w_t)((1 - u_{jt})\lambda_{jt})^{-1} \qquad (6.14b)$$

Both of these expressions are positive, so that areas with higher λ_{jt} will have both higher parasuicide rates for both groups, as well as higher unemployment rates.

This model is compatible with Platt's findings. Notice that what is being measured by a positive estimated a_{1s} coefficient on area unemployment is not the effect of anticipated unemployment (since $a_{2s} = 0$), but the effect of the predisposing characteristics. Suppose that $a_{1u} = a_{1e}$ and $a_{0u} = a_{0s}$. Thus, since also $a_{2s} = 0$ ($s = u, e$) unemployment has *no* effect at all on parasuicide propensity $\pi_{iujt} = \pi_{iejt}$ (see (6.6)) even though m_{sjt} and u_{jt} are positively correlated. The correlation is induced by the unobservable area characteristic λ_{jt} via the selection effect.

Case (iii): $\beta_1>0$, $a_{2s}>0$. In this model anticipated unemployment also affects parasuicide propensities. Proceeding as before, we again distinguish the effects of unemployment variations due to demand (w_{jt}) and predisposing characteristics (λ_{jt}):

$$dm_{sjt}/dw_{jt} = a_{1s} (dx_{sjt}/dw_{jt}) + a_{2s} (\beta_0 + \beta_1 (dx_{sjt}/dw_{jt})) \qquad (6.15)$$

$$dm_{sjt}/d\lambda_{jt} = a_{1s} (dx_{sjt}/d\lambda_{jt}) + a_{2s}\beta_1 (dx_{sjt}/d\lambda_{jt}) \qquad (6.16)$$

If only w_{jt} varies (case (iiia)) across areas then (6.15) is relevant. The area unemployment rate varies at the rate β_0 with w_{jt} and so α_{1s} will pick up the effects of the omitted x_{sjt} variable. Since x_{sjt} declines with w_{jt}, α_{1s} will *underestimate* α_{2s}. If only λ_{jt} causes variations in unemployment rates (case (iiib)), then, since x_{sjt} increases with λ_{jt}, α_{1s} will *overestimate* α_{2s}.

If there is selection, positive correlations of employment status specific parasuicide or suicide rates with area unemployment rates need to be treated cautiously. There may be no true effect of unemployment; or the regression coefficient on area unemployment may be picking up employment status effects rather an anticipatory effects; or it may over or underestimate the anticipatory effects.

Difference in status-specific rates

Assume for simplicity that $\alpha_{1u} = \alpha_{1e}$, $\alpha_{2u} = \alpha_{2e}$, $\alpha_{3u} = \alpha_{3e}$. Then the expected difference in status specific parasuicide rates is (see (6.9)):

$$m_{ujt} - m_{ejt} = \alpha_{0u} - \alpha_{0e} + \alpha_1 (x_{ujt} - x_{ejt}) + \alpha_2 (u_{ujt} - u_{ejt})$$
$$= \alpha_{0u} - \alpha_{0e} + (\alpha_1 + \alpha_2 \beta_1) (x_{ujt} - x_{ejt}) \quad (6.17)$$

and the difference in the status specific proportions possessing the predisposing attribute is

$$x_{ujt} - x_{ejt} = \lambda_{jt} (1 - \lambda_{jt}) \beta_1 [u_{jt}(1 - u_{jt})]^{-1} \quad (6.18)$$

Differentiation of (6.18) will show that increases in λ_{jt} can increase or decrease $x_{ujt} - x_{ejt}$, but increases in w_{jt} will reduce this difference provided $u_{jt}<\frac{1}{2}$). Since increases in w_{jt} also raise u_{jt} this may explain Platt's finding that $m_{ujt} - m_{ejt}$ is smaller in areas with higher unemployment. Notice that this correlation will appear even if $\alpha_2 = 0$ and $x_{0u} = x_{0e}$ i.e., even if unemployment has no effect on parasuicide propensities.

Non-status-specific rates

The suicide or parasuicide probability for an individual, not conditional on employment status, is

$$\pi_{ijt} = (1 - u_{ijt}) \pi_{iejt} + u_{ijt}\pi_{iujt} \quad (6.19)$$

Thus the expected value for the population parasuicide rate, in area j, at time t, (with π_{isjt}, u_{ijt} given by (6.5), (6.7)) is[10]

$$m_{jt} = a_{0e} + a_{1e}x_{jt} + (a_{2e} + a_{0u} - a_{0e})u_{jt} + a_{3e}q_{jt}$$

$$+ (a_{1u} - a_{2e})u_{jt}^2 + (a_{1u} - a_{1e})x_{jt}u_{jt} + (a_{3u} - a_{3e})u_{jt}q_{jt}$$

$$+ [(a_{1u} - a_{1e}) + (a_{2u} - a_{2e})\beta_1]\beta_1\sigma_{xjt}^2 \qquad (6.20)$$

In this expression u_{jt}^2 is the square of the expected value u_{ijt} and σ_{xjt}^2 is the variance of the predisposing characteristic x_{ijt} in j at time t.

As (6.20) indicates, even if the true parasuicide or suicide model is simple and linear, the expected value of the observed population rate can be moderately complex, involving interaction and squared terms. Suppose that a simple linear cross-section regression is estimated with the area unemployment rate as the single explanatory variable. Will there be any omitted bias?

Consider the omitted area environmental variable q_{jt}. Even if q_{jt} is not correlated with area unemployment u_{jt} the interaction term $u_{jt}q_j$ will be. Only if the environmental variable also has the same effect irrespective of employment status ($a_{3u} = a_{3e}$) will there be no omitted variable bias.

The selection effect means that the unemployed are not a random sample of the working population in any given area. This can make inferences based on employment status specific data dubious because the unemployed, on average, have a higher level of the predisposing variable x_{ijt}. With data which are not employment status specific this kind of bias will not be present, but the dependence of unemployment probabilities on predisposing variables can still create problems. The expected area unemployment rate u_{jt} depends on the expected value of the predisposing characteristic x_{jt} as well as on area demand (w_{jt}) Taking the expectation of (6.7) gives $u_{jt} = \beta_0 w_{jt} + \beta_1 x_{jt}$. If the populations of different areas have different x_{jt}, then u_{jt} will be correlated with the omitted variable x_{jt} and the estimated coefficient on u_{jt} will be too large. If $a_{iu} \neq a_{ie}$ or $a_{2u} \neq a_{2e}$ then bias will also be present if the *variance* of x_{ijt} is correlated with unemployment across areas.

Even if the omission of the predisposing and area environmental variables does not create difficulties, the estimated coefficient on unemployment requires careful interpretation. If $a_{2u} = a_{2e}$ the unemployment coefficient will be an unbiased estimate of

$\alpha_2 + \alpha_{0u} - \alpha_{0e}$. It will not be possible to determine the relative magnitudes of the effect of employment status *per se* ($\alpha_{0u} - \alpha_{0e}$) and anticipation or fear of unemployment (α_2). If $\alpha_{2u} \neq \alpha_{2e}$ the estimated unemployment coefficient will also reflect the omitted variable u_{jt}^2, making interpretation even more difficult.

Over a short time period, it is highly plausible that neither the distribution of predisposing characteristics (x_{ijt}) within an area, nor the area environmental variable will change very much. If we assume that they are in fact constant, and we have two sets of cross-section data from reasonably close periods, we could estimate the change in the area suicide or parasuicide rates. This change would have an expected value of

$$
\begin{aligned}
m_{jt} - m_{jt-1} = [&\alpha_{2e} + \alpha_{0u} - \alpha_{0e} + (\alpha_{1u} - \alpha_{1e})x_j \\
&+ (\alpha_{3a} - \alpha_{3e})q_j](u_{jt} - u_{jt-1}) \\
&+ (\alpha_{2u} - \alpha_{2e})(u_{jt}^2 - u_{jt-1}^2)
\end{aligned} \tag{6.21}
$$

where x_j, q_j are the (constant) area means of the predisposing and environmental variable. The advantage of estimating an equation in differenced form is that the influence of the omitted predisposing attributes and environmental variables is removed. Even with selection effects and q_{jt} correlated with u_{jt} across areas, there is no omitted variable bias. The area unemployment rate u_{jt} may be correlated with x_{jt} and q_{jt}, but $u_{jt} - u_{jt-1}$ is not correlated with $x_{jt} - x_{jt-1}$, $q_{jt} - q_{jt-1}$ or $\sigma_{xjt}^2 - \sigma_{xjt-1}^2$, because all of these are constant (equal to zero). The true model predicts that the estimated coefficients on $u_{jt} - u_{jt-1}$ and $u_{jt}^2 - u_{jt-1}^2$ will be positive. Although this can be tested, it will not be possible to disentangle the various routes by which unemployment influences suicide or parasuicide propensities because estimation produces only two coefficients which are combinations of eight coefficient from the true model.

Time Series Analyses

Status specific rates

Platt has also recently presented some results on the relationship between employment status specific parasuicide rates and the unemployment rate for Edinburgh for 1968–83 (see especially Platt, 1985b). The parasuicide rate amongst the unemployed was negatively, and that amongst the employed was positively (but not significantly), related to the Edinburgh unemployment rate. The difference between the two parasuicide rates was negatively (but not significantly), related to the Edinburgh unemployment rate. By contrast the cross-sectional analysis found that the area parasuicide rate for the unemployed was positively associated with the area unemployment rate. Platt's explanation for the discrepancy is that there are area environmental variables (q_{jt}) which are cross-sectionally correlated with area unemployment rates. However, there is relatively little variation in these variables over time. Thus, in a time series analysis, the estimated coefficient on unemployment does not reflect the omitted environment variables, and so is smaller, and less significant, than in a cross section analysis.

An alternative explanation can be given in terms of the selection effect. As we noted above in discussing (6.15) and (6.16), differences in unemployment rates can be due to differences in demand factors or the average level of predisposing characteristics. Over time it is likely that demand differences are relatively larger than they are cross sectionally. As we saw in discussing (6.15) and (6.16), demand variations can lead to smaller parasuicide variations than those arising from variations in the average of the predisposing variable. Thus we would expect the cross-section estimated unemployment coefficient to be larger than the time series coefficients.

Platt found that the proportion of parasuicides accounted for by the unemployed increased with the unemployment rate over time. This empirical relationship is not support for a positive effect of unemployment of parasuicide propensity. It will also occur if in fact unemployment had no effect at all on parasuicide propensity.

Suppose that the parasuicide probability is a constant, unaffected by employment status, the level of unemployment the individual's environment or his personal characteristics (in terms of (6.5) $a_{ou} = a_{oe} = a_o$; $a_{ks} = 0$, $k = 1, 2, 3$ and $s = u, e$). The expected proportion of parasuicides at time t who are unemployed will be:[11]

$$\sum_j \sum_i \pi_{iujt}\, u_{ijt} \left[\sum_j \sum_i \left(\pi_{iejt} \left(1 - u_{ijt}\right) + \pi_{iujt}\, u_{ijt} \right) \right]^{-1}$$
$$= a_o \sum_j \sum_i u_{ijt} \left[\sum_j \sum_i a_0 \right]^{-1} = \sum_j \sum_i u_{ijt}\, n_t^{-1}$$
$$= u_t \tag{6.22}$$

which is the expected unemployment probability at time t. Since u_t and the actual unemployment rate will differ only by a (small) error with a expected value of zero, the finding, that the proportion of parasuicides who are unemployed is strongly positively correlated with the unemployment rate, cannot be taken as strong evidence of any effect of unemployment on parasuicide propensities.

Population attributable risk

This is the difference between the population suicide rate and the suicide rate for the employed. Platt (1985b) found that the population attributable risk for parasuicide increased as the unemployment rate increased. This indicates that the unemployed are more prone to parasuicide at any point in time but does not establish why this should be so. In particular it does not rule out the possibility that the population attributable risk is due solely to selection.

To see this assume that $\alpha_{0u} = \alpha_{0e}$, $\alpha_{1u} = \alpha_{1e} = \alpha_1 > 0$, $\alpha_{2s} = \alpha_{3s} = 0$ $(s = u, e)$ and $\beta_1 > 0$, so there is selection for unemployment. The expected value of the population attributable risk will be just $\alpha_1(x_t - x_{et})$ where x_{et} is the expected value of the predisposing characteristic, conditional on employment status and x_t is the expected value over the whole population. Assume plausibly that x_t is constant over time. Then, drawing on our discussion of the cross-section case, increases in unemployment caused by reductions in demand will reduce x_{et}. There will be a positive correlation between population attributable risk and the unemployment rate, due solely to selection.

Non-status-specific analyses

Because of the difficulty of obtaining employment status specific data most analyses using aggregate time series have been concerned with the relationship between the suicide or parasuicide rate for a population as whole and the unemployment rate. For Edinburgh for the period 1968–83, Platt (1985b) found that there was significant positive correlation between parasuicide and unemployment rates in the same year, but the relationship became weaker as longer lags on the unemployment rate were tried. He also noted that when the 1968–83 period was split into two equal parts the correlation became negative for the second half of the period.

In a multiple regression analysis for England and Wales for 1955–76, Brenner (1985) discovered that suicide rates were significantly positively associated with the unemployment rate three years previously, the difference between the current and previous period unemployment rate, the number of business failures, spirits consumption (both in absolute terms and as a proportion of alcohol consumption) and the annual change in the number of divorces three years previously. Significant negative factors were trend real per capita income, the number of hours worked one to two years previously and beer consumption two years previously.

I have discussed at length elsewhere (Gravelle, 1984) the problems which can arise with time series analysis of unemployment and mortality, but two comments can be made on these studies. In any exercise of this kind, if an investigator runs many regressions, the conventional tests of significance do not mean very much. It is essential to test the fitted model by examining its structural stability within the period over which it was estimated or its forecasting ability outside this period. As Platt (1985b) shows, a good fit over the estimation period may conceal considerable changes in the relationship being examined.[12] The second, more specific, reason for being cautious in interpreting Brenner's results is that he does not attempt to examine, or even refer to, the implications of the detoxification of domestic gas which occurred within this period. Other studies have shown that it is likely that detoxification had a considerable but transitory effect on the suicide rate during the 1960s (Kreitman and Platt, 1984).

An apparent advantage of using data which is not employment-status specific is that there will not be selection into, or out of, the unit of observation (the whole population). Assuming again that (6.5), (6.7) depict the true model, the expected value of the suicide rate at time t across all areas will be:[13]

$$
\begin{aligned}
m_t =\ & a_{0e} + a_{1e}\, x_t + (a_{2e} + a_{0u} - a_{0e})u_t + a_{3e}\, q_t \\
& + (a_{2u} - a_{2e})u_t^2 + (a_{1u} - a_{1e})u_t\, x_t + (a_{3u} - a_{3e})u_t\, q_t \\
& + [a_{1u} - a_{1e} + (a_{2u} - a_{2e})\beta_1]\beta_1\, \sigma_{xt}^2 + (a_{2u} - a_{2e})\beta_0^2\, \sigma_{wt}^2 \\
& + [a_{1u} - a_{2e} + (a_{2u} - a_{2e})2\beta_1]\beta_0\, \sigma_{wxt}^2 \\
& + (a_{3u} - a_{3e})\beta_0\, \sigma_{wqt}^2 + (a_{3u} - a_{3e})\beta_1\, \sigma_{xqt}^2
\end{aligned}
\tag{6.23}
$$

where x_t, u_t, q_t are the expected values, over all individuals and areas, of x_{ijt}, u_{ijt}, q_{jt}; σ_{xt}^2, σ_{wt}^2 are the variances of x_{ijt}, w_{jt} and σ_{wxt}^2, σ_{wqt}^2, σ_{xqt}^2 are covariances. This expression differs from its analogue (6.20) in the cross-section case in the last four terms. These do not appear in (6.20) because within a given area and period w_{jt}, q_{jt} are constant. As with the cross-section equation, the simple linear individual employment status specific suicide propensities lead to fairly complex expressions for expected suicide rates over the whole population. Even if there is no selection effect ($\beta_1 = 0$), lack of information on the predisposing variables x_{ijt} can still lead to omitted variable bias via the terms involving the mean, variance and covariances of x_{ijt}.

Fortunately, it may not be necessary to attempt to estimate (6.23). First, if we assume that the true model has $a_{ks} = a_k$ for $k = 1, 2, 3$ and $s = u, e$, then all but the first four terms of (6.23) are zero. It is plausible that there will be little variation through time in the population mean of the predisposing variable x_{ijt}, so that x_t can be regarded as constant. Thus the selection effect ($\beta_1 > 0$) will not create a correlation between u_t and x_t and the lack of information on x_t will not bias estimates of the coefficient ($a_2 + a_{ou} - a_{oe}$) on u_t. If the area environmental variable q_{jt} does not vary over time or has a mean q_t which is not correlated with u_t then it will not produce potential omitted variable bias either.

Second, (6.22) is greatly simplified it if is the case that the joint distribution of the predisposing (x_{ijt}), area environmental (q_{jt}) and demand (w_{jt}) variables is invariant over time in certain respects. If the means x_t, q_t, the variances σ^2_{xt}, σ^2_{wt} and the covariances σ^2_{wxt}, σ^2_{wqt}, σ^2_{xqt} are constant, the terms involving them can be subsumed with the constant term a_{oe} in (6.22):

$$
\begin{aligned}
m_t = A_0 + [a_{2e} + a_{0u} - a_{0e} + (a_{1u} - a_{1e})x \\
+ (a_{3u} - a_{3e})q]u_t + (a_{2u} - a_{2e})u_t^2
\end{aligned}
\tag{6.24}
$$

when x, q are the constant means of x_{ijt}, q_{jt}. Even in this, not implausible, case it will not be possible to distinguish quantitively the various routes by which unemployment affects suicide propensity.

Because suicide is a rare event the quantification of the effects of unemployment on suicide will have to be based on the analysis of aggregate, population level data. Aggregation is usually to be avoided because much of the information present in the individual level data is lost. In this case, however, aggregation is not only a necessity, it can be a virtue. As we have seen, the bias caused by selection effects will be reduced in aggregate studies, more so with time series than with cross-sections. With this in mind, we turn next to an empirical analysis of suicide rates over the period 1923–81.

3. AN AGGREGATE TIME SERIES STUDY: SOME PRELIMINARY RESULTS

In this section we use some of the arguments of earlier sections in a preliminary analysis of the relationship between the annual age adjusted suicide rate for men aged 25–64 in Great Britain and the unemployment rate, over the period 1922–71. We amend the model discussed in Sections 1 and 2 and use it to guide the choice of estimating equations, to interpret the empirical results and to assess the implications of using incomplete or inadequate data.

The estimating equation is derived from the following model of individual suicide probability:

$$\pi_{isvt} = \gamma_{0s} + \gamma_{1s}\, y_{st} + \gamma_{2s}\, u_t + \gamma_{3s}\, D_{t-1}$$
$$+ \gamma_{4s}\,(y_{st} - y_{vt-1}) + \gamma_{5s}y_t + \gamma_{6t}y_t^2 + \gamma_{7s}u_t^2 \qquad (6.25)$$

where π_{isvt} is the probability that i commits suicide in period t given that he has employment status s in t and v in $t-1$ $(s, v = u, e)$, $y_{st}(y_{vt-1})$ is the income of i if in employment status $s(v)$ in period $t(t - 1)$, D_{t-1} is an employment status indicator dummy variable with $D_{t-1} = 1$ or 0 as the individual was employed or not last period, and $y_t = (1 - u_t)\, y_{et} + u_t y_{ut}$ is average income in period t.

This version of (6.2) differs from that used earlier in a number of respects. It contains no predisposing characteristic or area environmental variables. As we suggested in Section 2, these variables can be ignored if it is assumed that they are constant over time or are uncorrelated with observed variables such as the unemployment rate. The resulting empirical model may explain less of the level or variation in suicide, but the estimated coefficients on included variables will not be biased. The current period income y_{st} is included, since an increase in current income would be expected to raise J_t^0 and reduce suicide probability. Note, that by not indexing current or past income on i, it is being assumed that all individuals in the same employment state have the same income. If π_{isvt} was not linear in y_{st}, this assumption would have a simplifying effect on the estimating equation and lead to bias because of the omission of terms involving the higher moments of the income distribution. The D_{t-1} variable is an attempt to capture the effects of previous employment history. If $\gamma_{3e}, \gamma_{3u} < 0$, this would indicate that duration of unemployment affected suicide probabilities. If $\gamma_{3e} = 0$, $\gamma_{3u} > 0$, then the shock of becoming unemployed raises suicide propensity. The income change variable $y_{st} - y_{vt-1}$ also attempts to pick up adjustment costs. The u_t, u_t^2, y_t, y_t^2 terms are included to reflect anticipatory effects. They are based on the assumption that individuals have myopic expectations of future unemployment and average incomes and that these expectations have a non-linear effect on suicide propensity (possibly because of non-linearities in utility functions).

The expected suicide mortality rate is:

$$m_t = (1 - u_t)E\pi_{ievt} + u_tE\pi_{iuvt} \tag{6.26}$$

and, assuming that employment status is serially independent (so that $ED_{t-1} = 1 - u_{t-1}$) we have

$$
\begin{aligned}
m_t = {} & (\gamma_{0e} + \gamma_{3e}) + (\gamma_{0u} - \gamma_{0e} + \gamma_{2e} + \gamma_{3u} - \gamma_{3e})u_t \\
& + (\gamma_{2u} - \gamma_{2e} + \gamma_{7e})u_t^2 + (\gamma_{7u} - \gamma_{7e})u_t^3 - \gamma_{3e}u_{t-1} \\
& + (\gamma_{3u} - \gamma_{3e})u_tu_{t-1} + (\gamma_{5u} - \gamma_{5e})\,u_ty_t \\
& + (\gamma_{6u} - \gamma_{6e})u_ty_t^2 - (\gamma_{4u} - \gamma_{4e})u_ty_{t-1} \\
& + (\gamma_{1e} + \gamma_{5e})y_t + \gamma_{6e}y_t^2 - \gamma_{4e}y_{t-1} \\
& + \gamma_{4e}\,(1 - u_t)y_{et} + (\gamma_{1u} - \gamma_{1e} + \gamma_{4u})u_ty_{ut}
\end{aligned}
\tag{6.27}
$$

The estimating equation actually used differs from (6.27) in three ways. First, it has been suggested that suicide rates decline during wartime because external threats promote political integration.[14] To test this hypothesis we include a dummy variable W_t, with $W_t = 1$ for 1939–45 and $W_t = 0$ in all other years. Second, the detoxification of town gas has been alleged to reduce suicide rates. This is allowed for by the crude device of an integer variable G_t which is zero up to 1957 and increases by one in each year from 1958 to 1974 and is constant thereafter. Finally, in the absence of information on the income of the employed and unemployed the last two terms in (27) have been omitted from the estimating equation. If u_t is not correlated with y_{ut} or y_{et}, $(1 - u_t)y_{et}$ will be negatively correlated with u_t and u_ty_{ut} will be positively correlated with u_t. This creates the possibility of omitted variable bias. The estimated coefficient on u_t would pick up the effects of both omitted variables. If γ_{4e}, $\gamma_{4u} > 0$ and $\gamma_{1u} > \gamma_{1e} > 0$ the estimated u_t coefficient would be biased upward by the omission of u_ty_t and downward by the omission of $(1 - u_t)y_{et}$. Thus the net omitted variable bias on the estimated u_t coefficient may be fairly small. The correlations of $(1 - u_t)y_{et}$ and u_ty_{ut} with y_t could be positive or negative and thus omitted variable bias also may not be large in estimated coefficients involving y_t.[15]

Results

Table 6.1 presents the results from estimating (6.27) (plus the war and detoxification variables and without the last two terms). The first two columns give the results for the full equations. Column 1 has a low DW statistic indicating positive first order serial correlation amongst the residuals. Although such serial correlation tends to inflate t-statistics, it is remarkable that none of the estimated coefficients is significant at even the 10 per cent level. In column 2 allowance was made for first order serial correlation by use of the Hildreth-Lu search procedure.[16] The results are still not impressive in terms of explanatory power. None of the coefficients (apart from the serial correlation coefficient) are significant and the $\bar{R}^2$ of 0.40 is low for a time series regression. Indeed, the F statistic is too small to be significant at the 1 per cent level.

Columns 3 and 4 are the results from OLS and HILU estimation of a restricted version of the basic estimating equation. In this version all the interaction and power terms are dropped so that suicide is hypothesised to be linearly related to current and previous period income and unemployment. Once again there is evidence of strong positive serial correlation in the residuals from the OLS equation (column 3) and the use of HILU leads to a large fall in the explanatory power of the equation. What is interesting about these results is that some of the estimated coefficients are significant and of the sign predicted by the suicide model. In both versions the detoxification of town gas does appear to be associated with a reduction in the suicide rate. Unemployment also now appears to be linked positively with the suicide rate. In the OLS equation current unemployment rate is significant, but in the HILU equation it is the previous period's unemployment rate. In neither equation is income or the war a significant influence on the suicide rate.

The fact that the restricted equations in columns 3 and 4 have significant coefficients, whilst the full equations in columns 1 and 2 do not, is possibly due to multicollinearity. The variables dropped from the full equations to produce the restricted equation are power or interaction terms, which will be correlated with each other and with the other terms involving unemployment and income. Thus in columns 1 and 2 it is difficult to separate the effects of the collinear variables. In columns 3 and 4 the unemployment and income terms are probably reflecting the influence of the omitted power and interaction variables.

The restricted equation also appears to be structurally unstable. In

TABLE 6.1 *Suicide model with myopic expectations*

	(1) OLS 1923–1971	(2) HILU 1923–1971	(3) OLS 1923–1971	(4) HILU 1923–1971	(5) HILU 1923–1946	(6) HILU 1947–1971
Constant	−62.1 (−0.16)	−124.5 (−0.37)	168.3 (5.08)	122.2 (1.43)	107.2 (0.69)	26.23 (0.32)
u_t	13.1 (0.31)	−4.79 (−0.09)	7.21 (3.29)	2.3 (1.47)	1.69 (0.76)	8.67 (1.52)
u_t^2	−2.46 (−1.56)	−0.5 (−0.48)				
u_t^3	0.06 (1.03)	−0.60E−2 (−0.16)				
u_{t-1}	−4.66 (−0.89)	0.388 (0.1)	3.03 (1.49)	5.12 (3.43)	5.52 (2.57)	4.42 (0.65)
$u_t u_{t-1}$	0.449 (0.92)	0.562 (1.59)				
$y_t u_t$	0.116 (0.89)	0.97E−3 (0.01)				
$y_t^2 u_t$	−0.96E−4 (−1.2)	−0.2E−4 (−0.23)				
$y_t - u_t$	−0.024 (−0.43)	0.312 (0.83)				
y_t	0.534 (0.49)	0.815 (0.93)	0.156 (1.03)	0.035 (0.36)	0.083 (0.45)	0.028 (0.35)
y_t^2	−0.21E−3 (−0.29)	−0.47E−3 (−0.86)				
y_{t-1}	−0.105 (−0.47)	−0.072 (−0.48)	−0.163 (−1.05)	0.039 (0.41)	0.023 (0.13)	0.152 (1.3)
W_t	19.7 (1.9)	−5.32 (−0.5)	−5.39 (−0.58)	−12.3 (−1.35)	−14.16 (−1.14)	
G_t	0.609 (0.08)	−0.102 (−0.02)	−3.24 (−1.95)	−6.47 (−1.8)		−9.36 (−2.89)
Rho		0.9 (14.3)		0.9 (14.3)	0.9 (9.9)	0.7 (4.8)
DW	1.11	1.78	0.58	1.87	1.83	1.38
R^2	0.93	0.4	0.9	0.4	0.36	0.32
F	51.8	2.6	69.76	5.47	2.29	2.01
SER	13.57	10.76	16.83	10.75	14.46	7.43

TABLE 6.2   *First difference runs (dependent variable:* $m_t - m_{t-1}$*)*

	(1) OLS 1923–1971		(2) OLS 1923–1946		(3) OLS 1947–1971	
Constant	−1.33	(−0.61)	−1.76	(−0.52)	−0.62	(−0.19)
$u_t - u_{t-1}$	1.71	(1.09)	1.13	(0.53)	11.11	(1.94)
$u_{t-1} - u_{t-2}$	4.64	(3.10)	4.96	(2.35)	0.43	(0.10)
$y_t - y_{t-1}$	0.074	(0.73)	0.131	(0.76)	0.045	(0.36)
$y_{t-1} - y_{t-2}$	0.066	(0.69)	0.052	(0.32)	0.102	(0.82)
$W_t - W_{t-1}$	−13.11	(−1.46)	−14.62	(−1.22)		
$G_t - G_{t-1}$	−6.04	(−1.53)			−7.78	(−1.89)
DW	2.07		2.08		1.83	
$\bar{R}^2$	0.30		0.28		−0.12E−2	
F	4.39		2.51		0.995	
SER	11.13		14.68		7.94	

columns 5 and 6 the restricted equation has been estimated separately for the period 1923–46 and 1947–71. Previous year's unemployment is significant in the earlier period, but not the later, and detoxification is significant in the later period. The estimated relationship is clearly different for the two sub-periods, indicating that results from one period may not hold outside that period. The $\bar{R}^2$ is still rather low and the F statistic is insignificant at the 5 per cent level in both cases.

Differencing is an alternative to HILU as a method of allowing for first order serial correlation in the residuals. Table 6.2 reports the results from estimating the restricted model of Table 6.1 in terms of changes in the variables. The results are not greatly different from those in Table 6.1 where HILU was used. The change in unemployment one period previously is significantly related to the change in the suicide rate over the full period and in the first sub-period. In the second sub-period the current unemployment change is significant (at 10 per cent) but the previous period's is not. Detoxification also has an effect which is significant at the 10 per cent level. The overall performance of the equations is again rather poor and they do not account for much of the variation in suicide rates.

Non-Myopic Expectations

The estimating equations are derived from a very simple probability model (6.25) and this may partly explain the fact that the equations, account for only 40 per cent of the variance in the suicidal rate. The model is based on the plausible assumption that expectations of future unemployment rates and income affect suicide probabilities. Expectations have been assumed to be myopic, i.e., future unemployment and income are expected to be equal to their current values. This is a naive method of forming expectations. Let us suppose that individuals are somewhat more sophisticated and adjust their forecasts each period. Assume that in each period the forecast is adapted in proportion to the previous period's forecast error. Thus in the case of the forecast unemployment rate u_t^f we have

$$u_t^f - u_{t-1}^f = (1 - \lambda)(u_{t-1} - u_{t-1}^f) \tag{6.28}$$

which is equivalent to

$$u_t^f = (1 - \lambda)u_t + \lambda(1 - \lambda)u_{t-1} + \lambda^2(1 - \lambda)u_{t-2} + \ldots \tag{6.29}$$

and similarly for the forecast level of income y_t^f. Assuming that the suicide probability is

$$\pi_{isvt} = \gamma_{0s} + \gamma_1 y_t + \gamma_2 y_t^f + \gamma_3 u_t^f, \tag{6.30}$$

we get, via the Koyck transformation,[17]

$$
\begin{aligned}
m_t &= \gamma_{0e} + (\gamma_{0u} - \gamma_{0e})u_t + \gamma_1 y_t + \gamma_2 y_t^f + \gamma_3 u_t^f \\
&= \gamma_{0e}(1 - \lambda) + (\gamma_{0u} - \gamma_{0e} + \gamma_3(1 - \lambda))u_t - (\gamma_{0u} - \gamma_{0e})\lambda u_{t-1} \\
&\quad + (\gamma_1 + \gamma_2(1 - \lambda))y_t - \gamma_1 \lambda y_{t-1} + \lambda m_{t-1}
\end{aligned} \tag{6.31}
$$

Table 6.3, column 1 shows the results of estimating this equation by OLS. The equation appears to perform much better than those in Table 6.1 and 6.2 which are based on myopic expectations. The $\bar{R}^2$ is high, there is no evidence of residual serial correlation and the coefficients generally have the anticipated signs. The estimated coefficients in column 1 yield the following values of the coefficients in the theoretical model.[18]

$$\lambda = 0.744, \qquad \gamma_1 = 0.204$$
$$\gamma_{0u} = 258.22, \qquad \gamma_2 = -0.33$$
$$\gamma_{0e} = 255.48, \qquad \gamma_3 = 6.01$$

132

TABLE 6.3 *Non-myopic expectations and auto-regressive models*

	(1) OLS 1923–1971		(2) OLS 1923–1971		(3) OLS 1923–1971		(4) OLS 1923–1971		(5) OLS 1923–1971		(6) OLS 1923–1946		(7) OLS 1947–1971	
Constant	65.15	(2.48)	5.21	(0.65)	10.24	(1.07)	89.24	(4.8)	66.46	(3.85)	116.3	(2.11)	−19.07	(−0.57)
u_t	4.27	(2.81)									3.88	(1.77)	8.94	(1.58)
u_{t-1}	−2.04	(−1.33)									−1.04	(0.47)	−1.59	(−0.22)
y_t	0.12	(1.19)									0.1	(0.52)	−0.018	(−0.16)
y_{t-1}	−0.152	(−1.47)									−0.183	(−1.01)	0.109	(0.79)
m_{t-1}	0.745	(7.29)	1.2	(8.34)	1.18	(8.01)	0.598	(7.03)	0.679	(8.13)	0.656	(3.76)	0.679	(3.5)
w_t	−8.11	(−1.31)			−0.526	(−0.98)							−4.59	(−2.25)
G_t	−0.391	(−0.33)	−0.24	(−1.62)	−0.231	(−1.57)	−3.15	(−2.56)			−10.29	(−0.82)		
m_{t-2}														
DW	1.93		1.93		1.93		0.81		0.86		1.89		1.7	
$\bar{R}^2$	0.95		0.94		0.94		0.62		0.58		0.91		0.87	
F	141.6		343.9		229.4		40.12		66.03		35.28		16.86	
SER	11.25		13.22		13.22		32.14		33.98		15.05		6.9	

Of these only γ_1 has the wrong sign and note that $\gamma_{0u} > \gamma_{0e}$ as required by the model. Alternatively, only the estimated coefficients on current and previous period income have the wrong sign, but not significantly so. Notice, however, that the detoxification of town gas does not appear to have reduced the suicide rate significantly.

The estimated long run effect of a permanent 1 per cent increase in the unemployment rate is $\gamma_{0u} - \gamma_{0e} + \gamma_3 = 8.75$ extra suicides per 1 million of the population. This is about 4.4 per cent of the average age adjusted suicide rate for males aged 25–64 over the period 1923–71 and the elasticity (evaluated at the mean unemployment (4.29 per cent) and suicide rate) over 1923–71) is about 0.20. Put another way: with a male GB population aged 25–64 of 13.5 million in 1984, the model predicts that the long run effect of a 1 per cent increase in the unemployment rate would be an extra 118 suicides per year in this part of the population.

The remaining columns in Table 6.3 suggest that the results in column 1 should be treated cautiously. In columns 2 to 5 are estimates from simple models which assume that the suicide rate is primarily stochastic, following either a one or two period autoregression. The two AR(2) models in columns 2 and 3 are reasonably good (and much simpler) alternatives to the adaptive expectations economic model of column 1 in that they explain nearly as much of the variation in suicide rates. The addition of a detoxification variable in column 3 does not improve the performance of the AR(2) model significantly. The AR(1) models in columns 4 and 5 are rather less satisfactory. Their $\bar{R}^2$ are smaller and they exhibit first order serial correlation in the residuals. Detoxification is significant in column 5 but the DW statistic still indicates serially correlated residuals.

Columns 6, 7 are the results of estimating the column 1 model separately over the periods 1923–46 and 1947–71. The model performs reasonably well in both sub-periods but the coefficient on current unemployment is insignificant in the post-war period and only just significant at the 10 per cent level in the earlier period. Detoxification is significant when the postwar period is examined separately. A Chow test indicates that the estimated coefficients do not differ significantly between the two periods. The Chow test's validity is undermined, however, by the fact that the estimated error variances appear to be different in the two sub-periods. The null hypothesis of equal variances is rejected at the 1 per cent level against the alternative that the variance is smaller in the second sub-period.

A further test of the adequacy of the simple non-myopic economic

TABLE 6.4   *Forecast and actual suicide rates*

	Actual	Forecast	
		Economic Model (Table 6.3, col. 1)	Stochastic Model (Table 6.3, col. 2)
1972	124.1	138.2	131.8
1973	130.2	125.0	123.5
1974	126.4	118.4	132.3
1975	130.5	118.9	126.3
1976	134.7	127.0	132.1
1977	137.3	127.7	136.2
1978	139.7	144.3	138.3
1979	149.3	138.5	140.6
1980	155.4	145.1	151.5
1981	164.2	149.8	156.6
R^2		0.57	0.85
$\xi(10)$		8.13	1.81

model of suicide is its forecasting ability over the post-sample period 1972–81. Table 6.4 compares the actual suicide rates with those forecast using the estimated coefficients from the economic model (from column 1, Table 6.3) and the AR(2) model (from column 2, Table 6.3). The chi-square forecast test statistic (Harvey, 1981, pp. 179–81) for the economic model is 8.13 and for the AR(2) model is 1.81, so that both models are compatible with actual post-sample suicide rates. Both models typically under-forecast the actual suicide rates, but it is clear the AR(2) model has smaller forecast errors. The R^2 for actual and forecast values is 0.57 for the economic model and 0.85 for the AR(2) model. There does not seem to be any strong reason for preferring the economic model of suicide to the stochastic AR(2) alternative on the basis of these results.

4.   CONCLUSIONS

Selection is probably not a serious problem in aggregate time series analysis, but there are many other difficulties (Gravelle, 1984). The more obvious ones which should be specifically borne in mind in interpreting the preliminary results in Section 3 are:

1. many variables have been omitted from the regressions. These

include: measures of unemployment duration and the incomes of the employed and unemployed;
2. data for different countries and different ages have been aggregated and it is unlikely that suicide propensities are uniform;
3. since mortality probabilities are bounded above and below, estimation of linear mortality functions could be misleading and other functional forms, such as the logistic should be considered;[19]
4. only a limited range of diagnostic statistics and tests has been applied to the results;
5. the estimation procedures were chosen for simplicity and may be inefficient or inconsistent.[20]

Some of these problems will be tackled in subsequent work, but I suspect that the qualitative conclusions will not be greatly affected. Watkins (1985) has suggested that policy relevant propositions, especially those made by social scientists, should be clearly labelled to indicate the degree of uncertainty attached to them. He provides and defines eight labels, from 'almost certain' to 'highly unlikely'. The proposition that increases in unemployment rates lead to increases in suicide rates can best be described as 'plausible', in that the 'evidence is suggestive, but far from strong' (Watkins, 1985, p. 28). In particular, I do not feel that the evidence enables us to say whether unemployment has direct or merely precipitating effects on suicide, or whether the whole population or just the unemployed are affected. Nor do I think it is possible at the moment to reliably quantify the impact of unemployment on suicide.

APPENDIX: DATA SOURCES AND DEFINITIONS

Suicide rate (m_t): suicide rate per million for men aged 25–64 in Great Britain, age adjusted using 1951 population weights. Sources: *Registrar-General's Statistical Review: England and Wales*; *Annual Report of Registrar-General, Scotland*; *Annual Abstract of Statistics*.

Unemployment rate (u_t): total unemployed as a percentage of the total working population of the United Kingdom. Sources: C. H. Feinstein, *National Income, Expenditure and Output of the United Kingdom, 1955–1965*, London, 1972; *British Labour Statistics Yearbooks*; *Department of Employment Gazette*.

Income (y_t): real personal disposable income at 1975 prices per head of the UK population. Sources: Feinstein; *National Income and Expenditure* Blue Books; interpolation for 1938–46.

War (W_t): dummy variable, 1939–45: value 1, other years: value 0.

Gas (G_t): trend variable with value 0 prior to 1958, increasing by 1 in each year 1958–74, then constant in subsequent years. (The percentage of carbon monoxide in domestic gas was about 13.5 per cent in 1957, 12 per cent in 1960, 0 per cent in 1974).

NOTES

I am grateful to John Rigg and Shirley Spillane for their painstaking research assistance.

1. The families of the unemployed are also likely to be affected, but we will ignore this complication in the rest of the paper.
2. See Gravelle (1984), Stern (1983) for fuller discussions of estimation problems.
3. In this, and in all subsequent similar equations, the relationship will be assumed to be exact and error terms will be ignored. The conclusions reached concerning selection effects are not dependent on this simplifying assumption.
4. Suicides are 1 per cent of deaths in England and Wales. In 1982 there were 4279 suicides in England and Wales. This is 1 per cent of deaths or about 1 per 10 000 people per year. See Bulusu and Alderson (1984) for a summary of postwar trends.
5. The panel study of Sheffield school leavers does control for selection bias by measuring mental health before and after entry into the labour market. The mental health of those with jobs was better than for those without. This is unlikely to reflect selection because there was no difference in mental health between the two groups prior to leaving school (Banks and Jackson, 1982). The sample is too small to be useful for a study of suicide.
6. Using Bayes Theorem the probability that a suicide is unemployed is $\pi_{iujt} \, u_{ijt}(\pi_{ijt})^{-1}$ and the probability that a live control is unemployed is $(1 - \pi_{iujt})u_{ijt}(1 - \pi_{ijt})^{-1}$. Subtracting the latter from the former, rearranging and averaging over all n suicides gives (6.8).
7. Parasuicide is defined as non-fatal deliberate self-harm and is not synonymous with failed suicide. It has many similarities with suicide as an indicator of individual distress and can be analysed in the same way. See Platt (1984) for a discussion and references to the literature.
8. The unconditional probability that $x_{ijt} = 1$ is λ_{jt}, the unconditional unemployment probability for i is $(\beta_0 w_{jt} + \beta_1 1)\lambda_{jt} + \beta_0 w_{jt} (1 - \lambda_{jt}) = \beta_0 w_{jt} + \lambda_{jt}\beta_1$ and the conditional probability of unemployment given $x_{ijt} = 1$ is $\beta_0 w_{jt} + \beta_1$. Hence the use of Bayes Theorem for the probability of x_{ijt} conditional on i being unemployed, gives (6.10a). The expected value of x_{ijt} conditional on i being employed (6.10b) is similarly derived.

9. The constant a_{0s} will estimate a_{0s} plus the average of the area fixed effects $a_{1s}\lambda_{jt} + \sigma_{3s} q_{jt}$.
10. The expected value of the parasuicide rate in area j at time t is $\Sigma \pi_{ijt} n_{jt}^{-1}$ where n_{jt} is the number of individuals in j at t. Writing, $\pi_{ijt} = \pi_{iejt} + u_{ijt} (\pi_{iujt} - \pi_{iejt})$ then gives m_{jt} as the sum of the first, second, third, fourth and seventh terms in (6.20) plus:

$(a_{1u} - a_{1e}) \Sigma u_{ijt} x_{ijt} n_{jt}^{-1} + (a_{2u} - a_{2e})\Sigma u_{ijt}^2 n_{jt}^{-1}$.
Now $\sigma_{xjt} = (1/n_{jt})\Sigma(x_{ijt} - x_{jt})^2 = (1/n_{jt})(\Sigma x_{ijt}^2) - x_{jt}^2$
and $u_{ijt} = \beta_0 w_{jt} + \beta_1 x_{ijt}$. Hence $(1/n_{jt}) \Sigma u_{ijt}^2 = \beta_1^2\sigma_{xjt} + u_{jt}^2$
and $(1/n_{jt}) \Sigma u_{ijt} x_{ijt} = \beta_1 \sigma_{xjt}^2 + u_{jt} x_{jt}$

Substituting in and rearranging gives (6.20).
11. The expected value of a ratio of random variables is not the ratio of their expected values as shown by (6.22). However (6.22) can be regarded as a first order approximation and second order terms will be of the same order as the variances. For large populations these will be small.
12. See also Gravelle, Hutchinson and Stern (1981).
13. The derivation of (6.23) is similar to that of (6.20) except that there are area variations in w_{jt} and q_{jt} to be allowed for.
14. Marshall (1981) discusses the hypothesis and finds no support for it in an aggregate time series analysis for the United States.
15. We can also ignore the omitted terms if $\delta_{4u} = \delta_{4e}$ so that employment status does not alter the marginal effect of current income or the change in income.
16. These results arise from a HILU procedure with large steps (0.1). They are not sufficiently impressive to justify a finer search.
17. See Johnston (1984, ch. 9) on adaptive expectations and the Koyck transformation. Note that by assuming the same adjustment parameter for changes in y_t^f and u_t^f we have ensured that all parameters can be estimated.
18. The dependent variable is suicides per million.
19. Non-linearities in the probability function will raise problems of aggregation.
20. In Table 6.3 the presence of heteroscedasticity and the inclusion of a lagged dependent variable via a Koyck transformation may make OLS inappropriate, but OLS has the advantage of being a fairly robust procedure.

REFERENCES

Balusu, L. and Alderson, M. (1984) 'Suicides 1950–82', *Population Trends*, 35, 11–17.

Banks, M. H. and Jackson, P. R. (1982) 'Unemployment and Risk of Young People: Cross-Sectional and Longitudinal Evidence', *Psychological Medicine*, 12, 789–98.

Brenner, M. H. (1985) 'Economic Change and Mortality by Cause in Selected

European Countries', in Westcott, G., Svensson, P. G. and Zollner, H. F. K. (eds), *Health Policy Implications of Unemployment*, Copenhagen: WHO.

Fox, A. J. and Goldblatt, P. O. (1982) *Socio-Demographic Mortality Differentials: Longitudinal Study 1971–75*, London: HMSO.

Gravelle, H. S. E. (1984) 'Time Series Analysis of Mortality and Unemployment', *Journal of Health Economics*, 3, 297–305.

Gravelle, H. S. E., Hutchinson, G. and Stern, J. (1981) 'Mortality and Unemployment: A Critique of Brenner's Time Series Analysis', *Lancet*, ii, 675–9.

Harvey, A. C. (1981) *The Econometric Analysis of Time Series*, Deddington: Philip Allan.

Johnson, J. (1984) *Econometric Methods*, 3rd edn, London: McGraw-Hill.

Kreitman N. and Platt, S. (1984) 'Suicide, Unemployment and Domestic Gas Detoxification in Great Britain', *Journal of Epidemiology and Community Health*, 38, 1–6.

Marshall, J. R. (1981) 'Political Integration and the Effect of War on Suicide: United States, 1933–1976', *Social Forces*, 59, 771–85.

Moser, K. A., Fox, A. J. and Jones, D. R. (1984) 'Unemployment and Mortality in the OPCS Longitudinal Study', *Lancet*, ii, 1324–9.

Platt, S. (1984) 'Unemployment and Suicidal Behaviour: A Review of the Literature', *Social Science and Medicine*, 19, 93–115.

Platt, S. (1985a) 'Suicidal Behaviour and Unemployment: A Literature Review', in Westcott, G., Svensson, P. G. and Zollner, H. F. K. (eds), *Health Policy Implications of Unemployment*, Copenhagen: WHO.

Platt, S. (1985b), 'Parasuicide and Unemployment Among Men in Edinburgh 1963–1983', paper presented at Centre for Economic Policy Research, Workshop on Health and Unemployment, 1 February.

Platt, S. and Kreitman, N. (1984) 'Trends in Parasuicide and Unemployment Among Men in Edinburgh, 1968–1982', *British Medical Journal*, 289, 1029–32.

Stern, J. (1983) 'The Relationship Between Unemployment, Morbidity and Mortality in Britain', *Population Studies* 37, 61–74.

Watkins, S (1985) 'Recession and Health: A Literature Review', in Westcott, G., Svensson, P. G. and Zollner, H. F. K. (eds), *Health Policy Implications Of Unemployment*, Copenhagen: WHO.

7 Economic and Health Consequences of Reduced Smoking

JOY TOWNSEND

INTRODUCTION

It is a formidable undertaking to speak on the economics of smoking in Bristol where the British cigarette industry began, and in the University that I understand was founded by Imperial Tobacco. Despite this awesome milieu, I shall attempt to face some of the implications of the industry and its products.

The habit of smoking tobacco as cigarettes has not a long history. It has largely developed through the first half of this century. Before then, tobacco was smoked mostly as pipes or cigars. The new cigarettes were easy to use, could be sociably proffered to others, could be bought and consumed practically anywhere, were very cheap and were considered modern and sophisticated. The fatal factors for health were that, being so cheap and acceptable, people smoked, not the odd one, but twenty or so a day and, consciously or not, smokers tended to inhale the smoke, as indeed did non-smokers.

Britain already had tobacco interests and together with the USA quickly became a world leader, both in manufacturing and in consuming cigarettes, so that by the early 1960s over half the adult population were regular cigarette smokers.

I shall consider here what happened after this juncture; the publication of major medical findings concerning smoking, the responses to these and the resultant present patterns of smoking and health. I shall then discuss the economic impact of reducing smoking on taxation, health costs, the industry and employment. I shall discuss the cost effectiveness of different programmes aimed at saving lives and finally a package policy for reducing smoking.

By the late 1930s some doctors were beginning to suspect that the rapid rise in lung cancer deaths was related to the new habit, but it was not until after the Second World War that these ideas were formally tested by the most extensive epidemiological studies probably ever undertaken. Sir Richard Doll and Austin Bradford Hill in their pioneering work, monitored the smoking habits and mortality of British doctors through the 1950s, later followed up to 1970. In America, similar studies were carried out on one million men and women by Hammond, on 290 000 American veterans by Dorn, and by 92 000 Canadian veterans by Best. The statistical power of this work was high because of the approximately equal number of smokers and non-smokers.

In the British study (Doll and Peto, 1976, vol. 2, pp. 1425–536), it was reported that cigarette smokers' age-standardised death rates from lung cancer were fourteen times that of non-smokers, from chronic bronchitis and emphysema were twenty-four times and coronary heart disease 62 per cent higher than non-smokers. All the studies reported similar findings. Smoking increased the risk of dying from many other diseases as well, such as cancers of the mouth and throat, bladder and pancreas. A recent study has also reported that children who are exposed to ten or more cigarettes a day during pregnancy have a 50 per cent extra risk of cancer and have twice the risk of getting leukaemia (Stejernfeldt *et al.*, 1986, vol. 1, pp. 1350–2).

In summary, it is now estimated that one in every four smokers dies prematurely because of smoking and on average loses about ten to fifteen years of life and often twenty, thirty or forty years. Britain has the highest lung cancer death rates in the world and among the highest for coronary heart disease and bronchitis. In Britain 100 000 people a year die from smoking, that is one in seven of all deaths. It is the major epidemic of this century and greatly outstrips any other cause of premature death. British men and women have paid a very high price for the smoking habits of the last seventy years (see Figure 7.1).

How are these mortality risks modified when a smoker gives up? The British doctors' study reported that when a smoker gives up, the excess risk is reduced by 40 per cent in the first ten years and by as much as 90 per cent after fifteen years. Those who stopped before they were thirty lost all the excess risk. So there are major benefits in giving up, and the damage is to a large extent reversible.

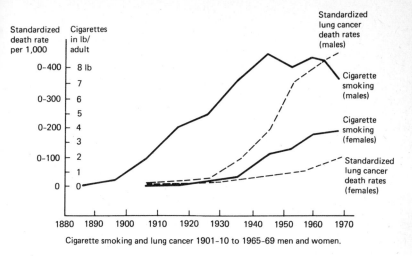

Cigarette smoking and lung cancer 1901-10 to 1965-69 men and women.

FIGURE 7.1   *Cigarette smoking and lung cancer 1901–10 to 1965–9, men and*
women
Source: Townsend (1978).

Also smokers' excess risk of dying is approximately proportional to
the amount they smoke. The average smoker loses about five and a
half minutes of life for each cigarette smoked (Royal College of
Physicians, 1977). So there are tangible benefits from smoking less or
even from giving up temporarily.

RESPONSE TO THE SCIENTIFIC EVIDENCE

Consumer

The medical evidence was widely publicised in 1962 in the Royal
College of Physicians report *Smoking and Health* and in 1964 with the
American Surgeon General's report. These were reported in the
media including feature programmes on television and made a major
impact. In Britain smoking fell by some 5 per cent after each report,
but this was only temporary and it quickly picked up again. There was
little impact overall and none on women's smoking which was rising
rapidly at the time. The studies had mainly concerned men.

Government

The government response was modest. Cigarette advertisements were banned on TV from 1965 and the industry agreed on a code to moderate advertisements but there was no specific legislation. This inaction was not necessarily due to indifference or inaction on the part of ministers, but where their policies were seen as a threat to the treasury or other interests, bills were shelved or ministers moved. (There is a lively discussion of this in Peter Taylor's book *The Smoke Ring* (1984 chs 4 and 8).)

Industry

The industry responded by setting up the Tobacco Research Council to check out the research. It was suggested that if there was a harmful agent it could be removed to render the cigarette safe. But the search for the safe cigarette was costly and unsuccessful. It appeared that there was no safe cigarette, at least no such saleable product.

The industry in Britain prepared for a large fall in demand. Companies diversified widely into related industries but mostly into new growth areas such as poultry, eggs, fast foods, potato-crisps, frozen foods, paper and boards, brewing and hotels. By 1973, 28 per cent of Imperial Tobacco sales were non-tobacco, as were 25 per cent of BAT's sales and 12 per cent of Gallahers' sales. There was some reduction in demand but not of the order anticipated. The companies have recently diversified further including into the insurance industry.

The industry has tended to keep the initiative in their own hands by having voluntary agreement with the government about advertising and have countered the effects of restricted direct advertising by sports sponsorship, by which means they have in effect achieved widespread television coverage. One benefit of agreements has been the reduction in the tar content of cigarettes, which has been achieved, at least until recently.

Health Publicity

So through the 1960s the health publicity was mostly media reporting of the major British and American epidemiological studies. The effect on smoking was significant, as we have noted, but mostly temporary.

However, from the mid and late 1970s things changed. Organisations such as ASH, Health Education Council, Scottish Health Education Group and more recently, the BMA have, together, provided sustained health information on the effects of smoking, support to health professionals and schools and a zealous monitoring of the advertising restrictions on the industry. *They* have kept the health issues in the public eye, provided materials to doctors and hospitals and have largely been the advocates for the country's health on this issue often when the health ministers have been unable or unwilling to take the part.

Legal Action

Recently in the USA there have been several cases where smoking victims have claimed compensation from the tobacco industry. None have yet succeeded but there are many more in the pipeline. In Britain, a patient with Buerger's disease is considering filing a case against Imperial Tobacco.

SMOKING PROFILES: SMOKING BY SOCIAL CLASS, SEX AND AGE

Class and Sex

The reduction in smoking over the last two decades for men and the last decade for women, has not been evenly spread between income groups and social classes. Before the anti-smoking health publicity of the early 1960s, there was very little difference between the smoking habits of different social classes in the UK. Around 60 per cent of men and 45 per cent of women in each social class smoked cigarettes (see Figure 7.2).

Since that time the pattern of smoking has been characterised by a widening divergence in smoking between members of different social classes, an overall increase in the number of cigarettes smoked per smoker and a narrowing of the difference in men and women's smoking habits. By 1984 49 per cent of unskilled working men (social class 5) smoked cigarettes, while only 17 per cent of professional men (social class 1) still did so. Percentages of smokers in social classes 2–4 range in between the two. For women the pattern is similar with about

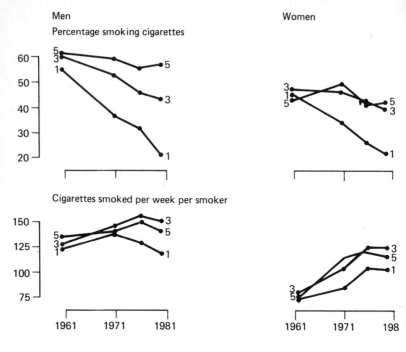

FIGURE 7.2   *Cigarette smoking by social class and sex*
Source: Townsend (1987).

40 per cent social class 3–5 remaining smokers compared with 15 per cent social class 1 (professional single women or wives of professional men). Smokers in social class 1 also smoke considerably fewer cigarettes than other smokers, as is shown in Figure 7.2.

Smoking in the UK over the last twenty years has therefore become predominantly a lower class phenomenon. This is reflected in smoking related mortality shown in Table 7.1. An unskilled working man (social class 5) is seen to be three times more likely to die of lung cancer as a professional man and 25 per cent more likely to die of ischaemic heart disease. These differentials are not all explained by smoking

TABLE 7.1 *UK Mortality rates for smoking related diseases per 100 000 of population aged 15–64 (standardised for age)*

	Social class	men	Women (married)
Lung cancer	1	37	12
	3	77	18
	5	100	22
Bronchitis	1	12	4
	3	35	12
	5	63	19
Ischaeric	1	173	27
Heart disease	3	213	54
	5	218	68

SOURCE: OPCS *Occupational Mortality 1970–2.*

differences, but smoking is a major contributor and also multiplies the risk of other diseases such as pneumoconiosis, bronchitis and asbestosis for which lower-class workers are already at greater risk.

Age

Although it has been the professed policy of successive British governments to try to discourage young people from starting to smoke, there has been little reduction among young adults and it is perhaps surprising to see (Table 7.2) that the same proportion of men and

TABLE 7.2 *Cigarette smoking by sex and age, 1984 (percentage smoking cigarettes)*

Age	Men	Women
16–19	29	32
20–24	40	36
25–34	40	36
35–49	39	36
50–59	39	39
60+	30	23

women in their twenties are smoking as in their fifties, although the middle-aged smokers smoke at a higher rate. A government survey has reported that 27 per cent of fifteen-year-olds are regular smokers (Dobbs and Marsh, 1985).

ECONOMIC EFFECTS OF REDUCING SMOKING

Despite all the scientific evidence smoking is still a widespread habit, although now only one in three adults smoke in Britain rather than one in two. Before looking at policies to reduce smoking and their economic consequences, it may be useful to discuss whether there is an economic case for intervention. Is there an argument for intervention or is it enough to say that there is a risk, smokers are aware of it, they are adults and are free to make their own mistakes?

Addiction

Firstly, economic analysis generally assumes the individual to be the best judge of his own welfare and to spend his money to maximise it. This is the assumption of most economic tools. Cigarettes however, are strange consumer goods. As Stepney says (*New Society*, 1983) 'A lot of smokers behave in a way which suggests they are more or less nicotine addicts. Such smokers may have started off in control – using nicotine – but later have been taken over by the drug.' Most smokers want to give up the habit. McKennell and Thomas in a government survey in 1967 found that 67 per cent had tried to stop smoking or wanted to stop. A UK government opinion poll in 1978 found that 68 per cent of cigarette smokers wanted to stop and 67 per cent would approve tougher curbs on smoking. Most smokers start smoking as adolescents, before the age of maturity, before they can legally buy cigarettes or make other commitments such as marriage, and they continue smoking through their life. An OPCS study in England and Wales (Dobbs and Marsh 1985) reported that 19 per cent of 11 to 16 year-olds smoked, 11 per cent of them regularly on average 47 cigarettes a week and that 27 per cent of fifth-year children were regular smokers. These children were below the age at which they were legally allowed to buy cigarettes. The National Cancer Institute found that 95 per cent of US adult smokers began to smoke before they were 21. Most smokers therefore are recruited *before* they are adult into a habit which they later try to give up but cannot.

Addiction may so influence or distort the addict's pattern of demand that the individual's total welfare is lower than it would be without the addiction. A person may choose to take a drug, but he does not choose to be a drug addict.

Ignorance

There is no longer the near complete ignorance that obtained before the 1960s but nevertheless the risks associated with smoking, the reduction of risk by stopping smoking and the outcomes of these risks, have been shown to be erroneously perceived, and underestimated by consumers.

Externalities

Thirdly, there is the problem of externalities. Externalities of smoking will include extra health care costs *not paid* by the smoker, costs of caring for dependents when a smoker dies prematurely or is sick, fires caused by smoking and general smoke nuisance and hazard.

These three problems of addiction, ignorance and externalities mean that the smokers' welfare may well be diminished by his smoking habit, that there may be costs of smoking not borne by the smoker, and that there is a case for intervention that is not simply paternalist.

POLICIES TO REDUCE SMOKING

The main policy instruments available to reduce smoking are taxation, health information, restrictions on advertising and fourthly restrictions on where smoking is allowed. Let us first look at taxation.

James I of England was a serious anti-smoking campaigner. He raised the tax on tobacco, not by a mere 5 per cent but forty fold from Elizabeth I's 2d per pound to a full 6s 10d per pound. This fierce fiscal attack followed the publication of his 'Counterblaste to Tobacco' of 1604 and put the price of tobacco above that of silver. It was intended to stamp the habit out once and for all; which it did not.

TABLE 7.3   *Retail price index for cigarettes relative to price of all goods and services (1980–1)*

1948	1.587
1950	1.549
1955	1.213
1960	1.217
1962	1.252
1965	1.331
1966	1.307
1967	1.262
1968	1.278
1969	1.318
1970	1.261
1975	1.068
1980	1.000
1981	1.104
1982	1.174
1983	1.196
1984	1.264

Now, as then, tax makes up a large part of the price of cigarette (73.5 per cent of price at present) and smokers are not greatl responsive to changes in price. For a 1 per cent increase they will dro smoking by only about ½ per cent. In 1947, cigarette tax was raised b 43 per cent in order to increase revenue, reduce imports and hel deflate the economy. Since then the real price and tax rate have mostl drifted down with inflation (see Table 7.3). There have been periodi tax increases but the price remains below that of the postwar leve Neither the present nor previous governments have had a clear polic concerning cigarette tax. In the late 1970s when reducing inflation wa the top priority of the government, there was reluctance to raise th tax, and it was argued that an increase would be inflationary in th short term because cigarette prices figure in the retail price index which in turn is used as a basis for wage negotiations. However, in 198 the then Chancellor, Sir Geoffrey Howe, imposed one of the larges tax increases in postwar years putting up the price by 10 per cent in year. The reason was not clear although it was reported that th Chancellor had himself recently stopped smoking. From 1981 to 198 the tax was increased annually by more than the rate of inflation. Th effect of raising taxes is also to raise revenue. The tax revenue elasticit is $1.0 - \frac{T}{P}e$ where $\frac{T}{P}$ is the proportion of tax in the total price and e is th price elasticity of demand. Tax revenue will *increase* with a pric

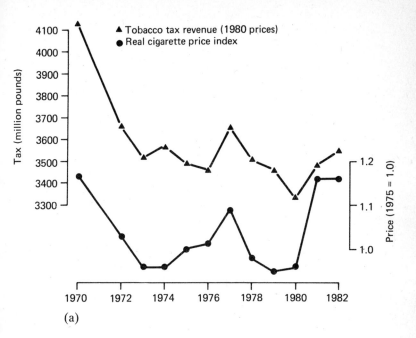

(a)

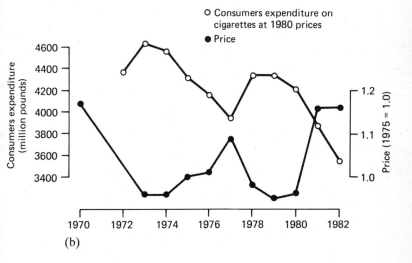

(b)

FIGURE 7.3   *Tobacco tax revenue and cigarette price change*

increase as long as $e < \frac{p}{T}$ which is about 1.4 for cigarettes and no study has suggested it is anywhere near as high as this. Figure 7.3(a) shows how the real value of tobacco tax revenue has risen and fallen with real changes in cigarette prices and demonstrates clearly not only that tax revenue rises with a tax rise but also that it can fall dramatically if tax does not keep up with inflation. Figure 7.3(b) shows how responsive consumption is to price changes.

An important aspect of taxation is that it impinges differentially on different income groups. Low income groups smoke more but they reduce their smoking more in response to tax increases. I argue therefore that the downward drift in real cigarette prices over the last twenty years in Britain has effectively *increased* the smoking levels of lower socioeconomic groups relative to social classes 1 and 2 and has been a major factor in the divergence in social class smoking. It has largely negated the effects of health education. If real cigarette prices were raised to the immediate post war level, it is likely that the differential in social class smoking would be considerably reduced.

Between 1980 and 1984, UK cigarette prices, mostly determined by tax rose by as much as 26 per cent in real terms. Consumption fell by a massive 20 per cent. At the same time, cigarette tax revenue rose by 10 per cent and provided an extra £435 million of government revenue.

The effect of putting up cigarette tax has always been to both *increase* the governments revenue and to *decrease* consumption, particularly amongst the young and among manual workers who have the highest smoking and mortality rates. So tax is operating as an effective ally of preventive medicine.

Even so, in 1986 a cigarette still cost only about 7p which compared very favourably with the price of a drink, chocolate bar, a packet of crisps or most other similar expenditures, and it is little wonder they are smoked in such quantity.

Long Term Tax

How important is cigarette revenue to the government, and can it tolerate other measures which reduce smoking without increasing revenue? In the later 1940s, cigarette tax was a major source of government revenue, providing over one third of all expenditure tax and 16 per cent of all government revenue. The same is not true today. In 1984 it provided only 4 per cent of government revenue. The whole structure of the economy has changed and other taxes such as VAT and petroleum revenue tax have become of greater value. Cigarette tax halved in importance from 1947–67 and halved again since then. By the end of the century it could be a minor source of tax.

Cost-Effectiveness of Health Education Programmes

Unfortunately there are too few of my worthy health economist colleagues around and most expenditure in the health service is not methodically evaluated or indeed evaluated at all. For example large and rapidly increasing amounts of money are spent on cancer chemotherapies, many of which have not been evaluated and 'many of them with very serious side effects and most having no more than a marginal effect at the present time on increased survival' (Bodmer, 1985).

For some health care where there is evidence of medical efficacy, the cost per patient may not be examined or may be considered by some to be very high, such as for renal dialysis or transplant programmes. Proper evaluation in the health field is difficult, because decision-making is in most cases diversified down to the single consultant and because outcomes of treatment are mostly unknown. The patient usually attends the hospital, receives treatment and goes home and is only rarely followed up in a way that would allow any evaluation of cost or benefit. Nor is other government expenditure much better analysed in any formal way. The methodology may be there, but it is only rarely used to determine specific expenditure.

Public Information programmes to reduce smoking are rather better placed because:

1. Decisions on expenditure are not highly devolved, most of the expenditure is likely to be decided centrally at a national, regional or district level.
2. There is firm evidence of its potential effectiveness in achieving its aim of reducing smoking.
3. There is evidence that success in reducing smoking will result in reduced morbidity and mortality.

It is often difficult to pick out the effects of one campaign when other factors are changing. Prices may be going up or down, incomes may be rising, advertising or unemployment may be changing. One way to try to tease out these different effects is by econometric analysis and this has been used to measure the effects of mass media programmes in the

USA and in Britain. In the USA, Hamilton (1972) found that health education had a significant effect over the period 1953–70 and was a much more effective deterrent from smoking than advertising was a stimulant and this was clearly appreciated by the tobacco companies.

Hamilton estimated that the broadcasting of anti-smoking advertisments in 1968–70 reduced cigarette consumption by 14 per cent per year. Warner (1977) estimated the reduction as an overall 17 per cent. For the UK one can clearly see from Figure 7.4 the effects of the RCP reports and the TV ban on cigarette advertising. Atkinson and Skegg (1973) estimated that these reduced men's smoking in 1962 and 1965 by 5 per cent and by a similar amount in 1971.

The Stanford Heart disease programme may have resulted in a reduction of smoking of 5.5 per cent still effective some two years later. In Australia there have been reported reductions of 6–11 per cent from New South Wales mass media campaigns. Mass media interventions in

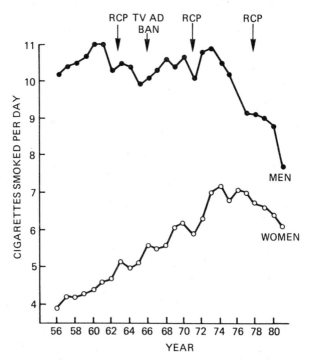

FIGURE 7.4   *Health education and cigarette consumption*
Source: Townsend (1985).

smoking have not always been as successful and of course the success is likely to be a subtle reaction between the methodology of the programme and the receptiveness of the particular audience and by its nature will have a large element of variation and unpredictability. But the potential effectiveness is very clearly demonstrated both on a national and on a local basis.

These econometric studies are the most subtle at picking out effects on a national basis using annual or quarterly data. However, a different technique will be required to try to assess the effectiveness of a particular campaign. Such a specific analysis may be needed for one of two reasons:

1. to work out the most effective way of spending a budget for smoking control programmes to maximise their effectiveness;
2. to assess how much to allocate to smoking control compared with other programmes.

Cost effectiveness analysis (CEA) may be the most useful in this context. This is essentially a comparative analysis either explicitly or implicitly in that it offers a comparison with alternative means of achieving an equivalent outcome.

Typical evaluation of health education campaign

The essence of a CEA is to decide on a homogeneous outcome which needs to be precisely defined. There will of course be several different outcomes but ideally some calculus should be sought by which each significant outcome can be defined in terms of another. For example, the primary aim of the campaign may be to get smokers to stop smoking. It might be agreed for example that 'having given up' may be defined as abstinence for one year, which is the indication of long term cessation used in most studies (Jarvis *et al.*, 1982; Russell *et al.*, 1979). Another outcome of the campaign may be that some smokers stop but only temporarily. A third outcome may be that some smokers reduce their smoking and again this may be quantified in terms of an average period of time and an average amount.

The evaluation could be generalised by translating these outcomes into say 'years of life saved' Alan Williams's QALYS. Such a generalised outcome might easily be compared with the outcome of quite different programmes.

This technique was used to assess the effectiveness of the campaigns round National No-Smoking Day 1985. Surveys were undertaken before and three months after the campaign. Assessments were made from those who had given up and those who had reduced their smoking, using the epidemiological results of the British Doctor's Study. It was estimated (Townsend, 1986) that 1889 years of life were saved by the campaign at a cost of £375,000 or £199 per life year saved. Alan Williams has estimated that the cost of saving a year of life by the simple means of a GP advising his patient to give up is about £167 per life year saved.

Now if we compare these figures with the cost of £800 per life year saved by coronary artery bypass for severe angina or £5000 per life year saved by heart transplant we see there is an overriding argument for more resources to go to smoking control programmes.

THE TOBACCO INDUSTRY AND EMPLOYMENT

There are three major British companies in the industry: British American Tobacco (BAT), the biggest tobacco company in the world is a British owned company but does not sell in the UK; Imperial Tobacco which has about half of the British market; and Rothmans International which is the third British Company and like BAT has extensive overseas operations. Another company with a large slice of the British market is Gallahers which is wholly American owned by American Brands. These companies, together with a further two US companies, dominate the world market, between them controlling about three quarters of world production, excluding the Soviet bloc and the People's Republic of China.

BAT is Britain's third largest company and Imperial is now the sixth largest. It is a formidable industry, but on the employment side it does not offer opportunities of the same order of magnitude. It is one of the most capital-intensive industries in the world, and in 1984 employed only 22 000 workers in Britain or 0.1 per cent of the workforce, half of them in Bristol and Nottingham. Employment is geographically concentrated, but even locally in Bristol and Nottingham represent less than 5 per cent of the workforce. Employment in the industry has fallen by a half since 1970, mostly from within the female labour force. This contraction has been not so much in response to a fall in sales but rather in response to more highly capital-intensive technology and faster machines. New machines introduced use less than half the labour and have been the main reason for plant closures and employment cut-backs. Manpower planning agreements have been negotiated between trade unions and the four major tobacco firms to enable ex-tobacco workers to undertake retraining with a view to finding employment in one of the firm's subsidiaries. Apparently, this has not been very effective in practice (Commission of the European Communities, 1982).

Although the industry complains loudly at any proposed measures to reduce smoking, the profits of the British Tobacco industry appear to have increased in recent years despite the fall in sales. The industry is enterprising and resourceful and has responded by increasing its activities in other expanding areas. Such further diversification could only have the effect of increasing employment, as alternative employment of resources is unlikely to be as capital intensive. This is not to deny the personal difficulties of specific job losses.

An undesirable trend in the industry is the exporting of the smoking problem by turning to third world markets which have little in the way of protective legislation.

Costs of Smoking in the Workplace

In recent years studies have reported that non smokers also suffer health risks by breathing other people's smoke both in the home environment and at work, and it has been estimated for the UK that about 200 lung cancer deaths per year are attributable to passive smoking.

TABLE 7.4   *Exposure of non-smokers to tobacco smoke*

Estimated daily annual average probability of a non smoker being exposed to tobacco smoke %		*Estimated daily average exposure to tobacco smoke particles*
At home and work	39	2.27 mg of tobacco smoke particles.
Neither	14	0.00
Work only	23	1.82 mg
Home only	24	0.45 mg
	100%	

Source: Repace (1983).

The workplace is the arena where non-smokers are most likely to find themselves in a smoking environment, and have least choice of absenting themselves from it. James Repace (1983) has estimated for the USA that only 15 per cent of non-smokers of working age escape passive smoking and that on average workplace exposures are about four times higher than domestic exposures, being equivalent to about one and a half medium tar cigarettes a day per non smoker (Table 7.4).

Smokers in the Workforce

A TUC survey of mainly manual workers found the results registered in Table 7.5. Marsh and Matheson (OPCS 1983) report that 79 per cent of smokers, 84 per cent non-smokers and 78 per cent of ex-smokers thought that non-smokers have the right to work in air free of tobacco smoke.

TABLE 7.5   *Percentage of smokers in the workforce*

Non smokers	37
Ex smokers	25
Smokers wanting to stop	22
Smokers not wanting to stop	16
Total	100%

These surveys suggest there is likely to be a high degree of agreement with work place non smoking policy. A survey of one hundred top companies in the UK carried out by the Louis Harris Group in 1982, reported that only 6 per cent have a formal smoking policy. However 51 per cent thought smoking should concern the employer; more of the large firms than the small thought this (only 24 per cent for those employing less than 1000 people).

There will inevitably be costs involved in the introduction of a new policy. These may be simply the labour costs involved in the negotiations, but may include signage, costs of segregated facilities or they may include costs of counselling smokers. Campbell's Soup Co. USA with 32 000 employees estimated costs of $70 per smoker with a 20 per cent success rate for which they estimated a short run benefit of £240 *pa* and a 60 per cent annual return on investment. This was a serious counselling input with a very high success rate.

Firms who have introduced smoking restriction in the workplace have reported savings in maintenance costs relating to cleaning, redecorating and repairs of between 10 per cent and 50 per cent, and increased productivity amounting to between 5.5 per cent and 25 per cent. For the USA, Marvin Kristein has estimated (or underestimated as he says) that the average smoker costs an employer about £5700 (1985 value) per year and that more than half these costs could be recaptured in the medium to short run by smoking cessation programmes in the workplace. He concludes that it would pay employers to invest at the very least up to £150 per year for each smoker.

A GOVERNMENT PROGRAMME FOR REDUCING SMOKING

Health Costs

The main costs of smoking to the economy are through:

1. premature death;
2. sickness absence through smoking induced illness;
3. excess health costs of smokers; and
4. fires and other damage caused by smoking.

A decade ago Atkinson and Townsend (1977) put forward a three pronged policy package aimed to reduce smoking by 40 per cent. First, by a 50 per cent rise in price to reduce smoking by 20 per cent, second, a sustained health education programme of £10 million a year to effect a further 10 per cent reduction and third, a curtailment of advertising to reduce smoking by a further 10 per cent. The estimated effects of this are given in Table 7.6.

We estimated, using a dynamic model of the lifetime use of health services by smokers and non smokers, that 250 000 hospital-bed days would be released annually in the phase-in period and 500 000 (0.5 per cent of total bed-days) thereafter. General-practitioner consultations would be saved in the phase-in period (about 250 000), but as the new non-smokers and lighter smokers aged, they would consult more, resulting in a net extra 500 000 consultations (one-third of 1 per cent of total consultations) by the end of the century.

There are large differences in sickness-absence rates between smokers and non-smokers particularly for men; the proposed package

TABLE 7.6   *Estimated effect on Government Budget of a 40% reduction in cigarette smoking in 1976 (at 1972–3 prices and rates) phased in during 1976–80*

	£ million per annum		
	1976–80	1986–90	1996–2000
Savings:			
Hospital inpatient stay (net)	3	6	6
General-practitioner consultations (net)	1	0	−1
Sickness benefit (net)	24	48	49
Widows' benefit	3	18	27
Costs:			
Retirement pensions	−4	−33	−60
Health education	−10	−10	−10
Net effect (excluding tax revenue)	17	29	11
Extra tax revenue	85	85	85

SOURCES: DHSS Social Security Statistics, 1973; Health and Social Security Statistics, 1973; Social Security Pensions Bill, 1975.

was to save a net 15 million days' sickness absence in the early years, rising to 30 million days per year.

Government Revenue

As the reduction in smoking would be brought about partly by increased taxation, the programme would actually increase government revenue by 17 per cent. The other measures such as health publicity were estimated to reduce demand without any offsetting rise in tax, although there would be some tax paid on the goods bought instead of cigarettes. The net effect, however, was estimated to be a rise in revenue of £85 million (1971–3 prices).

We did not attempt an overall cost-benefit assessment but collected together the implications for the government budget which were likely to be of immediate concern to policy-makers. In the case of the health service, the benefit of a reduction in, say, the demand for hospital beds was not likely to be realised in cash terms, for the beds would probably be used by other patients. However, in order to put some value on the release of hospital beds it was useful to look at saving in terms of average cost per in-patient day. Similarly, for general-practitioner consultations in terms of average cost per consultation.

The main elements on the plus side of the table were the savings on sickness benefits and widows' benefits and the extra tax revenue. In contrast, the potential savings to the health service appeared quite small. The main increase in expenditure was to be on health education and retirement pensions. Overall, even including the extra retirement pensions, there was to be a small net saving in government spending, with a substantial increase in the tax revenue.

Smoking could therefore have been reduced by 40 per cent with a net improvement in the budget position, added to which would be the main benefit, the massive reduction in avoidable illness and premature death.

A substantial part of this programme was in fact put into operation. Over this time the government *did* put money into health education, not as much as was asked for, but it was spent very effectively. The real price was raised by 18 per cent: about a third of that asked for. Little however was done to restrict advertising. The results of this dual policy of increasing Health Education and raising the price of cigarettes has been to reduce consumption by nearly 20 per cent. About 8 per cent has been due to the price increases (given the price elasticity of demand for cigarettes of -0.5) and about 12 per cent due to health education and public information.

Public opinion has fundamentally changed over this time. The public information campaigns have set the climate to make tax increases publicly acceptable because of their agreed health benefits.

A further 20 per cent rise in price together with a curtailment of advertising and continued health education, would result in a further 20 per cent reduction in smoking without detriment to the budget. If we are interested in improving health and longevity there is no more cost-effective way of reducing mortality and morbidity in this country than by further reducing cigarette smoking and the means to do this are available.

REFERENCES

Annual Abstract of Statistics (1983) CSO.

Atkinson, A. B. and Skegg (Townsend), J. L. (1973) 'Anti-Smoking Publicity and the Demand for Tobacco in the UK', *Manchester School*, 41, 265.

Atkinson, A. B. and Townsend, J. L. (1977) 'Economic Aspects of Reduced Smoking', *Lancet*, ii, 492.

Bodmer, W. F. (1985) 'Understanding Statistics', *J. Roy. Statist. Soc.*, 148, 2, 69–81.

Catford, J., Nutbeam, D. and Woolaway, M. C. (1983) 'Giving Up Smoking – Are We Giving Up?' *British Medical Journal*, 287, 1375–6.

Central Statistical Office (1982) *National Income and Expenditure*, London: HMSO.

Commission of the European Communities (1982) *Implications of Further Harmonisation of the Excises on Manufactured Tobacco*, Brussels: COM(82) 61.

Dawson, R. F. F. (1971) *Current Costs of Road Accidents in Great Britain*, Road Research Laboratory, Department of the Environment.

Department of Health and Social Security (1973) *Report on Hospital Inpatient Enquiry*, London: HMSO.

Dobbs, J. and Marsh, A. (1985) *Smoking Among Secondary School Children in 1984*, London: HMSO.

Doll, R. and Peto, R. (1976) 'Mortality in Relation to Smoking: 20 Years Observations on Male British Doctors', *British Medical Journal*, 2, 1525–36.

Hamilton, J. L. (1972) *Review of Economic Statistics*, 54, 104.

Jarvis, M. S., Raw, M., Russell, M. A. H. and Feyerabend, C. (1982) 'Randomised Controlled Trial of Nicotine Chewing Gum', *British Medical Journal*, 285, 537–40.

Johnson, J. (1975) Unpublished paper summarised in *Tobacco*, London.

Kristein, M. M. (1983) 'How Much Can Business Expect to Profit from Smoking Cessation', *Preventive Medicine*, 12, 358–81.

Laing, E. T. (1983) Unpublished report, Health Education Council.

Lee, P. N. (1976) *Statistics of Smoking in the UK*, London: Tobacco Research Council.

Lewitt, E., Coate, D. and Grossman, M. (1981) 'The Effects of Government Regulation on Teenage Smoking', *Journal of Law and Economics*, 24, 3.

Marsh, A. and Matheson, J. (1983) *Smoking Attitudes and Behaviour*, London: HMSO.

McGuinness, A. J. and Cowling, K. G. (1975) 'Advertising and the Aggregate Demand for Cigarettes', *European Economic Review*, 3·11.

McKennell, A. C. and Thomas, R. K. (1967) 'Adults and Adolescents' Smoking Habits and Attitudes', *Government Social Survey*, London: HMSO, p. 97.

Office of Population Censuses and Surveys (OPCS) (1974) *Mortality Statistics from General Practice*, London: HMSO.

OPCS (1978) *Occupational Mortality 1970–72*, London: HMSO.

OPCS (1983) *Cigarette Smoking: 1982 to 1984*, London: HMSO, GHS 81/82.

Repace, J. L. (1983) 'The Dosimetry of Passive Smoking', in Proceedings of the 5th World Conference on Smoking and Health, Winnipeg, Canada.

Repace, J. L. (1985) *Canadian Medical Association Journal*, 133, 737–8.

Royal College of Physicians (1983) *Health or Smoking*, London: Pitman.

Russell, M. A. H., Wilson, C., Taylor, C. and Baker, C. D. (1979) 'Effective General Practitioners' Advice Against Smoking', *British Medical Journal*, 2, 231–35.

Stejernfeldt, M., Berglund, K., Lindsten, J. and Ludvigsson, J. (1986)

'Maternal Smoking during Pregnancy and Risk of Childhood Cancer', *Lancet*, i, 1350–2.

Stepney, R. (1983) 'Why do people smoke?' *New Society*, 28 July 1983.

Stone, R. (1945) *Journal of Royal Statistical Society*, 198, 286.

Taylor, P. (1984) *Smoke Ring: The Politics of Tobacco*, London: The Bodley Head.

The Louis Harris Group (1982) *Company Policy on Smoking*.

Townsend, J. L. (1978) 'Smoking and Lung Cancer; A Cohort Data Study of Men and Women in England and Wales 1935–70', *Journal of the Royal Statistical Society, Series A*, 141(1), pp. 95–107.

Townsend, J. L. And Meade, T. W. (1979) 'Ischaemic Heart Disease: Mortality Risks for Smokers and Non-Smokers', *Journal of Epidemiology and Community Health*, 33, 243–7.

Townsend, J. (1985) 'Cost Effectiveness and Mass Media Programmes of Smoking Control', in *Smoking Strategies and Evaluations in Community and Mass Media Programmes*, eds. J. Croften and M. Wood, London: Health Education Council.

Townsend, J. (1987) 'Cigarette Tax, Economic Welfare and Social Class Patterns of Smoking' *Applied Economics* 19, 355–65.

Wald, N. J. (1978) 'Smoking as a Cause of Disease', in *Recent Advances in Community Medicine*, ed. A. E. Bennett, Churchill Livingstone.

Warner, K. E. (1977) 'The Effects of the Anti-Smoking Campaign on Cigarette Consumption', *American Journal of Public Health*, 67, 7: 645–50.

Weiss, W. L. (1985) *The Smoke Free Workplace*, Buffalo: Prometheus Books.

8 The Economic Evaluation of High Technology Medicine: The Case of Heart Transplants

MARTIN BUXTON

1. INTRODUCTION

The rate of development of medicine and clinical practice never ceases to astonish and impress the outside observer. The speed of adoption and dissemination of new techniques can be very rapid. Coronary artery bypass graft surgery was first introduced in the USA as recently as 1967. It is now a common operation worldwide with annual rates in the USA of well over 100 000 operations. Similarly, what is today at the boundaries of technical possibility may very rapidly become commonplace.

But there is a growing international recognition that there is a huge difference between what is technically possible and what is socially desirable (Jennett, 1986). There is a widening gap between what is technically achievable and what can be afforded. Using Professor Williams's terminology, we need to identify those technologies from which the value obtained by society is greater than the value that society has to sacrifice in order to provide them. For, any technological development for which the opportunity cost (the sacrifice) is greater than the benefit (the value derived) is likely to represent *economically* a step backwards however brilliant the *technical* leap forward. The advance of technology imposes a constant need to evaluate what is being done, or is being proposed, in such economic terms. Economic evaluation of high technology medicine is not without its problems, but has now been successfully carried out for a number of programmes both here in the UK and abroad. This paper uses the case of the evaluation of heart transplantation as an illustrative example, and from it attempts to indicate a number of more general lessons for the evaluation of medical technology.

2.   EVALUATING HEART TRANSPLANTATION

The world's first human heart transplant operation was performed by Dr Christiaan Barnard in South Africa on 3 December 1967, and the first in the UK in May 1968. But only four UK transplants had been carried out in the UK when in January 1979, following a voluntary moratorium, Mr Terence English established the current programme at Papworth, and in January 1980 Mr Magdi Yacoub established the current programme at Harefield. By 31 August 1986 the two centres had carried out a total of well over 450 heart transplant operations and about 80 heart-lung transplants.

Most of the initial funding of these programmes was from charitable sources but there were considerable pressures to provide specific and continuing NHS support for them. However the programmes were not without their critics. As the number of UK heart transplant operations began to grow in the early 1980s the two programmes were the focus of much debate and media attention. Proponents heralded them as offering patients the miracle of a new lease of life; critics claimed they were unduly expensive and unproven interventions, offering at best a qualitatively poor and restricted existence, and diverting resources from more important uses in the NHS. The ensuing debate merely served to highlight the paucity of systematic information on the costs and benefits of the procedure.

In 1981 the Department of Health and Social Security, following research proposals from the Department of Community Medicine at the University of Cambridge and the Health Economics Research Group at Brunel University, funded a study of 'The Costs and Benefits of the Heart Transplant Programmes at Harefield and Papworth Hospitals.' The three year prospective study was completed in December 1984 and the final report published in full (Buxton *et al.*, 1985).

The focus of its attention was on the *costs* (principally to the health service): measuring the opportunity cost of the resources used, and the patient *benefits* in terms of the twin parameters of survival and quality of life. It had to do this in the absence of a formal control group: the evaluation was essentially observational – monitoring the existing programmes – rather than interventional in the sense of influencing therapy. No randomisation was possible, nor indeed any of the other methods of establishing a formal basis of comparison. The interest was in comparing the effect of transplantation with normal routine management, but the effects of the latter – this is, what would have happened without transplantation – had to be inferred.

3. THE MAIN FINDINGS

Since the full report of the study has been published, it is not my intention to attempt to rehearse all its findings here. However a brief summary may be useful in helping to focus on a number of the general issues it highlights.

Survival

By 30 September 1984, a total of 221 patients had been transplanted on the current UK programmes – 135 at Harefield and 86 at Papworth. The 'typical' transplant recipient was male, forty-two years old, with ischaemic heart disease, and had undergone no previous cardiac surgery. Having waited sixty days after being accepted as a transplant candidate he received an orthotopic transplant where the donor heart came from a male aged twenty-four. Taking the combined experience of the two centres, one year patient survival was approximately 70 per cent; two year survival, 61 per cent, and three year survival, 52 per cent. The study found no statistically significant difference between the overall survival probabilities from Harefield and Papworth.

Univariate grouping of survival data by various recipient and donor characteristics indicated that there had been a significant improvement in survival following the introduction of the new immunosuppressive drug cyclosporine in 1982. In addition there was evidence that the age of the donor affects recipient survival, with 'older' donors offering poorer prognosis. Multivariate analysis also gave some limited evidence that there was a small upward time trend in survival since

1979 which was independent of the influence of the introduction of cyclosporine.

Subsequent – and as yet unpublished – analysis of more recent data up to 30 September 1985, shows that overall rates have continued to improve with, at that stage, one year survival for the combined data from the two programmes of 72 per cent; two year survival, 67 per cent; three year survival, 59 per cent, and four year survival, 53 per cent. One year survival for those patients transplanted since the introduction of cyclosporine in 1982 had risen to 78 per cent, closely comparable to the experience at Stanford, USA.

The view of the transplant surgeons has always been that the procedure extends life. In the clinical literature the basis for this conclusion stems from the comparison of survival from transplantation (for those who were transplanted) with survival from acceptance onto the transplant programme to death (for those who did not receive a transplant). (For such a comparison in the US and UK clinical literature see Pennock *et al.*, 1982; British Cardiac Society, 1984.)

There is an inherent bias in such a comparison. The non-transplanted group cannot be considered as a fair control group since the principal reason a transplant candidate does not receive a heart may be that he or she dies before a donor can be found: the waiting time may tend to filter out the 'bad risk' candidates.

Part of this bias can be removed by considering the acceptance-to-transplant period of patients *who are eventually transplanted* as a valid component of survival without transplant. The resulting comparison clearly supports the view that the operation is life-extending, but the magnitude of this extension depends crucially on assumptions about long term survival of transplanted patients (O'Brien, Buxton and Ferguson, 1987).

However this comparison ignores any *systematic* selection bias by the surgeons between patients, when a donor heart becomes available. If surgeons select the 'sicker' waiting patients (as seems to be the case) and the sicker patients have a poorer prognosis (as our subsequent analysis suggests), the comparison above may underestimate the positive survival effect of transplantation (ibid.).

Quality of Life

Historically the success of treatment interventions has been judged almost exclusively on the basis of survival. In recent times, however, there has been a growing awareness that the output of health care is as much about improving the quality of life as about increasing its length. With respect to heart transplantation, a number of early commentators had indicated that the procedure produces significant improvements in the recipients' quality of life.

In the UK study we adopted a dual approach to the identification and measurement of quality of life. To provide quantitative estimates of health status differences between individuals and through time, patients completed the Nottingham Health Profile (NHP) (Hunt, McEwen and McKenna, 1986). This is a fairly widely tested and utilised questionnaire measure of patients' subjective perceptions of their health state. The NHP was completed at regular intervals both before and after transplant. In addition a number of semi-structured interviews were undertaken with candidates and recipients in order to investigate certain aspects of health and life style in greater detail.

The NHP measures subjective health status by asking for yes/no patient responses to a carefully selected set of thirty-eight simple statements relating to six dimensions of social functioning: pain, energy, physical mobility, sleep, social isolation and emotional reactions.

Formal analysis of the NHP data indicated that patients showed:

1. whilst waiting for transplant, no spontaneous improvement on any dimension and a deterioration with respect to social isolation;
2. a marked and statistically significant improvement in quality of life relating to each of the six dimensions when three-month post-transplant scores were compared with their pre-transplant scores;
3. no evidence of systematically increasing or decreasing quality of life over time after three months post-transplant.

In summary, the evidence indicates a significant 'once and for all' upward shift in all dimensions of quality of life as a result of transplantation. NHP data for a 'normal' population is available. Although formal statistical comparisons could not be undertaken with these data, comparison of mean scores shows that the quality of life enjoyed by patients after transplant is very similar to that of their respective age-groups within the normal population.

Costs

Whilst neither the survival nor quality of life data showed important differences between the two centres, considerable differences existed in the length of stay in hospital. For example, in the first nine months of 1984, the average length of stay at assessment (prior to acceptance for transplant) at Harefield was 8.9 days whilst at Papworth it was 3.4 days. Conversely during the same time period, for the stage from transplant to discharge home, the average length of stay at Papworth was 44.4 days in hospital plus 1.5 days in local accommodation, whilst at Harefield it was 13.2 days in hospital plus 12.4 days in flats provided in Harefield village.

The costing carried out involved very detailed recording, on a patient-specific basis, of the resources used in relation to the transplant programmes, not only during the period from transplant to discharge, but also in the important selection processes prior to acceptance, during the waiting period between acceptance and transplant, the donor operation, and the long-term care and follow-up of transplant recipients (analysed in terms of six-month periods after transplant). These analyses paid particular attention to the costs of nursing, and involved recording the nursing dependency of patients both on the ward and in intensive care.

Not surprisingly the differences in length of stay were reflected in costs, with estimated average costs (July 1983–June 1984) at assessment of £1180 at Harefield and £429 at Papworth; whilst for the stage from transplant to discharge home the costs were £11 158 at Papworth and £6181 at Harefield. These figures exclude the costs of the transplant surgeons themselves which, with certain other costs, were treated as an overhead to each programme.

However, not only were there differences in costs between Harefield and Papworth but also important changes over time have occurred, reflecting changes in patient management, particularly declining length of stay. The analysis of costs was able to show how, for example, at Harefield the costs of the first six-months after (including the costs of the recipient operation) fell from £16.2 thousand for patients transplanted in the first half of 1982 to £10.4 thousand for patients transplanted in the second half of 1983.

4. PROBLEMS

This study is by no means unique, and interestingly a rather similar study of heart transplantation was simultaneously carried out in the USA (Evans *et al.*, 1984), and that study produced a number of very similar results. Both of these, and recent studies of various other medical technologies, show that sound evaluation is now quite achievable. However there are still a number of problems which need carefully to be considered.

Measurement and Valuation of Costs and Benefits

Traditionally the NHS has been criticised for failing to produce good data on the costs of individual patients, or relevant patient groups. This situation is slowly improving with the introduction of various forms of speciality costing and clinical budgeting. Even in their absence, as was the case in the heart transplant study, ad hoc systems can be instituted to attribute costs to individual patients or small groups of patients. There are problems still of differences between studies in costing methodology but these are diminishing. Our study, and much more general information on, for example, variations in length of stay between hospitals suggests to me that a much greater problem may now be the variations in cost between different hospitals for the same procedures or treatments. This raises, for technologies carried out at many different hospitals, questions as to the extent to which costs can be generalised from one centre (or even a small number of centres) to the country as a whole.

For benefits, the problems of measurement and valuation are still much greater. Survival (or length of life) as one aspect of benefit is conveniently clear-cut and sophisticated statistical techniques are available for its analysis. Quality of life is a much more difficult concept to measure and value. However, for many health economists part of the excitement and challenge of the topic lies in developing and improving our techniques for measuring and valuing different health states and quality of life. The NHP we used represents a step towards this objective. Other scales and measures have, and are being, developed (Culyer, 1983; Teeling-Smith, 1983). A body of knowledge is being built up on values for different health states elicited from the public (Torrance, 1986). Nevertheless at the moment some caution is still needed particularly in making comparisons between studies.

The Context of Evaluation

The ideal context for a rigorous economic evaluation is normally seen as being alongside a formal randomised clinical trial, in which differences in costs and benefits between a group of patients receiving the intervention under evaluation and a randomised control group can be accurately determined. However technology in normal medical practice is not quite like technology in the formal trial situation. In the medical literature, it is normal to distinguish between 'efficacy' and 'effectiveness'. 'Efficacy' is defined as the capacity of a medical intervention to achieve a desired outcome in the ideal settings of a test or trial for a well-defined patient group when used by doctor and patient exactly as intended, and after allowance for any placebo or hawthorne effects, and 'effectiveness' as the extent to which an intervention achieves the desired outcome in normal practice. It is important that economic evaluation realistically measures cost *effectiveness* rather than cost *efficacy*. Thus whilst the heart transplant study had the theoretical disadvantage of being a study of a service, without strictly defined protocols and with for example changing patient selection criteria, it had the practical advantage of being an evaluation of a prototype service rather than a formal trial situation. As a result it is likely to be a better indicator of the effectiveness of a future more routine service.

The Timing of Evaluation

However, even when presented as briefly as I have done here, the changing nature of the costs and benefits of this new technology is apparent. If evaluation is to be carried out on new technologies, then it must accommodate, and illuminate the nature of, the changing resource usage of, and benefits from, the technology. This problem is often used as an argument for delaying evaluation until a more settled or established technology has emerged, but this is a dangerous line because the technology becomes established and the administrative and political scope for cutting back on an accepted programme is far less than the scope for constraining a programme at an earlier stage. It's always too early until, unfortunately, it's suddenly too late' (Buxton, 1987).

But it is not just a question of when to start an evaluation but also for how long to evaluate. Obviously the cost-effectiveness of heart transplantation (or any other such intervention) will depend very much on long-term survival. Yet the pressure for necessary decisions and the inherent momentum of development means that it is rarely possible to carry out such economic evaluations over more than a two or three year period. But medium-term survival and/or quality of life, and medium-term costs (say 3–15 years) are crucial to the cost-effectiveness and social value of many health care interventions.

The Need to Monitor

The problems of timing and of change suggest that the concept of evaluation as being a one-off single point-of-time process, to help make a once-and-for-all decision is, inappropriate. The concept must become much more one of a process of initial evaluation and subsequent *monitoring*. This monitoring needs to take account of a number of factors which may lead to substantial changes to the cost or effectiveness of the intervention. Again taking the case of heart transplantation as an illustration a number of important changes have taken place.

1. *Detailed Changes in the Relevant Technology*. The most important of these was the introduction of cyclosporine as a much more effective immunosuppressive agent. This has led to a significant improvement in observed survival, but there is a concern about the long-term cytotoxicity of the drug.
2. *Detailed Changes in Patient Management*: generally through increased experience it has become possible to reduce considerably lengths of stay as a whole and the very costly period of stay in intensive care. In addition, by organisational change it has been possible to introduce at each centre accommodation for patients ('flats' at Harefield; 'mobile homes' at Papworth) which facilitates early discharge for patients by providing accommodation close to the units but without nursing support for a period immediately post-discharge. During their period in this accommodation patients can be seen regularly (but much more cheaply) as outpatients.
3. *Changes in Patient Selection*. In a non-trial context one of the most important elements of change can be explicit (or implicit) changes in the patient selection criteria. [In the case of transplantation this can in fact be seen as also including donor organ acceptance criteria.] Multivariate analysis has already indicated that a number of these may affect survival probabilities.

In addition to these three elements of practical changes, there is a fourth factor which is of a rather different nature.

4. *Changes in Available Information for Evaluation*: as time proceeds, data on longer-term follow-up of patients (including information on both costs and benefits) gradually becomes available.

Technology is not static and the evaluation techniques need to reflect this.

5. THE STATE OF THE ART: CAN IT HELP TO DECIDE PRIORITIES?

As researchers, it is easy to emphasise the problems that occupy so much of our time, and to suggest as a result that the evaluation techniques themselves are still at a research stage, and not yet ready for use in applied contexts. Our evaluation technologies, like medical technologies, are certainly still developing but they are of immediate use. Whilst advocating a more sophisticated concept of evaluation and monitoring, it is important to stress how little *basic* evaluation has been carried out. Heart transplantation is a notable exception in the UK, and interestingly an exception in several other countries as well (USA, Netherlands, Denmark) where similar evaluations have taken, or are taking, place. In contrast, liver transplantation, for example – and there are many other examples – has never been subjected to adequate economic evaluation. There are enormous and quite unacceptable gaps in our knowledge.

Such gaps need to be filled to inform the debate about health service priorities. Economists such as Professor Williams have strongly advocated an initial prioritisation criteria of (marginal) cost per QALY. With the current state of the art of evaluation such an approach is perfectly practicable, and desirable. No one, least of all the proponents of this approach, would suggest that as yet we have perfect and complete information on which to estimate such measures. Nor would they argue, I am sure, that no other factors need be taken into account. But such ranking of procedures and technologies provides a starting point against which special or exceptional cases need to be explicitly pleaded, and the implications of any data weaknesses explored. It is not, or should not be, acceptable any longer to ignore information on costs or benefits where such information exists and revert to emotional appeal, rhetoric or simple political expediency.

Nor should we be prepared as a society to devote significant sums of health service resources to programmes that have not been evaluated, however strong their appeal to the public when presented emotionally and dramatically in the media. It is the harsh reality that resources used for one technology in health care cannot be devoted to another. The opportunity cost of saving one life, or improving its quality, may be the inability to save, or improve, two elsewhere. We need to know what are its costs and benefits if we are to make sensible and socially justifiable decisions about medical technology.

REFERENCES

British Cardiac Society (1984) 'Report on Cardiac Transplantation in the United Kingdom', *British Heart Journal*, 52, 679–82.
Buxton, M. J. (1987) 'Problems in Economic Appraisal of a New Health Technology: The Case of Heart Transplants in the UK', in Drummond, M. (ed.) *Economic Appraisal of Health Technology in the European Community*, EC Series on Health Services Research, Oxford: Oxford University Press.
Buxton, M. J. *et al.* (1985) *Costs and Benefits of the Heart Transplant Programmes at Harefield and Papworth Hospitals*, DHSS Research Report No. 12, London: HMSO.
Culyer, A. J. (ed.) (1983) *Health Indicators*, London: Martin Robertson.
Evans, R. W. *et al.* (1984) *The National Heart Transplantation Study: Final Report*, Seattle: Battelle Human Affairs Research Center.
Hunt, S. M., McEwen, J. and McKenna, S. (1986) *Measuring Health Status*, Beckenham, Kent: Croom Helm.
Jennett, B. J. (1986) *High Technology Medicine: Benefits and Burdens*, 2nd edn, Oxford: Oxford University Press.
O'Brien, B., Buxton, M. and Ferguson, B. (1987) 'Measuring the Effectiveness of Heart Transplant Programmes: Quality of Life Data and their Relationship to Survival Analysis', *Journal of Chronic Diseases*.
Pennock, J. L. *et al.* (1982) 'Cardiac Transplantation in Perspective for the Future: Survival, Complications, Rehabilitation and Costs', *Journal of Thoracic and Cardiovascular Surgery*, 83, 168–77.
Teeling-Smith, G. (ed.) (1983) *Measuring the Social Benefits of Medicine*, London: Office of Health Economics.
Torrance, G. W. (1986) 'Measurement of Health State Utilities for Economic Appraisal', *Journal of Health Economics*, 5, 1–30.

9 Economic Analysis and Medical Research

MICHAEL DRUMMOND

1. INTRODUCTION

Significant amounts of scarce resources are devoted to medical research. In the United States, for example, around $5000 million was spent by the Department of Health and Human Services on basic and applied research in 1985, about 10 per cent of the total Federal research commitment (Office of Technology Assessment, 1986).

However, more importantly, medical research plays a significant role in shaping the health care system of the future. The lifecycle of health technologies can be depicted (as in Figure 9.1) as beginning with basic and applied research, leading to first human use, through to adoption of the technology in the health care system. At each stage policies can be applied to encourage more efficient use of the technology. For example, at the stage of basic and applied research, funding could be based on social priorities. At the stage clinical trials are being mounted one could consider undertaking economic analysis of the therapies being evaluated. In the later stages, when the technology is widely adopted, reviews of its use could be undertaken to assess whether it is being used only in clinical applications for which the benefits exceed the costs. There are therefore a number of issues that economists might help explore, namely:

How should medical research priorities be formulated?
How can medical research be most efficiently carried out?
How can medical research be more closely integrated with economic analysis?

The main focus of this paper is on the third issue, that of undertaking

173

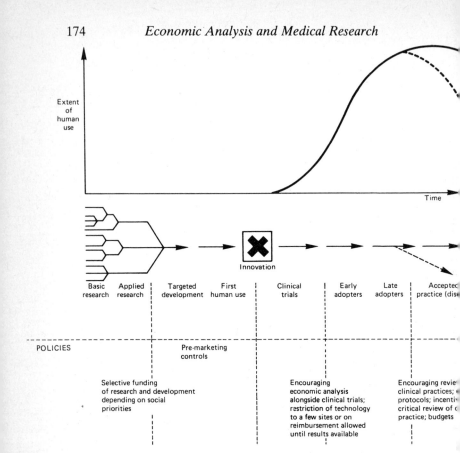

FIGURE 9.1 *The diffusion curve for health technology: choices and policies*
Source: Adapted from Banta *et al.* (1981).

economic analysis alongside controlled clinical trials. However, before concentrating on this issue a few comments will be made about the other two issues.

Medical research priorities are in the main formulated on the basis of the scientific merit of the proposals submitted for funding by researchers. Certainly scientific merit is an important *necessary* condition for funding to be given. However, whether it should also be a *sufficient* condition is much more open to question. In principle, economists would argue that decisions should be made based on the expected costs and benefits resulting from the research being carried out. For example, will successful research result in large gains in benefits because no satisfactory treatment currently exists for the

TABLE 9.1 *Overall proportion of burden of disease categories, averaged over the five indices*

Category	Indices Mainly Affected	Percentage of Total Burden
Mental illness and handicap	**1**, 2, 3, 4	13.60
Respiratory disease	**3**, 4	13.47
Ischaemic heart disease	4, **5**	6.59
Bone and joint disease	2, 3, **4**	6.38
Accidents and suicide	2, 3, **4**	6.25
Neoplasms	5	6.08
Digestive disorders	**2**, 3, 4	4.56
Neurological disorders	2	4.11
Cerebrovascular disease	1, **5**	3.74
Skin diseases	2, **3**	2.55
Urogenital disease	2	2.31
Total		69.64

Note: Where more than one index number is given for a category, the number corresponding to the most severely affected index is bold type. The indices are numbered as follows: 1. inpatient days; 2. outpatient referrals; 3. general-practitioner consultations; 4. days of sickness-benefit; 5. mortality, as loss of life-expectancy.
Source: Black and Pole (1975).

disease in question? Alternatively, will it lead to a more cost-effective treatment than those which already exist for a given disease?

Given the uncertainty surrounding medical research it may be difficult to estimate the expected costs and benefits at the outset. However, some initiatives have been taken. For example, Black and Pole (1975) suggested that medical research priorities should relate to the relative burden placed on the community by various diseases. They calculated five indices of burden (inpatient days, outpatient referrals, general practitioner consultations, days of sickness benefit and loss of life expectancy) and ranked diseases in terms of their impact on the indices (see Table 9.1). Although an important first step, Black and Pole's work does not show that the research effort should be concentrated on those diseases near the top of the list. One also requires information on the relative costs of reducing the burden from the diseases in question.

Another initiative worth noting is that of the Ministry of Health in Ontario (Canada), where requests for research monies are evaluated not only in terms of their methodological soundness but also in terms of whether 'the proposal is likely to have an important economic impact in reducing the costs or increasing the efficiency of health services'. Furthermore, the grant application has to 'provide, where appropriate, an adequate cost-effectiveness, cost-benefit or cost-utility analysis'.

Turning to the issue of carrying out medical research in the most efficient way, an obvious consideration is economies of scale. Research institutions may have large set-up costs in terms of equipment and trained personnel. Also, concentration of the research effort in a few locations may lead to more interchange between researchers and the possibility that a large number of patients could be enrolled in the research study quickly, enabling evidence on new medical therapy to be obtained as soon as possible and avoiding duplication of effort. On the other hand a larger number of research institutions might encourage more diversity of ideas and more competition.

Another important consideration is that of communication of research results, thereby influencing clinical practice. Mosteller (1981) has pointed out that there is often a large lag between the discovery of a research finding and this result bringing about a change in policy, the most extreme example being the time lag between the discovery that vitamin C prevented scurvy and the change in sailors' diets being implemented by the British Navy, a time lag of 264 years! There is therefore a case for examining the ways in which research findings are communicated and whether more systematic methods could be adopted. In some countries efforts are made to incorporate research advances in guidelines for clinical practice (WHO, 1981). Drummond and Hutton (1986) have pointed out that similar communication problems exist in relation to economic evaluation results for new health technologies.

However, the main issue addressed below is that of integrating economic analysis more closely with medical research, in particular controlled clinical trials. The questions that are considered are as follows:

what are the methodological issues involved in undertaking clinical trials?
what are the methods of economic evaluation?
what is the logic for integrating economic analysis more closely with clinical trials and is there much evidence of such an integration?
what are the major difficulties in achieving such an integration?
when should economic analysis be undertaken alongside clinical trials
how can economic analysis be best undertaken alongside clinical trials?

2. THE METHODOLOGICAL ISSUES INVOLVED IN UNDERTAKING CLINICAL TRIALS

The main objective of clinical trials is to assess whether therapies do more good than harm (Sackett *et al.*, 1985). It is possible to distinguish two types of trials. The first type is *efficacy* trials, where the therapy is assessed when delivered under ideal conditions. That is, those patients that are most likely to be helped would be selected from the overall caseload, the method of delivery of the therapy would be carefully monitored and patients with co-existing illnesses would be excluded from the trial. In efficacy trials, particularly those of new drugs, the new therapy will often be compared with a placebo (a tablet containing no active ingredient) so as to separate out the 'placebo effect', the fact that patients often improve merely when interest is taken in them and their illness. The other type of trial is known as an *effectiveness* (or management) trial. Here the interest is in assessing the therapy's effect when delivered under normal service conditions, warts and all. Here, a number of factors may lead to a lower level of success of the therapy; it may be incorrectly administered, patients may not comply with the therapy, or it may be given to inappropriate patients (i.e. those for whom the therapy is no better than doing nothing).

There are a number of key methodological issues in designing and carrying out clinical trials. The main issue concerns the method of allocating patients to experimental (i.e. new therapy) and control (i.e. placebo or existing therapy) groups. Ideally this should be done systematically, by randomisation of patients to the groups (i.e. on the toss of a coin, or by reference to random number tables). This minimises the chances that there will be any differences between the groups other than the method of treatment.

Other important issues concern the 'blinding' of assessors (and patients where possible) to the form of treatment, to avoid biased interpretation of changes in the patient's condition. Also the sample size needs to be large enough to detect the size of difference in clinical improvement that is being sought. (There are formal methods of calculating sample size.) Finally, the outcome measures used in trials may be biomedical measures (e.g. blood pressure), clinical measures (e.g. number of complications), or measures of functioning (e.g. ability to return to work). Increasingly clinical trials are including measures of improvements in the quality of life among the measurements made.

Most of these methodological issues are discussed in Sackett *et al.*

(1985). The main point to note here is that clinical trials are already complex, time-consuming and costly to design and carry out. Therefore, one needs to consider carefully the issue of adding yet another dimension, namely economic evaluation.

3. THE METHODS OF ECONOMIC EVALUATION

Economic evaluation builds on the clinical evaluation of health care programmes and treatments. It compares the resource inputs (costs) of programmes with their benefits. The general range of items that an economic evaluation would typically seek to include is given in Figure 9.2. First, it can be seen that an assessment of the economic efficiency of treatments requires examination of the changes in health service resource use brought about, in both the hospital and community care sectors. These changes will usually be in the direction of additional resources, although some programmes, notably prevention programmes, may lead to reductions in the use of other health service resources. Secondly, it is also important to examine the changes in other community resource use, such as the inputs to health care that might be made by other public agencies, voluntary agencies and the family. Such inputs are obviously important in assessing community care programmes for the elderly or mentally handicapped. Finally, assessment of efficiency also requires examination of the changes in health state brought about by health treatments. Here the inputs from medical research are obviously important, although the economist may wish to take matters further and *value* the improvements in health state, in terms of the changes in productive output of the patient (if he is able to return to work), or of that of members of the family (who may be nursing the sick relative). However, more importantly, the improvements in health state *per se* represent significant *economic* benefits, since individuals value improved health in its own right.

The different forms of economic evaluation are set out in Figure 9.3 (p. 181). It can be seen that they all consider costs, but differ in the extent to which they measure and value benefits. One form of analysis, *cost analysis*, considers only costs. This can only be used in situations where the improvements in health state brought about by the alternative treatments are identical. In *cost-effectiveness analysis* the benefits of the treatments are measured in the most convenient natural units, such as 'years of life gained' or 'cases successfully treated'. This

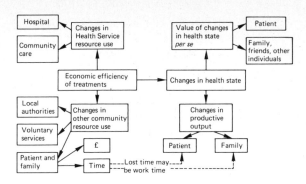

FIGURE 9.2   *The relevant changes in a comparison of the economic efficiency of treatments*
Source: Drummond (1980).

is a very useful form of analysis if it is accepted that the given objective (i.e. to treat a case of the disease in question) is going to be met.

Cost-benefit analysis is potentially the broadest form of analysis, since it attempts to measure all the benefits in money terms in order to make them commensurate with the costs. Therefore, in principle it can help determine whether a particular treatment objective is worth meeting. However, in practice cost-benefit analyses are often limited in scope, restricting their attention to benefit items that are easy to measure in money terms. They often ignore the intangible costs and benefits (C_3 and B_3 in Figure 9.3).

For this reason analysts are increasingly turning to *cost-utility analysis*, a form of cost-effectiveness analysis where the benefits are measured in quality-adjusted life-years (QALYs). Here improvements in health are valued, not in money terms, but relative to one another. These 'utility' values of health states are then used to weight the extra years of life gained from treatments or programmes, based on the quality of the life gained. This approach has obvious advantages in assessing those treatments, such as cancer chemotherapy or hypertension treatment, which extend life only at a price of some reduction in quality of that life (i.e. through the side effects of therapy). It also permits comparisons to be made across a wide range of health programmes, as outlined by Williams (1987).

Economic evaluation has now been widely applied in health care and several reviews are available (Drummond, 1981; Weinstein, 1981; Warner and Luce, 1982; Drummond *et al.*, 1986).

4. THE LOGIC FOR INTEGRATING ECONOMIC ANALYSIS WITH CLINICAL TRIALS AND THE EXTENT OF SUCH INTEGRATION

It was pointed out earlier that most health technologies follow a diffusion curve (as set out in Figure 9.1) where, following a short period of clinical research, there is rapid adoption of the new technology. It has been well documented that many health technologies are widely adopted before systematic evidence of their costs and benefits is available. Therefore, if governments and other agencies funding health care are to have good evidence upon which to base their decisions, it is important that this is assembled at the time the clinical research is taking place.

In addition, given the need to base economic evaluation on good medical evidence, it would be beneficial if the economic analysis were more closely integrated with clinical trials, the main vehicles for assembling good medical evidence about the impact of therapies. It may also be the case that clinical and economic researchers will learn something from each other through engaging in multidisciplinary work. A particularly fruitful area for such collaboration is in the measurement and relative valuation of different health states.

Given the potential advantages of undertaking economic analysis alongside clinical trials, it is surprising that this is not more often carried out. Some examples do exist in the literature. For example, Russell *et al.* (1977) investigated the effectiveness and efficiency of day-case surgery for hernias and haemorrhoids. A randomised controlled trial was carried out which showed that, for hernias at least, day case surgery resulted in equivalent medical outcomes to traditional inpatient surgery, as measured by number of complications and length of convalescence. The question was therefore whether day-case surgery used fewer resources. In terms of community care following discharge from hospital, it was found that the day-case patients had more visits from district nurses. However, day-case surgery offered the potential for more efficient use of beds in the hospital, which would generate financial savings if bed capacity were reduced or plans for expansion revised downwards. Alternatively, if bed capacity were to remain the same, additional benefits would be generated, as more patients could be treated. (Of course, it would be important that these patients were given effective therapies.)

Another economic evaluation undertaken alongside a clinical trial is that by Weisbrod *et al.* (1980), comparing community-based treatment

181

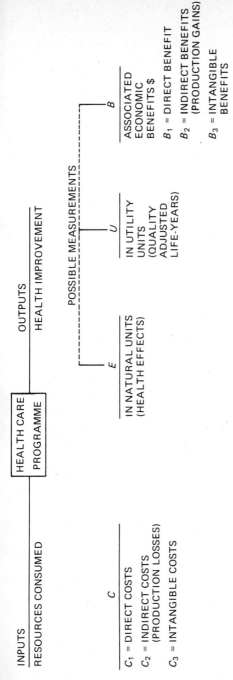

FIGURE 9.3 *Components of economic evaluation*

for some mental illness patients with a more traditional hospital-oriented treatment. The clinical variables measured included various aspects of clinical symptomology and adjustments to normal living patterns. In addition, a wide range of resource items was assessed, including not only the costs of the main care agency, but those of other health care agencies, other public sector agencies such as the police, and expenditure by the patient and family.

However, the integration of economic analysis with clinical trials is not as frequent as one would like. Culyer and Maynard (1981) point out that although many clinical trials had been carried out of cimetidine, a drug which aids the healing of duodenal ulcer, none formed a satisfactory basis for their economic evaluation. The existing trials were either too small, were inadequately controlled, evaluated alternatives (like a placebo) which were unlikely to be used in regular clinical practice, or incorporated an inadequate range of clinical measurements. For example, they would typically be restricted to biomedical outcomes and would not include measures of social functioning or quality of life. In the most recent review of economic evaluation in the health care field, eighteen of the one hundred studies were based on controlled clinical trials and a further twelve were based on some sort of prospective medical evaluation (Drummond *et al.*, 1986). The remaining studies used estimates of the key medical variables from the literature, which were based on research of variable quality.

5. THE CRITERIA FOR UNDERTAKING ECONOMIC ANALYSIS ALONGSIDE CLINICAL TRIALS

Clearly it would neither be possible nor appropriate for all clinical trials to incorporate economic analysis. It is therefore important to specify criteria for determining *when* it would be advantageous to consider undertaking economic analysis alongside a clinical trial.

This issue has been investigated by Drummond and Stoddart (1984). The criteria they gave for when to build economics into clinical trials were to select those trials where:

resource allocation decisions were likely to be made as a result of the trial (i.e. the trial was likely to be an influential one);
the resource consequences of adopting the new therapy were potentially large, either because the potential patient population

was large, or because there was a large unit cost difference between the new therapy and existing ones;

resource considerations were likely to be prominent in making decisions about adoption of the new therapy. (Indeed, on occasions the demonstration of economic as well as clinical benefit may be a prime motivation for undertaking the trial, e.g. as in trials of day-case or short-stay surgery.)

In order to assess the extent to which trials meeting the given criteria were incorporating economic analysis in a particular field, Mugford *et al.* (1986) selected a random sample of one hundred trials from the Register of Trials in Perinatal Medicine held by the National Perinatal Epidemiology Unit in Oxford (UK) (National Perinatal Epidemiology Unit, 1986). They found that economic analysis would have been indicated by at least one of the criteria in forty-eight of the trials. It was not performed in any of the trials concerned.

5. DIFFICULTIES IN UNDERTAKING ECONOMIC ANALYSIS ALONGSIDE CLINICAL TRIALS

Clearly there must be considerable obstacles to undertaking economic analysis alongside clinical trials if it is so infrequently performed. The most commonly cited difficulties are that:

the design of trials is already a time-consuming and costly activity, without incorporating yet another dimension;

economics expertise is not readily available, particularly in those medical research institutions where the clinical research would take place;

most trials are 'efficacy' trials. That is, they seek to establish whether the therapy does more good than harm when delivered under ideal conditions. These trials give results which are atypical of normal service delivery;

even those 'effectiveness' or 'management' trials which are carried out may themselves be atypical of normal service delivery and may not generate costs and benefits that would be found when the new therapy is more generally adopted;

the results of many trials are negative, and therefore it would be irrelevant to know the costs of a therapy that was not going to be adopted;

medical researchers may be uneasy about considering costs, as decisions about investments in health care programmes are better left to politicians.

It is therefore clear that some thought needs to be given to how best to integrate economic analysis with clinical trials if these difficulties are to be overcome.

7. METHODS OF INTEGRATING ECONOMIC ANALYSIS WITH CLINICAL TRIALS

Drummond and Stoddart argue that many of these difficulties could be overcome by careful selection of the trials for economic analysis, and by 'phasing in' the economic analysis as more is known about the likely clinical benefits from the new therapy. The main elements of a phasing policy are that:

in early trials some tentative cost estimates should be made of the likely cost of the new therapy (compared to existing ones) and the likely economic benefits should it work;

in a given trial, meeting the criteria outlined above, emphasis should be placed on collecting data that would be difficult or costly to collect later, e.g. the length of stay of patients, any special tests or therapies they receive, their place of discharge, any use of community services when patients are discharged to home, patients' own costs in obtaining care;

towards the end of the trial, when the clinical evidence is more clear, detailed economic analysis should be performed, calculating cost-effectiveness or cost-utility estimates and extrapolating the results of the trial to different settings. For example, what would be the net economic impact if the therapy were more widely adopted?

8. CONCLUSIONS

Medical research represents a significant investment of the community's scarce resources. In addition, today's medical research plays an important role in shaping the health care system of the future Economic analysis has a contribution to make in setting priorities for medical research funding, in examining the efficiency of the research carried out and in generating evidence on the costs and benefits of new health care programmes and treatments.

However, new medical technologies often become widely adopted without systematic examination of their costs and benefits. In addition, there is a lack of integration between economic analysis and clinical trials, the main vehicle for evaluating medical therapies.

In this paper some of the difficulties of achieving a better integration between economic analysis and clinical trials have been discussed. Some proposals have been made for selecting those trials which would benefit from economic analysis and recommendations made for phasing in such analysis, as more is known about the clinical benefits of new therapies.

REFERENCES

Banta, H. D., Behney, C. and Willems, J. S. (1981) *Toward Rational Technology in Medicine*, New York: Springer & Co.

Black, D. A. K. and Pole, J. D. (1975) 'Priorities for Biomedical Research: Indices of Burden', *British Journal of Preventive and Social Medicine*, 29(4), 222–7.

Culyer, A. J. and Maynard, A. K. (1981) 'Cost-effectiveness of Duodenal Ulcer Treatment', *Social Science and Medicine*, 15C, 3–11.

Drummond, M. F. (1980) *Principles of Economic Appraisal in Health Care*, Oxford: Oxford Medical Publications.

Drummond, M. F. (1981) *Studies in Economic Appraisal in Health Care*, Oxford: Oxford Medical Publications.

Drummond, M. F. and Stoddart, G. L. (1984) 'Economic Analysis and Clinical Trials', *Controlled Clinical Trials*, 5, 115–28.

Drummond, M. F. and Hutton, J. (1986) 'Economic Appraisal of Health Technology in the United Kingdom', *Centre for Health Economics Discussion Papers No. 11*, York: University of York.

Drummond, M. F., Ludbrook, A., Lowson, K. V. and Steele, A. (1986) *Studies in Economic Appraisal in Health Care: Volume Two*, Oxford: Oxford Medical Publications.

Mosteller, F. (1981) 'Innovation and Evaluation', *Science* 221, 881–6.

Mugford, M., Chalmers, I. and Drummond, M. F. (1985) *Controlled Trials in Perinatal Medicine: When is Economic Analysis Appropriate?* Oxford: National Perinatal Epidemiology Unit.

National Perinatal Epidemiology Unit (1986) *A Classified Bibliography of Controlled Trials in Perinatal Medicine, 1940–1984*, Oxford: Oxford University Press.

Office of Technology Assessment (Congress of the United States) (1986) *Research Funding as an Investment: Can we Measure the Returns?* Washington, DC: Government Printing Office.

Ontario Ministry of Health (1981) *Health Personnel and Research Grant Programs 1981/82*, Toronto: Ministry of Health.

Russell, I. T., Devlin, H. B., Fell, M., Glass, N. J. and Newell, D. J. (1977) 'Day Case Surgery for Hernias and Haemorrhoids: A Clinical, Social and Economic Evaluation', *Lancet*, i, 844–7.

Sackett, D. L., Haynes, R. B. and Tugwell, P. (1985) *Clinical Epidemiology: A Basic Science for Clinical Medicine*, Boston and Toronto: Little, Brown & Co.

Warner, K. E. and Luce, B. R. (1982) *Cost-Benefit and Cost-Effectiveness Analysis in Health Care: Principles, Practice and Potential*, Ann Arbor: Health Administration Press.

Weinstein, M. C. (1981) 'Economic Assessments of Medical Practices and Technologies', *Medical Decision Making* 1(4), 309–30.

Weisbrod, B. A., Test, M. A. and Stein, L. I. (1980) 'Alternative to Mental Hospital Treatment: Economic Cost-Benefit Analysis', *Archives of General Psychiatry*, 37, 400–5.

Williams, A. H., 'Health Economics: The Cheerful Face of the Dismal Science', reprinted as Chapter 1 of this volume.

World Health Organization (Regional Office for Europe) (1981) 'Guidelines for Health Care Practice in Relation to Cost-Effectiveness', *Euro Reports and Studies 53*, Copenhagen: WHO.

10 Markets and Health Care

ALAN MAYNARD

1. WHAT IS THE PROBLEM?

Scarcity and the Failure to Evaluate Practice

The failure to recognise some basic economic rules generates confusion and the waste of much scarce intellectual and political resources in markets for health care worldwide. These basic rules are not complex and when recognised might defuse the superficial rhetoric of policy debate and highlight the inefficiencies inherent in existing health care policies.

The basic economic assumption, which contributes to the subjects' reputation as a 'dismal science', is that resources are finite. Always and everywhere resources are limited, competing demands have to be rationed and valuable and productive ways of using resources have to be foregone. The process of rationing in health care is particularly controversial, in part because sectional interests face opportunity costs (when they lose out and may die as a consequence) in the rationing process and in part because of the reluctance to accept the ubiquitous nature of scarcity.

In the health care system, public (NHS) and private market decisions have to be made about who will die and who will live in what degree of pain and discomfort. Obviously if less was spent on Trident, on education, on videos, on cabbages, on nuclear power, or on roads, more resources would be available to provide health care. However such switches in the allocation of resources public and private, would merely ease the rationing problem. Rationing cannot be abolished because the capacity to delay the one certainty in life, death, and

187

improve the quality of life exceeds our capacity to finance it and this gap may be widening due to scientific and technological advance.

A health authority with a finite budget has to make choices about how to spend its resources. It can save lives by dramatic interventions such as the transplanting of hearts, kidneys and livers. It can improve the quality of life of working men and women by repairing hernias and varicose veins. It can care for physically and mentally handicapped children and provide a better supply of Zimmer frames and incontinence pads for the elderly.

The choices between these and thousands of other options in health care have to be made because of scarcity and they impose opportunity costs inevitably: given a limited budget more transplants for kidney patients will involve forgoing improving care for the elderly, the handicapped and the people in the workforce.

At present these choices are made on the absence of scientific evidence about the costs and benefits of alternative ways of spending health care resources. Given scarcity, the objective of policy must be to use resources efficiently: i.e. maximise benefits and minimise costs. In order to make efficient choices, the decision maker needs to evaluate options in relation to the following rules:

1. (a) if total costs exceed total benefits, abandon the project;
   (b) if total benefits exceed total costs, adopt the project and research out of the efficient level of output in relation to rule 2
2. (a) if marginal benefits (MB) exceed marginal costs (MC) increase output;
   (b) if marginal costs (MC) exceed marginal benefits (MB) decrease output;
   (c) until costs and benefits at the margin are equal (MC = MB)

In many health care systems the nature of costs and benefits, total and marginal, are unknown because of the failure to evaluate health care options scientifically. The total cost of repairing a hernia includes public sector costs to the NHS and to local authority social services and private sector costs arising from the effects of the procedure on the patient and his/her family, members of whom may provide scarce caring time during the patient's recovery. All these costs, public and private, need to be identified and provided to the decision maker to be weighed with the benefits of the procedure and against the costs and benefits of rival interventions.

The quantification of the benefits arising from health care expenditures is more complex. Health care expenditures finance the provision of inputs, such as nursing and doctor time, bed time and drugs, which when combined provide processes of care or health care activities such as inpatient hospital stays, outpatient visits and GP consultations. These inputs and activities may improve health status.

The output of the health care system is the creation of additional life-years and the improvement of the patient's quality of life after the health care intervention. A composite measure of these characteristics is the quality-adjusted life-year or QALY and estimates of the QALYs created by alternative procedures are now being produced by researchers (e.g. Williams, 1985a, b in Britain; Torrance, 1986 in Canada; and in the USA, for instance Sandberg, 1985).

However this novel approach to valuing health care outcomes is controversial. It makes explicit and subject to argument what was once implicit and largely uncontroversial and accepted by consumers. It raises issues about the accuracy and sensitivity of measures of the quality of life and begs the question of whether the methods used by different researchers are compatible, i.e. would these measures generate similar results when used to evaluate the health state of a given group of patients?

Such issues can only be resolved by further research. Until such work is carried out and augmented by better cost data, it will not be possible to identify the cost-QALY characteristics of competing therapies. Existing work offers some provocative insights e.g. a budget of £20 000 could provide one year of life at full quality (i.e. one QALY) if spent on hospital dialysis for renal failure patients or over twenty-six QALYs if spent on hip replacements or over 119 QALYs if spent on GP advice to stop smoking according to Williams's results (see Table 10.1).

These results are derived from crude cost and QALY data for a limited list of procedures. Similar but independent work in the USA is producing similar 'league tables' of the productivity of competing ways of spending health care resources (see Table 10.2). Slowly such data may illuminate the cost-benefit (QALY) characteristics of competing procedures and if incorporated into prospective trials and if calculated for a list of important (in terms of cost, innovation or some other characteristics) procedures, would be important guides to resource use.

So is the problem in health care the failure to evaluate? It is without doubt the primary problem. Until the efficiency of competing therapies is identified, it will be difficult for decision-makers to identify the efficient way of using scarce resources. However even if the ideal

TABLE 10.1 *Cost per QALY data (at 1983–4 prices, £s)*

Hip replacement	750
Pacemaker implantation for atrioventricular heart block	700
Valve replacement for aortic stenosis	900
CABG for severe angina with LMD	1040
CABG for severe angina with 3VD	1270
CABG for moderate angina with LMD	1330
CABG for severe angina with 2VD	2280
CABG for moderate angina with 3VD	2400
CABG for mild angina with LMD	2520
GP advice to stop smoking	167
GP control of hypertension	1700
GP control of total serum cholesterol	1700
Kidney transplant	3200
Heart transplant	8000
Hospital haemodialysis	14000

CABG = Coronary Artery Bypass Grafts
LMD = Left Main Vessel Disease
3VD = Three Vessel Disease
Source: Williams (1985a, b).

TABLE 10.2 *Cost per QALY estimates (North American results at 1983 prices, $)*

CABG for left main coronary artery disease	4200
Neonatal intensive care (1000–1499 gms)	4500
T4 (thyroid screening)	6300
Treatment for severe hypertension in males aged 40 years plus (diastolic 105mm Hg)	19100
Treatment for mild hypertension (94–105mm Hg)	19100
Estrogen therapy for post-menopausal symptoms in women without prior hysterectomy	27000
Neonatal intensive care (500–999 gms)	31800
CABG for single vessel disease, moderately severe	36300
School tuberculin testing programme	43700
Continuous ambulatory peritoneal dialysis	47100
Hospital dialysis	54000

Source: These studies are taken from a range of studies reported in Torrance (1984).

pattern of resource allocation could be identified, the problem then would be that you 'can lead a horse to water but you can't make it drink'.

Perverse Incentives in the Health Care System

At present incentives in the NHS tend to be perverse because of the compartmentalisation of the health care system and because of security of tenure for the main resource allocators in the health care system, the doctors.

Health care is provided by a variety of public and private agencies who are subject to rules concerning provision and finance. The hospital budget – hospital and community health services (HCHS) – is cash limited and allocated by budget formula (RAWP) which seeks to equalise the financial capacity of health authorities. The primary care budget – the family practitioner services (FPS) – is demand-determined (that is, the result of the number of doctors and their decision-making about care, especially prescriptions) and not RAWPed, with the result that financial capacity and the provisions of primary care are very uneven (Birch and Maynard, 1986). The local authority social service (LASS) budget is cash limited and provided unequally due to the different priorities of the constituent parts of the local government system. The social security (SS) budget, which finances care for the elderly, the mentally handicapped and the mentally ill in private residential and nursing homes, is open ended. The provision of caring services by households is affected by local (especially female) labour markets and the behaviour of statutory services in largely unknown ways.

The primary decision-maker in the NHS (i.e. HCHS and FPS) part of this system of health care provision is the doctor. In the hospital system the doctor is pressed to reduce lengths of stay, thereby shifting the costs of care out to FPS, LASS, SS and household budget holders, and shift costs in other ways: e.g. shifting drug and CAPD fluid costs on to FPS budgets by refusing to prescribe (generic) hospital products on discharge and obliging GPs to prescribe for patients, usually with high-cost branded products.

Hospital managers can shift costs on to the social security (SS) budget by discharging, for instance, elderly, patients into private nursing homes and transferring the costs of their care from the NHS budget on to the SS budget. Other patients, for instance the physically and mentally handicapped and the mentally ill, can be 'budget-shifted' in this manner too, leaving HCHS budget holders with resources to allocate into other types of care and cure.

The general practitioner (FPS-financed) can reduce demands on his caring services by diverting patients into the hospital (HCHS) system. Referrals by GPs may vary by as much as twenty-five fold (Acheson (1985)) with some GPs referring one in four of their patients to hospital outpatients and the HCHS budget. The causes of these variations in practice may be supply availability or such factors as GPs shifting costs on to the HCHS budgets to create time for them to indulge in other types of work and leisure.

Local authority decision-makers can shift costs on to households by low levels of home help and other provision. They can 'privatise' their statutory obligations to provide Part 3 accommodation (1948 National Assistance Act) and shift the finance of care for some of the elderly on to the social security budget.

The interactions between these parts of the NHS and the rest of the health care system are many and various but, once again, their costs and benefits are not evaluated: e.g. the efficient levels of GP referral are unknown. Most community care 'packages' for the mentally ill, the mentally handicapped and the elderly have unknown costs and benefits because of the failure to evaluate. Not only is it impossible to identify the efficient mode of care for any client group, it is difficult to move patients between the 'compartments' of the system to efficient provision. Patients tend to get 'locked in' to different parts of the system with no reference to cost minimisation or the appropriateness of care in relation to dependency or maximising possible improvements in health status.

This inflexibility is affected by the nature of the doctor's contract. GPs and hospital consultants are appointed for life and in the case of the latter they are employed by one authority (the Region) and paid by the authority in which they work (the District). The processes of performance norm setting, peer review, and medical audit are weak. As a consequence, if better evaluation identifies a practitioner to be deficient in his practice, it would be difficult to change his performance other than by moral suasion. Such persuasion may be forceful but may not always be effective with the result that inefficient practices can be institutionalised.

So what is the problem? The first problem is the lack of evaluation which is explored further by Michael Drummond and Martin Buxton elsewhere in this volume. However, even if efficient therapies can be identified, the problem of incentives and producer behaviour remain. The NHS, like other health care systems, has incentive systems which induce behaviour which are inefficient.

2.   WHAT IS THE PROPOSED SOLUTION?

Would it all be better if the NHS were abolished and replaced by the 'market'? It is important to realise that a market is merely a network of buyers and sellers who may be privately and publicly financed and who may be employed by public or private agencies. So one proposed solution to the inadequacies of the NHS in terms of lack of evaluation and perverse incentives is the creation of a private market in which private producers provide care which is financed largely by private consumers, augmented, usually in an undefined way, by public finance.

One of the characteristics of a market is that its price mechanism generates signals which indicate the measurement of value to consumers and the measurement of cost to producers. These signals provide the decision makers, consumers and producers, with the information relevant for efficient decision-making. If, at a price that clears the market, medical practice is profitable, more people will enter the medical profession, and thus supply will be demand responsive. If medical practice offers poor rewards to practitioners, people will leave it, and stop entering it until the system stabilises. In this theoretical world, competing suppliers will keep down prices in an effort to find a market for their services, and well informed patients will find the most cost-effective type of treatment. Prices, reflecting supply costs and demand values, will motivate providers and consumers to use resources efficiently.

However, for a variety of reasons these signals may be poor measures of value and cost in a market for health care. In a private health care market consumers will purchase insurance. Indeed, in some health care markets this purchase is subsidised by the government permitting premiums to be offset against taxes (in the USA the income tax forgone through medical care insurance offsets is over $20 billion, a large subsidy to the non-poor. Tax concessions reduce the price of insurance and encourage consumption, as do employer provision and subsidisation of such cover as part of 'fringe benefits'. Once the consumer or his employer has purchased such insurance, the cost of consuming health care in the absence of copayments or deductibles, is zero. Thus the consumer has little incentive, apart from own time, to economise: the opportunity cost of using health care is met largely by the insurer.

This problem is referred to in the US literature as moral hazard and the consequence is that the third party (insurer) pays for health care. Neither the consumer-patient nor the doctor-provider has an incentive to economise in their use of scarce health care resources. The problem of moral hazard occurs also in the National Health Service where the exchequer, rather than the insurer in the private case, meets the cost of health care. However, this is not the only problem which is shared by the public and private health care sectors. Another is the asymmetry of knowledge and its consequences for decision-making.

Typically, patients are uncertain about diagnosis, treatment and prognosis. So although the initial decision to seek medical advice is that of the patient, once she enters the medical system she will delegate decision making to the doctor. The doctor becomes the patient's agent because she is regarded by the patient as the 'expert', better informed about diagnosis, treatment and outcome. The consequence of the delegation of the demander's role to the doctor is uncertain. The doctor may act neutrally and treat the patient in relation to her knowledge of the productivity of care. Alternatively she may use her demander's role to generate employment and income for herself and other health care workers.

Thus the consequence of the asymmetry of information is that the doctor-agent may be able to induce or reduce demand for her services depending on whether the doctor gets utility from income or leisure. Furthermore because of moral hazard, this cost of such induced demand has little effect on the behaviour of either the producers or patients, the third party meets the cost of such inefficient practices.

Another characteristic of all private (and public) health care markets is occupational licensure, i.e. the control of entry into the profession and its standards of practice by medical trade unions. The effects of such organisations on the rewards of practitioners over the life cycle is debated but appears to be that of raising the rate of return in comparison to other professions. As Adam Smith (1776) remarked

> People of the same trade seldom meet together, even for merriment
> or diversion but the conversation ends in a conspiracy against the
> public or in some contrivance to raise prices.

The inflated returns to medical practice may be an insurance against quackery as argued by Arrow (1963) or a return to monopoly power as argued by Friedman (1963), or be the result of both factors. The non-pecuniary effects of licensure are the conservative control of medical education – which fails to inculcate a spirit of scientific enquiry in many practitioners – and weak monitoring of the performance of practitioners over the life cycle. Professional monopoly power has costs and benefits and is a powerful limitation on the flexibility of the market mechanism; so powerful that many libertarians advocate its abolition (Friedman, 1963).

It is not surprising that the combined effects of moral hazard, third party pays, the agency (physician induced demand) relationship and licensure, have generated 'cost containment crises' in many health care systems. These problems, and the associated welfare losses arising from subsidised, zero price consumption, have led researchers and policy makers to search for remedies to these market 'failures'. The distortions inherent in actual market structures have been such that the ideal characteristics of the private market mechanism have proved to be theoretical and unobtainable in working health care systems.

3. WITHER MARKETS?

The fundamental characteristics of public and private health care systems, in particular moral hazard, licensure and the agency relationship, are such that the proposed solutions to the problems of the NHS offered by the market alternative appear to produce problems very similar to those inherent in the NHS. This conclusion is verified by the experience of all health care systems (see, e.g. McLachlan and Maynard, 1982): inherent in public and private health care systems are characteristics which lead to a failure to evaluate the input–output relationship and to the existence of perverse incentives which induce consumers and producers to act without due regard to costs and QALY benefits.

The future use of market mechanisms in public and private health care markets is dependent on their proven ability to achieve the objectives of policy. The objectives of the NHS were set out by the Churchill administration in the 1944 White Paper.

the Government . . . want to ensure that in the future every man and woman and child can rely on getting . . . the best medical and other facilities available; that their getting them shall not depend on whether they can pay for them or on any other factor irrelevant to real need.

This statement can be interpreted as advocating the allocation of health care resources on the basis of need or maximising improvements in health status (QALYs) regardless of the willingness and ability to pay of patients. Thus the NHS budget is to be used to maximise benefits or QALYs and the rationing of care and the choice of patients will be related to the QALY inducing response of using scarce resources to treat alternative patients.

The Thatcher government, ambiguous at times about its health care goals, has, perhaps for vote maximising reasons, apparently adopted this collectivist ideology. Thus Mrs Thatcher said in a speech to the 1982 Conservative Conference, reiterated in the 1983 Election Manifesto:

> The principle that adequate health care should be provided for all regardless of ability to pay, must be a foundation of any arrangements for financing health care.

If this collectivist (NHS) policy goal is accepted as given, the relevant policy question is how, if at all, can the market mechanism be used to facilitate the achievement of NHS targets? This type of question is not unusual in economics and in the Soviet bloc there has been an animated debate for decades about the role of markets in centralised economies. In economic theory the debate about this role is even older with, for instance Lange and Taylor (1938), exploring 'socialism by price guidance' nearly fifty years ago.

The Thatcher government's use of the market mechanism within the NHS has been very conservative. There has been much controversy over the putting out to competitive tender of catering, cleaning and laundry services. Much of this controversy has centred over job losses and cost savings but the central issue is the efficiency of the policy which is unfortunately unknown. While the government is collecting data about cost reductions, and these seem substantial (in excess of £50 million by mid-1986) there has been no attempt to measure the effects of the policy on the quality of services provided for patients.

At a superficial level it is evident that this policy will produce real savings (i.e. reduced costs for the same quality of service) because it has obliged health authorities to analyse these services systematically for the first time in many years. This analysis was absent previously because of the gross undermanagement of NHS resources inherent in the ignorance induced by inadequate evaluation of health care processes and health outcomes.

Given its apparent and possibly real effects it is surprising that the competitive tendering policy has not been extended to other services. At the Regional level, computer and architectural services are obvious candidates to be set up as 'profit centres' and hived off, charging Districts and Region for services offered. At the District level pharmacy, radiology and other diagnostic services (e.g. pathology) could be put to the market test: e.g. can the NHS provide pharmacy services at a cost lower than, for instance, Boots? The logical extension of such policies is for health authorities to put clinical and caring services out to tender.

It is this logical extension from which Enthoven (1985) starts. He envisages a publicly financed hospital health authority charged with pursuing NHS goals which could finance all care but provide none, having put it out to tender from competing public and private organisations. Elsewhere Maynard (1985a, b) has advocated experimentation, with the merging of the hospital (HCHS) and primary care (FPS) budgets and resource allocation being centred on the general practitioner. Thus patients would choose their GP annually and this choice would generate a payment by the NHS to the GP. In exchange, the GP would provide comprehensive health care, buying in hospital care on a tender-contractual basis from the most efficient provider, public or private.

Such arrangements might mitigate the effects of the compartmentalisation of the NHS but would require careful evaluation in relation to existing practices in experiments: i.e. the British government should finance the evaluation of the results of experimentation using prospective randomised trial techniques.

In the United States, such health care innovations have been evaluated scientifically. For instance Health Maintenance Organizations (HMOs), have been shown in prospective trials to reduce costs by up to 40 per cent compared to fee per item of service systems of provision (Manning *et al.*, 1984). However these benefits are acquired at a cost: it has been shown that the effects on health status for ill, poor patients in HMOs are inferior in terms of morbidity and the probability of mortality to that of similar patients in fee per item of service systems (Ware *et al.*, 1986). This is a not unexpected outcome when the latter system rewards intensive care. Thus controversy about the workings of the HMO has been illuminated by facts from careful trials.

Careful experimentation by the Rand Corporation in an experiment costing over £70m, has illuminated the effects of user charges on patient behaviour. An alternative market type innovative to the budgeting ideas of Enthoven and Maynard in the NHS is the use of prices to reduce patient utilisation and general public revenues. The advocates of such changes in the UK argue that this will reduce 'wasteful' consumption but its actual efficiency needs more careful evaluation using trials if subjective rhetoric is not to determine resource allocation.

The US experimentation has shown that even low user prices reduce utilisation (Newhouse *et al.*, 1981) and that the effects of reduced utilisation on the health status of patients is not always deleterious (Brook *et al.*, 1983). The health status results found only small differences at the end of the study between those receiving 'free' (zero price) care and those required to meet part of the costs of their bills. However, the health status measures that were used were limited, the participants in the experiment were relatively healthy adults under sixty-five and the follow-up period was quite short (three years for 70 per cent of the patients and five years for the rest). Relman (1983) concluded that the results do not indicate clearly the effects of cost sharing on the health of patients. However the Rand experiment was innovatory and with longer follow-up and better outcome measures the effects of user charges could be determined more fully.

Whilst something is known about the effects of prices on consumer behaviour, little of a systematic nature is known about the effects of prices or remuneration on producer behaviour. There is some general evidence about the effects of capitation payment, fee per item of payments and salaries on the behaviour of practitioners (e.g. Gray, Marinker and Maynard, 1986), but there is relatively little known about the effects of particular payment systems on the quantity and quality of activities of practitioners, let alone about the effects of such process on patient health status. Indeed concern about the effects of perverse incentives on producer behaviour inevitably brings attention back to the consideration of producer budgets in HMO-type institutions and the need for experimentation and carefully evaluated trials.

All these market-type innovations and indeed the whole of the move to more active management of the NHS following the Griffiths report, have the implication that doctor contracts will need to be made more flexible with practitioners' behaviour evaluated explicitly and tenure terminated if performance in terms of the processes of care provided and patient health outcomes is inadequate. Eight year rolling contracts i.e., a four-yearly review of performance and a roll-on or notification of contract withdrawal at year eight) for GPs and consultants would seem to be a sensible and efficient solution although undoubtedly the profession will use its trade union power to oppose such innovations.

Carefully designed and executed clinical trials could elucidate the costs and benefits of market-type innovations in the NHS and such elucidation is essential if decision making is to be informed by science rather than by rhetoric and prejudice. At present there is a considerable amount of innovation taking place in medical practices throughout the country but little attention is paid to the scientific evaluation of these practices. As a consequence fundamental questions about the costs and benefits of alternative medical therapies and of alternative incentive mechanisms remain unexplored but a major challenge to economists and other health service researchers.

The benefits to be gained from greater investments in health services evaluation appear to be considerable and account for Alan Williams's belief that health economics can be the optimistic science. In conjunction with other health-service researchers, economists can contribute to the identification of more efficient policies which will enable health service managers and doctors to produce more QALYs per unit of health care expenditure, but this contribution with regard to provider and consumer behaviour requires ambitious and thoughtful evaluation of which are continually being implemented in an ad hoc and unevaluated way in the National Health Service.

REFERENCES

Acheson, D. (1985) 'Variations in Hospital Referrals', in G. Teeling-Smith (ed.), *Health, Education and General Practice*, London: Office of Health Economics.

Arrow, K. (1963) 'Uncertainty and the Welfare Economics of Medical Care', *American Economic Review*, 53, 941–73.

Birch, S. and Maynard, A. (1986) *The RAWP Reviews: Rawping the UK and Primary Care*, Discussion Paper no. 19, Centre for Health Economics, University of York.

Brook, R. H., Ware, J. E. and Rogers, W. H. (1983) 'Does Free Care Improve Adults' Health? Results from a Randomised Controlled trial', *New England Journal of Medicine*, 319, 1426–34.

Enthoven, A. C. (1985) *Reflections on the Management of the National Health Service*, Occasional Paper no. 5, Nuffield Provincial Hospitals Trust, London.

Friedman, M. (1963) *Capitalism and Freedom*, Chicago: University of Chicago Press.

Gray, D. P., Marinker, M. and Maynard, A. (1986) 'The Doctor, the Patient and their Contact', *British Medical Journal*, 292, 1313–15, 1374–6, 1438–40.

Lange, O. and Taylor, F. M. (1938) *On the Economic Theory of Socialism*, Minneapolis: University of Minnesota Press.

McLachlan, G. and Maynard, A. (eds) (1982) *The Public–Private Mix for Health: The Relevance and Effects of Change*, London: Nuffield Provincial Hospitals Trust.

Manning, W. G., Leckbowitz, A., Goldberg, G. A., Rogers, W. H. and Newhouse, J. P. (1984) 'A Controlled Trial on the Effect of Prepaid Group Practice on Use of Services', *New England Journal of Medicine*, 310, 1505–10.

Maynard, A. (1985a) 'Policy Choices in Health', in R. Berthoud (ed.), *Challenges to Social Policy*, London: Policy Studies Institute, Gower.

Maynard, A. (1985b) 'Performance Incentives', in G. Teeling-Smith (ed.) *Health, Education and General Practice*, London: Office of Health Economics.

Maynard, A. and Williams, A. (1985) 'Privatisation and the National Health Service', in J. Le Grand and R. Robinson (eds), *Privatisation and the Welfare State*, London: Allen & Unwin.

Newhouse, J. P., Manning, W. G., Morris, J. N., *et al.* (1981) 'Some Interim Results from a Controlled Trial of Cost Sharing in Health Insurance', *New England Journal of Medicine*, 305, 1501–7.

Relman, A. (1983) 'Is Cost Sharing Dangerous to your Health?' *New England Journal of Medicine*, 309, 1453.

Sandberg, S. I., Barnes, B. A., Weinstein, M. C. and Braun, P. (1985) 'Elective Hysterectomy: Benefits, Risks, and Costs, *Medical Care*, 23, 1067–85.

Torrance, G. W. (1986) 'Measurement of Health State Utilities for Economic Appraisal: a review', *Journal of Health Economics*, 5, 1–30.

Ware, J. E., Brook, R. H., Rogers, W. H., Keeler, E. B., Davies, A., Sherbourne, C., Goldberg, C. A., Camp, P. and Newhouse, J. P. (1986) 'Comparison of Health Outcomes at Health Maintenance Organisation with those for Fee for Services', *Lancet*, i, 1017–21.

Williams, A. (1985a) 'Economics of Coronary Artery Bypass Grafting', *British Medical Journal*, 291, 326–9.

Williams, A. (1985b) 'Screening for Risk of Coronary Heart Disease: Is it Worthwhile?', paper presented to a conference in Edinburgh, November, Centre for Health Economics, University of York.

Index